ON CITIES AND SOCIAL LIFE

THE HERITAGE OF SOCIOLOGY

A Series Edited by **Morris Janowitz**

Louis Wirth

ON CITIES
AND SOCIAL LIFE

Selected Papers

Edited and with an Introduction by
ALBERT J. REISS, JR.

The University of Chicago Press
Chicago & London

The University of Chicago Press, Chicago 60637
The University of Chicago Press, Ltd., London

© 1964 by The University of Chicago
All rights reserved. Published 1964
Midway reprint 1981
Printed in the United States of America

ISBN: 0-226-90242-0
LCN: 64-24970

Acknowledgments

An expression of appreciation is in order for Elizabeth Wirth Marvick, who assisted in selecting the papers for the original volume of Louis Wirth's papers and who generously aided in this one by preparing the biography of Louis Wirth. The cooperation of Mary Wirth in both these undertakings is gratefully acknowledged.

At the beginning of each chapter credit is given to the original publisher and copyright owners of Louis Wirth's essays. Thanks are due all of them for their generous permission to reprint them here.

Contents

Introduction

Sociology as a Discipline

SOCIOLOGY, for Louis Wirth, is a more or less organized body of knowledge about human behavior—"What is true of human behavior by virtue of the fact that always and everywhere men live a group existence?" Like others from the "Chicago school" of sociology, he held that the discipline of sociology consists of three divisions, loosely defined: demography, ecology, and technology; social organization; and social psychology.

The field of *demography, ecology, and technology* is concerned with the physical, biological, and situational base of human living, and the techniques and tools that man evolved which

In preparing this introduction, I have relied heavily upon a variety of sources including Wirth's published papers, course notes, and memories of discussions with Wirth. I am particularly indebted to Bendix's excellent paper, "Social Theory and Social Action in the Sociology of Louis Wirth," *American Journal of Sociology*, LIX (May, 1954), 523–29 and to Wirth's autobiographical statements in Howard Odum, *American Sociology: The Story of Sociology in the United States through 1950* (New York: Longmans, Green & Co., 1951), pp. 227–33. Unless otherwise stated, direct quotation is from transcriptions of his lectures made by students in his classes, 1945–52. All page references to Wirth's essays are to this volume, unless otherwise indicated.

affect his environment. These circumstances or factors constitute
the preconditions of existence at particular times. They are ma-
terially ascertainable conditions. At the other pole is *social psychology*, a field concerned with personality and collective behavior. It constitutes the study of the "subjective aspect of culture,"
the psychic states, attitudes, and sentiments of persons as well as
communication, public opinion, consensus, ideas, and collective
action. The main field is *social organization*, concerned not only
with systems of social life but all their constituent elements, such
as groups, associations, communities, institutions, and classes.

Sociology is to be regarded as both a general and a special
social science:

> Sociology . . . is a general social science in the sense that the
> questions it asks about human nature and the social order are of a
> kind that cut across different specific contexts and accent the group
> factor in human behavior . . . sociology is a specific discipline in that
> it focuses on the nature and genesis and forms of the human per-
> sonality and attitudes (social psychology); in that it is also con-
> cerned with the structuring of group life . . .[1]

As a special discipline, Wirth at times characterized sociology as
the "science of left-overs," a collection of special subjects dis-
carded by the other social sciences, e.g., social problems, the
family, and rural sociology. These special concerns he felt hin-
dered the development of a genuinely comparative sociology.

Of his own entry into sociology, he said:

> I was enthusiastic and radical in those days in a sense that I be-
> lieved a science of human behavior not only possible but indispen-
> sable. What I read in the course of my studies impressed me as rather
> disappointing. Through the inspiration and the help of . . . teachers
> . . . I was impelled to go on and do what little I could to make our
> knowledge in the field perhaps a little less disappointing to others.[2]

Wirth's papers stand as partial evidence of his success. Though
what sociologists *do* may often be disappointing, sociology is an
intellectually challenging subject matter.

[1]   Howard W. Odum, *American Sociology* (New York: Longmans,
Green & Co., 1951), p. 228.

[2]   *Ibid.*, p. 229.

Sociological Theory and Methodology

Louis Wirth regarded himself as a sociological theorist, though it is not possible to characterize his own sociological theory. He firmly maintained that sociology had not developed a body of knowledge that merited formulation as a theory. What he offered to others—both to students in classes and in his writings—therefore, was an analysis of sociological writings and of social reality as he saw it, and a strategy for the development of sociological theory. To students, his penetrating negative and critical stance generally emerged as contributing more to their own development than any positive one. This is not surprising perhaps since his own analysis remained essentially unsystematized. The essays in this volume thus do not provide an introduction to the work of a systematist, as that word is generally used. He would have been the first to deny that he was one. Rather, what the reader finds is a number of essays that illuminate several aspects of social life as he defined it, molded by a general perspective of consensus as the basis of social order.

Whether Wirth might have developed a more systematic sociological theory had he lived is perhaps a matter of idle speculation. Yet several things are worth noting in this connection. Though interested in questions regarding formal properties of any theory, what is called metatheory, he was skeptical of the possibilities for a systematic sociological theory. He had the humanist's regard for the central role of values in shaping and reshaping human events, and of history in the unending social drama. Though a political activist, he was disinclined to tackle the problems of politics theoretically. He approached such problems primarily through action research, research that is intimately tied to changing the social order rather than to a theoretical formulation about what that order is like.

The first step to be taken in developing a sound sociological theory Wirth maintained was to develop a coherent set of assumptions and a conceptual framework consistent with the group character of social life.

By theory, I mean the definition of interests of scholars, the assumptions with which they start, the conceptual framework in terms of which they analyze their materials, and the types of generalizations which they develop as they are related to other generalizations in the field as a whole or knowledge as a whole.[3]

He was rarely sympathetic with attempts to develop deductive sociological theory, speaking of all such endeavors as "mere exercises" in theory construction. As Bendix points out, Wirth contested the validity of most sociological theory on grounds that it was but proof of what had already been assumed.[4] "Most sociological theories," he would say, "ignore the most obvious and obscure thing about human beings, what it is they take for granted." He was especially disenchanted with theories based on a rational means-ends framework, since they failed to treat non-rational behavior as important determinants of behavior.

Theories of social action were generally dismissed on grounds that they focused only on people doing things, i.e., actually behaving, when failure to act was in his judgment an equally significant fact about human social life. Wirth steadfastly refused to limit sociological inquiry to the study of overt behavior or action, contending that values, ideas, attitudes, and motives are equally viable concepts in sociology:

. . . in the study of human social life generally, while it is desirable to concentrate on overt action—of which language itself is one form— it is not so irrelevant, as some have thought, to take account of what people say. For despite the deflections, distortions, and concealment of their verbal utterances, men do betray, even if they do not always accurately and completely reveal in them, their motives and their values.[5]

Yet he was clearly dissatisfied with most theories of motivation and values. He was particularly critical of psychoanalytic theory,

3   *Ibid.*, p. 230.

4   Reinhard Bendix, "Social Theory and Social Action in the Sociology of Louis Wirth," *American Journal of Sociology*, LIX (May, 1954), 525.

5   Louis Wirth, "Ideological Aspects of Social Disorganization," p. 59.

opposing it on grounds that it was incompatible with the group
nature of social life and personality in the context of a cultural
milieu. Despite his admiration for the Scottish moral philosophers, particularly Adam Smith, he contended that Smith failed
to utilize the fundamental insight developed in the *Theory of
Moral Sentiments,* that motivation arises through the sharing of
common sentiments, for his analysis of the market economy in
The Wealth of Nations. Notwithstanding his criticism of specific
theoretical formulations in *The Polish Peasant,* he was perhaps
more sympathetic to Thomas and Znaniecki's basic concerns in
developing a theory of motivation resting in values and attitudes
than were most of the critics of that work.[6] Though rejecting
Thomas and Znaniecki's formulation of the "four wishes," he
nevertheless expressed the view that critics had failed to provide
viable alternatives for their formulation. For he steadfastly maintained that ". . . if we do not have an understanding of . . . motives and values, we do not know men as social beings."[7]

Values are for Wirth an important concern in sociology for
two reasons. They are data of sociology necessary to know men
as social beings. But, they are also forces acting upon the sociologist in his study of human behavior. His own position on the sociologist's dilemma regarding facts and valuations in social science is closer to that recorded in Myrdal's *American Dilemma*[8]
than that of Weber,[9] as the hitherto unpublished piece, "On Making Values Explicit," in this volume makes clear. Writing to
Myrdal in 1939, he said: "Without valuations we have no interest,

[6]   See Part Two, "Transcript of the Conference Proceedings," in
Herbert Blumer, *Critiques of Research in the Social Sciences: I, An Ap-
praisal of Thomas and Znaniecki's, The Polish Peasant in Europe and
America* (Bulletin 44, New York: Social Science Research Council, 1939).

[7]   Louis Wirth, "Ideological Aspects of Social Disorganization," p.
59.

[8]   Gunnar Myrdal, *An American Dilemma: The Negro Problem and
Modern Democracy* (New York: Harper & Bros., 1944), Appendix 2,
pp. 1035–64.

[9]   *Max Weber on the Methodology of the Social Sciences.* Translated and edited by Edward A. Shils and Henry A. Finch (Glencoe, Illinois: Free Press, 1949).

no sense of relevance or significance, and, consequently, no object."[10] Summarizing his view of values in sociology for Howard Odum, he wrote:

we are, of course, as scientists, or would-be scientists, interested in understanding what is, rather than what ought to be. But it has been my experience that almost everything we do is tied up with the problem of values. Values determine our intellectual interests, the selection of problems for analysis, our selection and interpretation of the data, and to a large extent also our generalizations and, of course, our application of these generalizations. Therefore, I believe the sociologist, like other social scientists, must make greater efforts than physical and biological scientists to make explicit the value premises from which he proceeds.[11]

Wirth's theoretical position on values is therefore intimately tied to a methodological position. Even the critical examination of another man's contribution to sociology requires a knowledge of the theorist's background and perspective, an examination at the level of the sociology of knowledge. At the Social Science Research Council conference on Herbert Blumer's appraisal of Thomas and Znaniecki's *The Polish Peasant,* Wirth remarked:

. . . I would say one way to begin the analysis of a given theory is to inquire into the particular perspective which prompted this particular author to arrive at these particular conclusions or hypotheses. Having discovered that, i.e., what he took for granted, I would say, "Now suppose we take something else for granted, at what conclusions would we arrive?" . . . it might result in two opposing theories. Then I would ask, which one requires the most assumptions and which one is more consistent with what we already know?[12]

Just as it is difficult to characterize Wirth's scholarship in terms of a theoretical position, other than to say that he sought a body of verified knowledge for sociology, so it is not easy to characterize his methodological stance in terms of a recognized position or unified school. Close to the skeptics in his approach to any

10   Gunnar Myrdal, *op. cit.,* pp. 1063–64.

11   Howard Odum, *op. cit.,* p. 230.

12   *Critiques of Research in the Social Sciences: I, op. cit.,* p. 154.

question, he would have been among the first to question such a procedure, delighting in questioning the assumptions and presuppositions of any and all schools of thought. Given to phenomenological empiricism as was Robert Park, he argued against the pitfalls of "getting too close to the data." Perceiving the relational character of all knowledge, he advocated an assault upon the problem. "Knowledge of the unstated assumptions and premises of our own and other people's premises comprises the foundation of our intellectual house." For him, the sociology of knowledge, or of intellectual life, vied with established schools of epistemology in getting at truth—"a version of reality compatible with reality." He sensed a "real" order to the world, the way things are to human beings, but regarded the nominalist-realist controversy as a straw man.

Apart from the basic methodological position inherent in his sociology of intellectual life, Wirth advocated a union of intimate acquaintance with social life and *sociologically* contrived conceptions of that reality. He continually emphasized the importance of William James's distinction between knowledge of things and acquaintance with them. Acquaintance with things was most likely to stem from actual *experience* and *involvement* with reality. "In my work in theory, especially through my years of teaching it to graduate students, I have tried to emphasize that theory is an aspect of everything they do, and not a body of knowledge separate from research and practice."[13]

He was unimpressed with most cross-cultural work as a basis for the development of a scientific sociology. Such comparison, in his view, was essentially sterile, since it ignored the most important facts about human life—the changing course of human history and the ways in which societies are changed by civilization. A genuinely comparative sociology must be based in history.

Wirth had a predilection for typological classification, believing it to be the single most important prerequisite to the development of sociological theory. The ideal types of "urban" and "rural" ways of life developed in the essay on "Urbanism as a Way of Life"; of pluralistic, assimilationist, secessionist, and

13   Howard Odum, *op. cit.*, p. 230.

militant minorities in "The Problem of Minority Groups"; of hegemony, particularistic, marginal, and minority nationalism in
"Types of Nationalism"; and of social types of Jews in "Some
Jewish Types of Personality" reflect both his concern for the development of ideal types to facilitate theoretical analysis and his
insistence that these types be grounded in experience and observation of social reality.

He rejected the basic methodological distinction of German
sociologists between causal and meaningful relationships, suggesting it is a contradiction in terms. Undoubtedly Max Weber's
critique of the German school of Verstehen, together with Weber's reformulation of it, and his discussion of ideal type analysis
and causal imputation influenced Wirth's thinking. Skeptical of
Weber's analysis in *The Protestant Ethic and the Spirit of Capitalism,* he nonetheless sympathized with the method Weber used
to approach the problem. Weber's treatment of causal imputation,
by construction and verification of a historical individual—the
thing to be explained—was of special interest to him. He insisted
on viewing social reality in terms of "what would have happened
if an event had not taken place," or "what would happen if we
altered or changed these conditions." To understand social institutions, he regarded it as important to know what would be altered or disrupted if the institution were taken away. This, for
him, was the clue to its function. "We get an institution when we
know that its removal will slow up sets of behavior and understandings among people in a society."

Wirth readily questioned what other social scientists take for
granted. Students and colleagues alike were aware of his critical
skills. Educated men were not necessarily speaking intelligently
nor were they intellectuals. He was generally as impatient with
the grand theory as with the trivial empirical investigation with
precise measurement. Both were usually seen as pretensions that
disregarded the nature of social life. If anything could be said to
be characteristic of his highly perceptive and usually insightful
commentary on social life, it is that it arose from what he liked to
term a healthy skepticism, a continuous questioning of what is
known or of how things come to be known. "Nothing is ever self-

evident; it is not even evident." "The hardest thing to know is what people take for granted." "To say something is a law of nature is to confess ignorance, especially when it is applied to the realm of social life." "Our generalizations can be no more valid than the precision with which our concepts are formulated." "The more precise and unambiguous concepts in social theories become, the less valuable they are." Such statements convey both his impatience with assumptions or generalizations that are accepted without question by sociologists, and the way in which he tried to imbue others with a healthy skepticism.

Consensus

Wirth's theoretical writings center around the problem of consensus as the basis of social order. He defined a society or social group by its capacity to act together, or to take collective action. Collective action rests in "a set of common understandings, a system of reciprocally acknowledged claims and expectations." His presidential address to the members of the American Sociological Society emphasized that collective action rests in consensus.

I regard the study of consensus as the central task of sociology, which is to understand the behavior of men in so far as that is influenced by group life. Because the mark of any society is the capacity of its members to understand one another and to act in concert toward common objectives and under common norms, the analysis of consensus rightly constitutes the focus of sociological investigation.[14]

The most important thing to know about any aggregate of people belonging together, he contended, is "what they take for granted." The first task for sociology, therefore, he held, is to learn the unstated assumptions of people, the credo by which they live. These are the elements upon which there is consensus, a consensus which does not "rise above the level of consciousness." To know these things about organized entities, he insisted, requires that "we enter into their life." He often paraphrased

[14] Louis Wirth, "Consensus and Mass Communication," p. 20.

Kant's dictum: "one should not believe everything that people say, nor should one suppose they say it without reason."

That for Wirth the study of consensus was the central task of sociology is apparent from the way he treated the ends-means (teleological) problem. Although he viewed human beings as essentially goal-directed animals, the crucial fact about them, for him, was their collective pursuit of ends. Only rarely is behavior an individual pursuit. Goal-seeking requires organization and collective action which derives from consensus on ends to be pursued. The paradox this created for Wirth is that while ends cannot be pursued without organization, organizations may monopolize one's loyalties and the very conditions for freedom. He was deeply concerned with the establishment of consensus by democratic means in the mass society. He wanted to know not only what consensus is necessary for individual freedom to be realized but how much freedom is necessary to achieve a genuine consensus resting in voluntary agreement.

Wirth's concern with the analysis of consensus was by no means an interest in some static equilibrium, for consensus is treated as problematic in the social order. Yet he never probed the different meanings of consensus, formally regarding it in only two senses: (1) as a sufficient understanding of the symbols of others to permit communication rather than "talking past one another" and (2) as sharing of the same values. Consensus in the first sense might involve only "an agreement to disagree." A minimum condition for it he thought is tolerance, which in his elfin manner he described as a "suspicion that the other fellow might be right." Following Robert Park, he contrasted consensus in the second sense with symbiosis. "Symbiosis" was defined as a condition in which "men live together by virtue of sheer existential dependence upon one another" while "consensus" is that condition in which men agree with and mutually identify with one another.

His failure to explore the dimensions of consensus is readily apparent in the kind of questions he raised about consensus in the mass society. "The fundamental problem for modern society," he would say, "is how can so many people live together if they have so little in common in the way of moral values or sacred beliefs? How can a mass society exist with so little conseusus?" This manner of stating the problem led him to ignore the possibility that there may be more consensus in a modern mass society than in any previous ones, given the myriad consensually legitimate groups within it.

Wirth was particularly critical of simple explanations of the conditions for consensus. He did not regard contact and interaction as necessary and sufficient conditions for consensus. Though he regarded contact as a necessary condition for consensus, since only through confrontation with alternatives could choice be made, he argued that with contact one is as likely to get confusion and conflict as well as friendship and harmony.

Like Robert Park, Wirth saw society as resting on three main types of order. There is first a kind of equilibrium in which people compete with and struggle against one another, what Hobbes termed a *bellum omnia contra omnes*. This is the *symbiotic order*. Society is also a set of symbols or communications resulting in common understandings, a *cultural order*. Finally, society is a group of people accepting a set of common norms, rules of the game, common goals, and agreement upon the achievement of these goals. This was termed the *moral and political order*. For Wirth, these were different orders of *social cohesion*. They exist and grow up, one upon the other. A political order rests upon a cultural order, and there can be no political order without a competitive system. In his lectures, he often remarked, "If we look at a society as being a symbiotic system, a set of common understandings, mutual claims and expectations, and a system of norms, we can say that society exists wherever *consensus* exists among men. A society is as large as the area over which consensus prevails." Reference to the consensual base of society as the moral or political order was by no means a fortuitous choice of words. Wirth, unlike Park, saw the problems of consensus as political problems. The democratic selection of political means and the mobilization of people for a consensual order resting in a democratic creed or ideology was his idea of the "good society."

At times he approached the problem of consensus by first

asking what were the bases for concerted action. "On what bases do people coexist?" he would ask. His answer was that they coexist first of all in terms of physical contact and interdependence, an *ecological community*. A second basis for collective action is the division of labor and the struggle for a livelihood, an *economic base*. A consideration of *different or common interests* arising from needs that are incidental to living or working together is a third basis for collective action. The pursuit of interests gives rise to a fourth basis for collective action, the *normative basis*, or the moral area of life as it is regulated by common values. The realm of tradition, a *culture*, provides a fifth basis for collective action since it provides a common framework of language, ideas, sentiments, and the like. Although he argued that these account for man's coexistence, he concluded they do not deal directly with the problem of how men, although they are different beings, can act concertedly—how consensus is achieved. He emphasized that there is an important difference between the kind of order that arises from the fact that people have similar or parallel aims and that arising from their co-operation to achieve a common end which is seen and shared by everyone. Organizations based upon these two kinds of bonds were fundamentally different for him. In the one case he held that people act alike because they are and think alike while in the other, people work to implement commonly accepted goals even though they are not necessarily alike and may think and act differently as they work to achieve them.

Few issues were as confused in sociology, he thought, as that between "similarity" and "commonness" or between "parallelism" and "shared circumstances of living." He emphasized that people often live similar lives without common goals; they are culturally and socially distant, though spatially and economically interdependent. "A mere aggregate of peope does not constitute a social entity," he would say; "Unless people recognize they have the same goals or position in life and act accordingly, unless they develop a consciousness and a capacity for collective action based upon the consensus, they do not have a group life." Perhaps because of this artificial distinction between symbiosis and consensus and his own definition of widespread consensus as the basis for collective action, he was led to underestimate both how much social life is possible without consensus and how much the mass society is organized through consensually legitimated institutions. For Wirth, the main problems in achieving consensus in modern societies arose from the segmentation of values and interests and their lack of integration with one another, and from the failure of men to participate together in reaching common decisions. He viewed the modern world as atomized into a multiplicity of interests with people failing to communicate meaningfully with one another and to participate in common decision-making, and concluded that the main task of anyone who would forge a democratic consensus is less one of reconciling conflicting interests than of *generating participation in common decisions.* A main difficulty, he felt, in generating participation in the mass society is the fact that people are generally *excluded* from participation in decision-making. He often remarked: "Even if there is a so-called common man by virtue of the fact that as Lincoln said, 'God made so many of them,' there is no discounting the fact that they have little to say in making common decisions; today the common man has no power of original decision, judgment, or initiation." It seems clear that for Wirth democratic consensus lay less in consensually legitimated institutions that make decisions than in mass participation in making them.

Wirth viewed the dissociation of men from full and intimate participation in community life then as an integral aspect of the mass society. The problem of democracy in a mass society for him was how to encourage people to share in decision-making. He argued that today there is only a "superficial" consensus based on similarity and concentration of power whereas a "genuine" consensus is necessary, one based on communication and common participation in making common decisions. Like Dewey, he emphasized that society exists not only *through* communication but *in* communication. Central to an understanding of consensus, therefore, is an understanding of communication and its organization in societies. He was particularly concerned that communication through the mass media is a one-way process, with the media controlled by a small group of men, since he viewed the mass media of communication as a potential means of generating mass participation in common decisions in the mass society. His presidential address, "Consensus and Mass Communication" was devoted to this question.

Openly critical of those who nostalgically advocated a return to the "simple life," he maintained that such a situation is possible in modern societies only on the condition of terror. At the same time he was frankly skeptical about the possibility that men can be integrated in a common life in mass societies, emphasizing that the bases for agreement are ever-shifting. To what extent can we enlist the masses of men to participate in some functional activity when we have segmental interest groups, he would ask. In reply, he would say that uncoerced consensus requires some kind of constitution, minimal consensus to arbitrate our differences and a maximum communication of ideas and values. Above all he contended there should be competition in the marketplace of ideas if democracy is to survive. "Ideas and Ideals as Sources of Power in the Modern World" is an essay reflecting the importance that Wirth attached to them as a basis for building consensus for a world community.

Wirth never attempted any systematic theory which might be brought to bear on the problem of consensus as the basis of social order. He brought rather a point of view and illuminating discussion of the problem of achieving a democratically based consensus in the mass society. Analytically, he was disposed to view consensus in terms of several main questions: (1) How widely does consensus extend for a given universe of discourse? (2) What is the penetration of consensus? How pervasive or thoroughgoing is it? (3) What is its degree of integration? Is it segmental or comprehensive?

Social Organization

Wirth approached the analysis of social organization from a dual viewpoint: (1) that of *social structure or form* resulting from social interaction and (2) that of *social process* or dynamic qualities underlying any more or less enduring structure. A central task of sociology he contended is to understand how structure and process are interrelated in all social phenomena. He conceptualized social structures as forms of human activity. This led him to reject most current theories of social structure on the grounds that they dissociated structure and process. He suggested that, for example, if the concept of "association" were looked at as a verb rather than as a noun, one would ask with whom do people associate, and why, rather than what kind of associations do they form. Social organization for Wirth was both structure and equilibrium, and process and interaction.

Wirth emphasized also that an understanding of social organization required that it be compared with other "conditions," those of unorganization, disorganization, and reorganization. Like W. I. Thomas, he viewed such conditions in terms of social process. Much human activity he suggested is unorganized. A main task of sociology, therefore, is to investigate how organization comes into being. He asserted that under unorganized conditions, parts are readily observed but there is no order, regularity, or continuity—no organized relationship among them. He implied that the field of collective behavior in its concern with crowds, mobs, social movements, and related phenomena is generally concerned with this problem of how organization comes into being, although he did not limit the study of unorganized activity to these phenomena.

The concept of social disorganization, like that of social organization was given a normative basis.

. . . The degree to which the members of a society lose their common understandings, i.e., the degree to which consensus is undermined, is the measure of a society's state of disorganization. The degree to which there is agreement as to the values and norms of a society expressed in its explicit rules and in the preferences its members manifest with reference to these rules, furnishes us with criteria of the degree to which a society may be said to be disorganized.[15]

Like Durkheim and W. I. Thomas, Wirth did not regard all deviations from norms as prima facie evidence of social disorganization. He asserted that in a society there could be both wide differentiation in norms and deviation from them without dis-

[15]   Louis Wirth, "Ideological Aspects of Social Disorganization," p. 46.

organization, for in Thomas's terms "Social organization is not coextensive with individual morality, nor does social disorganization correspond to individual demoralization."[16] Societies were viewed as having the capacity to reconstruct and reorganize following disorganization. A focal concern in Wirth's own writing is the reconstruction of modern societies as literate and democratic ones.

Since Wirth viewed social organization and disorganization in terms of norms, he concluded that a main task of social organization was to discern those norms upon which consensus rests. In a Socratic vein he would inquire, "if it were not for norms, values and consensus, would there be mutual understanding, claims and expectations, or communication among men?"

"What we are after when we talk about social organization," he would say, "is something like a set of processes of interaction by means of which social entities retain their structure." To this he added, "There are as many kinds of social organization as there are varieties of human interests that can be expressed in an organized way." Interests for him, were irretrievably bound up with historical situations from which they emerge and are organized. There was for him, therefore, no study of social organization apart from a study of history.

He protested against sociological attempts to develop theoretical schemes in terms of some basic unit. Those who say a social act is the basic unit were reminded that there is no act apart from interaction and that means become ends and ends, means. Those who attempted to define a basic unit of social organization such as the family were brushed aside with the comment that any social group is a basic unit by virtue of its being a group. Nor would he regard persons as the basic unit of social organization: "Insofar as human beings are persons, they are always members of some kind of group; men are persons only by virtue of the fact that they are incorporated in some kind of social structure."

Discontented with much of the empirical work on social struc-

16   W. I. Thomas and F. Znaniecki, *The Polish Peasant in Europe and America* (New York: Alfred A. Knopf, 1927), II, 1129.

ture, he insisted that investigators failed to distinguish structural categories based on people having certain traits in common, such as income or opinion aggregates, from groups as collectivities based on a sense of belonging or solidarity and in sharing common values, claims, and expectations. He firmly maintained a distinction between social aggregates and social groups; groups were not "mere aggregates" but "corporate bodies moving toward common ends."

Wirth suggested that a main task of social organization is to develop a theory which orders and differentiates organized units or groups from one another. Although he never evolved such a theory, he addressed himself to the main criteria which might be used to differentiate types of organized units. In his lectures on social organization, he stressed the following criteria, which he did not see as mutually exclusive: (1) the social bond that holds people together; (2) their stratification or rank as a product of common interests or the roles people play in collective action oriented toward some common end; (3) the amount of difference in human behavior which may be attributed to the role the group plays in the life style of members; (4) the chronological priority the group has upon the formation of, or change in, personality; (5) the permanence of the group and the devices it has to insure or disrupt activity; (6) the transitory or permanent character of its organization; (7) size of the group; (8) the original *raison d'être* for the group, and whether forces other than these must reinforce it; (9) criteria for membership, particularly whether it recruits by appeal or ascription and the exclusiveness or selectivity of membership; (10) whether it is a *Gemeinschaftliche* or *Gesellschaftliche* group.

Sociology of Intellectual Life

A substantive area of considerable interest to Wirth was the sociology of knowledge. He liked to remark that it is ". . . a field which is misnamed and with the misnaming of which, unfortunately, I have had something to do. . . . It should rather be called the sociology of intellectual life."[17]

[17] Howard Odum, *op. cit.*, p. 231.

Wirth did little writing in this field, although he offered annually a course in "The Sociology of Knowledge" at the University of Chicago. His preface to Karl Mannheim's *Ideology and Utopia* discusses the major problems involved in the relationship of intellectual activity and social existence and concludes with a tentative outline of the major issues of the field.

For Wirth, the sociology of intellectual life ". . . historically and logically falls within the scope of general sociology conceived as the basic social science."[18] When systematically developed, the sociology of intellectual life should deal with a series of subject matters ". . . in an integrated fashion, from a unifying point of view and by means of appropriate techniques."[19]

The leading issues with which the sociology of intellectual life must concern itself, he thought, are these: (1) an elaboration of the theory of knowledge itself, particularly of knowledge as a social product, or of how the context of thought is socially determined by social conditions—the relational character of knowledge; (2) the discovery of the styles and modes of thought characteristic of historical-social situations, particularly the role of belief systems and ideologies, and their comparison across historical situations; (3) the effect of thought upon social life, including examination of whether we can intervene in the world and make a difference, and of how society allocates its resources for the cultivation of types of knowledge; (4) the study of the intellectuals, those whose special function it is to "accumulate, preserve, reformulate, and disseminate the intellectual knowledge of the group"; (5) the social organization of intellectual life, especially an analysis of its institutional organization.

Social Action

Louis Wirth began the quest for sociological knowledge with a fundamental question, "can we do anything about social life, or do we live in a matrix of social forces that elude under-

18 Louis Wirth, "Preface to *Ideology and Utopia*," p. 142.

19 *Ibid.*, pp. 142–43.

standing?" Or, in another vein, "What are the paths open to us in society for intelligent self-direction?" He once concluded his course on social organization with these words:

We must stay close to the reality of our own life in our own day. We must reshape our technical investigations to consider its problems and to provide the understanding that is needed for the formulation of an enlightened public policy.

Wirth belonged to a cohort of social scientists at the University of Chicago that contended the social sciences are policy sciences: Research without action or policy implications is sterile. Action based on social science knowledge is amenable to intelligent direction.

The central problem of sociology for Wirth, as already noted, is to understand consensus as the basis of social order. The analysis of consensus he argued requires not only an understanding of the conditions generating and stabilizing it but also of the bases for its manipulation. Time and again he emphasized that there is a distinction between knowing how a thing works and knowing how to put such knowledge to work—to know enough to act upon the basis of what is already known. Nowhere did he address himself more eloquently to this problem than when he spoke of the "suicide of civilization in the face of the new physical power":

There may be some among us who feel that we already have the knowledge to prevent disaster but that we lack the power to put that knowledge into effect. Such a claim, however, is a confession that we lack perhaps the most important knowledge that we need, namely the knowledge to unlock the power requisite to put our existing knowledge usefully to work.[20]

Wirth not only emphasized that some of the most important knowledge sociologists might gain was the knowledge of how to make things work, but also that this kind of understanding could best be gained by involvement in action to change things. Though value and fact might to a substantial degree be separated from one another, he counseled against the separation of social action from either one. Out of the myriad of problems to which sociologists might address themselves, they should, he felt, address them-

[20]   Louis Wirth, "Consensus and Mass Communication," p. 18.

selves to those which are relevant to the social life of man in contemporary societies. There was no room for "knowledge for the sake of knowledge" in his view of the world of social science. Wirth's "competent sociologist" was one who experiences the reality he investigates and assumes the full role of citizen as well as the role of scientist qua scientist. The professional sociologist he recommended should be a scholar in action.

Perhaps it is a temperamental trait rather than an orthodox turn of science to turn in a period of turmoil away from the problems of the world to the problems of science, and as we customarily say, to take the long view and devote oneself to the building up of a body of knowledge which may or may not be relevant to the problems of life but which satisfied ones intellectual curiosity. It is curious that the reputation of a realist goes to one who never thinks about reality and that the reputation of a social scientist goes to one as far away from the actual problems and aspirations of society as he can get.

Happy are those who can find this refuge. . . . The student of society will be plagued by the difficulties of achieving "objectivity," by the competition with common-sense knowledge, by the limits of his freedom and capacity to experiment, and by other serious and peculiar handicaps which trouble the natural scientist not at all. But the social scientist, whose very subject matter is the social world, can avoid studying the processes and problems of man in society only by pretending to be something he is not, or by lapsing into such a remote degree of abstraction or triviality as to make the resemblance between what he does and what he professes to be doing, purely coincidental.[21]

The interplay of scholarly interest, citizen role, and sociological expert or investigator are exemplified in Wirth's case both in his writing and in his public and professional life.

The main answer that Wirth gave to the question of what avenues are open to us in democratic societies for intelligent self-direction is that of planning. He regarded the planning process very much in Mannheim's sense as a technique of social organization. His own personal commitment to the central function of planning in mass societies is evident not only in his many writings on cities, regions, intergroup relations and tensions, unemploy-

21   *Ibid.*, p. 19.

ment, housing, and a broad range of social problems, but it is evinced by his active participation in planning programs and organizations. He founded the Chicago Community Inventory at the University of Chicago to gather information that could be equally useful to action agencies and social scientists. During Franklin D. Roosevelt's administration he served as a member of the Committee on Urbanism of the National Resources Planning Board and wrote a number of their reports. Much of the research and writing in their volume, "Our Cities: Their Role in the National Economy" is his. He served as Director of Planning for the Illinois Post-War Planning Commission, an organization he was active in founding and promoting. At the University of Chicago, he was actively involved in founding an interdisciplinary graduate program in planning and taught several seminars in planning.

His many writings on the urban community reflect his deep involvement in studying and influencing social life. Central to these concerns was an active interest and involvement in planning cities and the urban civilization. The now classic "Urbanism as a Way of Life" is a formulation of a sociological framework for the analysis of urban phenomena developed while a consultant to the Committee on Urbanism of the National Resources Planning Board.

Wirth's writings on minorities included in this volume reflect his interest in minority problems and race relations, whch he spoke of as his first and main love. He was a founder and director of the American Council on Race Relations and was active in preparing material presented to the U.S. Supreme Court in support of pleas to declare racial restrictive covenants unconstitutional and to desegrate the nation's schools. His "Problems of Minority Groups in War Time." "The Problem of Minority Groups," and "The Present Position of Minority Groups in the United States" are among the essays which reflect both a scholarly and a citizenly interest in these matters.

His interest in belief systems, nationalism, and ideology centered around the generic problem of how they undermine consensus as well as build it. Yet he wrote about these topics in terms of the contemporary world, their effect on achieving a "demo-

cratic social order and a society of nations." In "Ideological
Aspects of Social Disorganization," he tried to show that "through
the analysis of ideologies we may be able to discover the clues
that indicate the disintegration of our social structure and to spot
the areas of life where disorganization threatens to occur."[22] In
"Types of Nationalism," he examined the effect of national interest on the possibilities for a unified Europe. Deeply concerned
with the problem of establishing a minimum consensus for the
basis of world order in the face of mass destruction, he not only
wrote upon these topics but became involved with others in their
resolution. He was particularly interested in the role which the
United States might play in the contemporary world. The essay,
"Freedom, Power and Values in Our Present Crisis" deals with
the effect of the discrepancy between American ideals and reality
upon its leadership role in a world polarized by the two great
concentrations of power, the United States and the Soviet Union.

He was deeply concerned with maintaining conditions for free
exchange in the marketplace of ideas and promoted exchange
among intellectuals. For a good many years he participated frequently in the public broadcast discussions of the University of
Chicago Round Table. He was influential in the establishment of
the International Sociological Association following World War
II and served as its first president.

Though he firmly believed in social action he was not altogether optimistic about the prospects for bringing about the kind
of consensus and change he sought for democratic societies. To
the fraternity of democratic liberals, he observed that "it is almost impossible to live in either a revolutionary society or a reac-
tionary one and be a liberal."

Albert J. Reiss, Jr.

[22]   Louis Wirth, "Ideological Aspects of Social Disorganization," p. 58.

I. Social Organization

1

SOCIAL INTERACTION:

THE PROBLEM OF THE

INDIVIDUAL AND THE GROUP

THE CONTRIBUTION in the *American Journal of Sociology*'s symposium on "The Individual and the Group" variously attempts to formulate the central problem of sociological theory. That problem has been part of the philosophical heritage of the Western world since antiquity. It was the stock illustration in the dispute about logic between the nominalists and the realists during the scholastic period and was revived during the seventeenth and eighteenth centuries in the polemics concerning the state of nature and the social contract. In modern sociological theory under the influence of the discoveries of biologists, on the one hand, and of writers on collective behavior, on the other hand, it has reappeared in the attempt to discover the proper locus of sociological investigations. The atomistic point of view arising out of the biological and mechanistic tradition of the late nineteenth cen-

Reprinted from *Community Life and Social Policy*, ed. Elizabeth Wirth Marvick and Albert J. Reiss, Jr. (Chicago: University of Chicago Press, 1956), pp. 21–34, first published in the *American Journal of Sociology*, XLIV (May, 1939), 965–79.

tury led to the recognition of the individual organism as the solid reality constituting the unit of social life, and depreciation of "society" as a terminological construct or an irrelevant fiction. The interest developing out of folk psychology, which received its most pregnant expression in the writings of Lazarus and Steinthal, and which culminated in the work of the Durkheim group in France, led to an emphasis on society as an entity *sui generis*. This conception was in turn attacked on the ground that a society is nothing more than the individual members of which it is composed, that the behavior of actual individuals constitutes the whole of social life. In defense of this view it was pointed out that the culture of a group is something more than and different from the habits of the individuals composing it and that such social phenomena as language, mythology, religion, and other expressions of collective life cannot be understood adequately so long as attention is concentrated exclusively on the individual bearers of these cultural traits.

In the course of time it has become clear that no satisfactory solution to this problem could be obtained as long as the issue is stated in terms of "either/or." For certain analytical purposes it is well to regard the individual organism composing human society as the suitable and real unit; for others it is desirable to take the collectivity as the ultimate entity; but it should always be noted that neither the *individual* nor the *group* is adequate to comprise all the aspects of the life of man in society. As Cooley pointed out:

A separate individual is an abstraction unknown to experience, and so likewise is society when regarded as something apart from individuals. The real thing is Human Life, which may be considered either in an individual aspect or in a social, that is to say a general aspect; but it is always, as a matter of fact, both individual and general. In other words, "society" and "individuals" do not denote separable phenomena but are simply collective and distributive aspects of the same thing.[1]

Rather than settling the issue as to whether the individual or the group is the ultimate unit in terms of which social life must be

1   Charles H. Cooley, *Human Nature and the Social Order* (New York: Charles Scribner's Sons, 1922), p. 33.

analyzed, the main stream of sociological and social-psychological thought has forgotten this issue and proceeded to analyze social phenomena as complexes of the meaningfully oriented actions of persons reciprocally related to one another. This approach has based itself on the assumption that "society exists wherever a number of individuals enter into reciprocal relations with one another."[2] As sociology has turned from speculation to research, the fruitfulness of Simmel's suggestion that sociology finds its proper subject matter in the process of interpersonal relations has been effectively demonstrated.

The insistence upon social interaction as the focus of sociological interest not only has led to the abandonment of interest in the sterile individual-group controversy but has led to a marked advance in our understanding of the relation between personality and society. Personalities, according to this view, by playing more or less integrated roles in the groups of which they are members, manifest complexes of traits the locus of which is the concrete organism. The roles of the persons are systems of action, responses to claims and expectations on the part of the individual and his fellows. The structure or system of their interrelations when seen collectively constitutes the society which may be regarded as the bearer of a culture. This conception allows us to see more clearly the varied perspectives in terms of which social phenomena may be empirically analyzed.

In its most external aspect social life involves the distribution of the members of an aggregate in space. From this physical and superficial view of an aggregate we may proceed in two directions to explore further significant aspects of social life by means of the techniques of the specialized branches of social science that concern themselves with it. On the one hand, we can seek to discover what is true of such an aggregate by virtue of that fact that the constituent members are organisms of a certain sort, endowed with the impulses and organic traits characteristic of their species. On the other hand, we can ascertain what is true of the members

2   Georg Simmel, *Soziologie* (Leipzig: Duncker & Humblot, 1908), p. 5. Cf. Max Weber, *Wirtschaft und Gesellschaft* (Tübingen: J. C. B. Mohr, 1925), I, 1, 11–14; Talcott Parsons, *The Structure of Social Action* (New York: McGraw-Hill Book Co., 1937).

of such an aggregate by virtue of the fact that they are in interaction with one another, and in the process have built up what
we call a culture. Thus we come to see the peculiar relevance of
human ecology, biology, psychology, and social science in its
various branches to the understanding of the social life of man.
No single field of specialization can by itself be expected to reveal
more than a highly segmental aspect of the total reality, but each
can become more fertile than it would be in isolation by recognizing its own peculiar problems and interests and their relations
with all the others.

In the attempt to formulate an empirical science designed to
study social groups as products of participating individuals, Professor Znaniecki postulates the relation between individuals and
groups with hypotheses concerning " 'individuals-as-experienced-
by-themselves-and-other-individuals' in relation to 'groups-as-
experienced-by-participants-and-outsiders.' " He emphasizes the
fact that the individuals who participate in the activities which
bring the social group into being also become a part of the product which they have helped to create as group members. In analyzing this act of participation and its product, he points out that
every social role involves (1) a social circle composed of a set of
people of whom the performing person is the center and to whom
he bears definite relations; (2) the person's social self as conceived by this social circle and by himself, which undergoes
change in the course of interaction between himself and his fellows; (3) the person's status, as indicated by the "rights" which
his group assigns to him and which he expects of them; and (4)
the person's function, or his activities in response to the expectations of his social circle.

The isolation of these analytical elements in the social role is
helpful in formulating an attack on this complex phenomenon.
They should be seen, however, as having a highly variable content
under varying conditions of group structure and specific situations in which the person participates. Thus, for instance, an individual may not always be the center of a social circle, as
Professor Znaniecki seems to think he is. Indeed, it is precisely
because in some of his social circles he is not so centrally located

as in others, or as he conceives himself to be within that particular circle, that the individual comes to have successively varying and simultaneously divergent or conflicting conceptions of himself. The recognition of this fact would go far toward illuminating some of the more basic forms of personal maladjustment with which some of the other contributors to the symposium deal. Professor Znaniecki further points out that some of the more distinctively group phenomena, or collective aspects of personal behavior, leading to the characteristics which Sumner has so aptly described in his discussion of the in-group and the subjective aspect which has been set forth by Cooley in his analysis of the we-feeling, are to be seen in the emergence of group norms and values which crystallize into group institutions and organizations. It is in the variety of groups, the interrelations between groups, and the differential position of the person within these groups we must seek the explanation of the highly differentiated personalities emerging in our culture; and at the same time it is in the uniformities of group life and individual participation in and sharing of group norms that we must seek the clue to the uniformities of human behavior.

Professor Halbwachs places his discussion of individual consciousness and the collective mind in the matrix of the sociological theories which characterize the Durkheim tradition. In arguing against the classical fallacy of the isolated man, he makes use of the notion of collective representations which transcend individual consciousness as demonstrable bases of the primacy of the group. The basic datum of collective psychology is the group, with tendencies and representations common to various social milieus. According to this view, collective psychological states cannot be explained in terms of the individual but only in terms of the social structure, the customs, institutions, science, language, art, and technology which are reflected in each individual mind. Psychology, he holds, following Blondel, "must place [its] emphasis solidly on the psychophysiological and psychopathological data." These two points of view, by being placed in juxtaposition, would thus in a measure explain mental life in its entirety, "for our mind owes all that it is and all that it holds either to the organism or to social groups." But in addition he points out, following Tarde's statement that man is a social being grafted on to a biological being, that the individuality which results from this crossing between physiological and social elements cannot be completely explained either by the psychologist or by the sociologist, for it constitutes a unique phenomenon which can never be truly the object of any science.

Lest it be held that collective thought is a metaphysical entity, Professor Halbwachs asserts that it exists and is realized only in individual consciousness—"the states of consciousness of a greater or lesser number of individuals comprising the group" of which each separate individual carries on only a fragmentary portion. Because society comprises a collection of individuals who think, feel, and act in common, sociology deals first and foremost with psychological materials; but this does not exhaust its scope. Social solidarity presupposes certain conditions or techniques in the economic, religious, political, scientific, linguistic, and artistic realms which imply the presence not only of collective representations but which also have their physical counterparts ("morphology"). It was in this sense that Durkheim proposed to treat social facts as "things." Even such external facts as the physical distribution and mass of a group, which are the concern of the demographer, cannot be studied and explained without taking account of the states of mind people have about it. While sociology, therefore, is primarily concerned with group phenomena as they manifest themselves in visible forms in space, these physical manifestations are socially significant only because they are coupled with collective representations. Psychology and sociology thus turn out to be two polar approaches toward the phenomena of conscious life rooted in an organism and in a social milieu. For purposes of analysis they can be isolated, but in reality they occur only together.

Turning from the point of view of the sociologist to that of the psychologist, we find in Professor Woodworth's paper that the psychologists, conditioned as they are by the tradition of their discipline, are disposed to see the starting point of their investigations in the individual. There is, however, a thorough awareness of the inadequacy of the view that a social group is nothing more than the individuals composing it and that collective behavior is merely an aggregate of the reactions of individuals. Indeed there is a clear recognition in Professor Woodworth's paper that conduct in some of its most essential aspects cannot be adequately apprehended by directing one's attention to individuals as such. Although he does not explicitly state it in so many words, he seems to appreciate the relevance and implications of Josiah Royce's observation that there is a fecundity in aggregations, an emergent property which transcends the sum of individual reactions. Specifically, Woodworth points to the constraint imposed by group situations upon the individuals composing the group as an important factor in individual behavior. He perceives, however, that the group not merely exercises a restrictive influence upon the individual but presents him with opportunities for action of which he, as an individual, would inevitably be deprived. He goes so far as to say that there is a fundamental propensity for participation in environmental happenings which profoundly alters both the range and the character of human activity when viewed within the matrix of group life. Men are social precisely in the sense that they participate in the activities of the group. The view of human action which John Dewey has set forth in his *Human Nature and Conduct*[3]—namely, that the individual is not a mere passive entity reacting to an environment, but certain of his impulses make him an active agent in the discovery of the adjustment to and the transformation of his environment—appears to be quite congenial to Professor Woodworth's approach. With this in mind he suggests the study of teamwork in small groups of children as one of the most fruitful ways in which the laws of participation might be discovered.

The paper by Professor Blatz stands in sharp contrast to that of Professor Woodworth. He suggests a line of distinction between psychology and sociology to the effect that the former studies the individual whereas the latter studies the group. Roughly this distinction would be acceptable enough if it were clearly understood that there are no groups without individuals and that an isolated

3   New York: Henry Holt & Co., 1922.

individual without some measure of group participation is unknown to human experience. He denies the emergent properties of the behavior of individuals in various types of group situations and asserts that no new motives come into play in crowds, mobs, or other collectivities. (Apparently he recognizes no element of novelty even in such a mechanism as that of circular reaction, which has played so useful a role in the analysis of crowd behavior as undertaken by students of collective action.) Professor Blatz appears to be operating with the dichotomy, long since rejected by the sociologists, of the isolated individual on the one side and the dense physical assemblage of the crowd on the other. It is precisely this simplified version which sociologists have been attempting to correct by pointing out that the social situation is a factor in the determination of individual action in ways far more complicated and subtle than those which come into play in consequence of participation in a crowd.

Having divided individual behavior into two phases—that which represents an adaptation to the physical environment and that which represents an adaptation to the social environment—he claims both of these for the province of psychology and, by implication, leaves sociology out of the picture altogether. The motives which according to him determine an infant's behavior consist of attitudes of approach and withdrawal, the appetites (comprising hunger, thirst, elimination, rest, change, and sex), and the emotions arising in situations for which the individual feels unprepared. These three kinds of need, which he calls cultural, appetitive, and emotional, respectively, are considered basic, presumably because they are common to all individuals and remain operative throughout life. Professor Blatz does not recognize the existence in the infant of any form of behavior which is social in the sense of the manifestation of behavior indicating a social need.[4] He would begin to speak of social desires, though not needs, when the child has developed to a point of perceiving the

4   The distinction which Professor Blatz sets forth between "need" and "desire" requires further clarification. Needs are ordinarily conceived of as the conditions necessary for the survival of the organism, whether they become motives in action or not.

similarity between his own experience and that of others. This behavior, however, is not basic but wholly derived from the fundamental needs outlined above. As a result of the observation of the Dionne quintuplets, he notes no sign of the genesis of a behavior pattern which may clearly be interpreted as social before the age of twelve to eighteen months. At this point there come into play acts and responses to the acts of others which cumulatively mold the social consciousness of the child. In his analysis of the development of social behavior, Professor Blatz might have been aided considerably by the literature dealing with the social genesis of the self, especially the works of Mead and of Cooley. Particularly the work of the former on the distinction between physical and social objects, and that of the latter on the looking-glass self, would have enabled him to carry on his analysis with considerably greater discrimination and penetration than has been possible by the approach he has employed. And yet, despite his disregard of the sociological approach, in his improvisations of a theory to account for the genesis of personality he has to take account of factors which lead him beyond his original premises. Eventually he does recognize the significance of social interaction and the role of common standards in a community in affecting the behavior of the individual. Particularly when he comes to account for the highly differentiated behavior of different individuals who appear to be reacting to the same environment, as is the case with the Dionne quintuplets, he is confronted with the subtle influences of group symbols and differential individual interpretations thereof, which despite his insistence on the adequacy of the psychological approach lead him into the universe of sociological discourse.

Directing his attention to the problems of the individual and society as they appear to the student of child development, Professor Anderson traces the shift in interest from the older theories to the modern research on children's behavior in their group relations. He sees the personality of the child as the product of social interaction. The structuring of social behavior depends upon the initial organization of the individual, the content of the environment to which he is exposed, and the modifications resulting from his observation of the effects of his behavior on others. As the individual becomes incorporated in a social organization, there is a transition from the solitary and parallel play of the infant through the co-operative play of the child to the organized and differentiated social life of the adolescent. The complexity of the products of the social activity of the individual increases cumulatively with maturity. The circle of social attachments widens and becomes more selective with age. The range and effectiveness of the motivations emanating from the group increase correspondingly. Professor Anderson finds that the traditional dichotomies between competition and co-operation, between negativistic and rapport behavior, and between aggression and sympathetic behavior, upon which earlier studies proceeded must be given up in favor of the view that "in the process of socialization seemingly antagonistic tendencies develop together." He suggests that, in view of the striking results of recent research, personality traits, such as dominance and submission, be analyzed in terms of the differentiated roles which children play in the social groups in which they participate. The leading factors operating upon the total makeup of the child and conditioning his responses, according to Professor Anderson, are: (1) the content of the prevailing group behavior patterns; (2) the fluid and changing character of the child's social relationships; (3) the range of personal contacts with others; (4) the richness of materials which the environment permits; and (5) the opportunities for participation in a variety of activities far transcending those afforded by the school curriculum. On the basis of the results obtained in the attempts at experimental modification of social relationships, he concludes that both differentiated individual personalities and group activities must be seen as arising in a context of group relationships, so that the student of child behavior inevitably is led to the analysis of social interaction.

In the attempt to overcome the false dichotomy of individual versus group and the strict departmentalization of the sciences dealing with man in society, Professor Brown projects "field theory," which regards "socio-psychobiology as the basic science of human behavior." "Implicit in field theory is the idea that social behavior depends on the biological nature of the individual as an integral part of groups whose characteristics are intimately connected with cultural phenomena." The Freudian psychoanalysts, by having emphasized the importance of early emotional experiences, and the Marxian sociologists, by having stressed the dependence of social attitudes and behavior on the system of production and the individual's position in it in all cultures, have contributed to our more adequate understanding of these interrelationships. Field theory, Professor Brown believes, will aid us in formulating a systematic attack on the crucial research problems which lie along the lines where sociology, psychology, and biology meet and reveal the implications of their findings for one another.

This approach stems from the same movement and follows in its procedures the one set forth by Professor Lewin, namely, topological psychology, the central concept of which is that of "life-space."[5] He illustrates the fruitfulness of the structural approach by means of the analysis of adolescence. He would shift the focus of investigation from the individual conceived as a separated entity to the situation. This procedure, he holds, might become the "key-technique even for problems of individual psychopathology." But in his case as well as in that of Professor Brown, it should be noted that the soundness of the technique of observation employed has nothing to do with the conceptual apparatus of topological psychology. Nor is it clear just what the method of research would be for dealing with the problems they state, aside from the more or less analogical procedure of translating independently made observations into the language of field theory.[6]

Finding that such terms as "custom," "culture," "fashions,"

5   For an elaboration of this approach see Kurt Lewin, *Principles of Topological Psychology* (New York, 1936) ; and J. F. Brown, *Psychology and the Social Order* (New York, 1906).

6   The concepts of topological psychology appear to be only new names for already observed objects, and the mere changing of names produces no new insights. It does not, in other words, lead to the discovery of any problems additional to those which non-field-theoretical methodology would disclose, and it contributes no additional evidence relevant for the solution of these problems.

"conventions," "traditions," "institutions," "folkways," and "mores" have been used uncritically and inconsistently by various authors, Professor Allport undertakes to single out the central fact of "conformity" which is implicit in all of them and to treat them as variations of "large numbers of people acting under known conditions of their human and nonhuman environment." Conformity, Professor Allport argues, is not an "all-or-none" matter, as he believes students of culture and society have viewed it, although this view may help to locate the problem. Individual differences range widely over a continuum falling in a normal probability distribution. He advances the "J-curve hypothesis of conforming behavior" on the basis of which he proposes to study "custom situations" empirically, the units of which are variables, such as time, space, weight, velocity, etc. In addition to these empirical continua, he proposes to study non-empirical continua, namely, those measuring trends or traits of personality, or those measuring purpose fulfilment. In any field of conformity he would "apply a scale whose steps are variations of behavior which represent successive recognizable degrees of fulfilment of the 'accepted common purpose,' ranging from the prescribed or 'proper' act, which most completely fulfils the purpose to that which gives it the least recognizable amount of fulfilment." In this way he hopes to show in what areas of social life conformity exists, in what way individuals are conforming, how much they conform, what variations of conformity occur, who wishes the mass of people to conform, what conformity means to them, what influence they have, and what conformity means to the people who practice it. While this may give us an operational definition of custom, it is not likely to throw any light upon the process of cultural change or upon the manner in which custom is related to the society that is its bearer, and particularly the motives prompting different individuals in what appears to be the same society and exposed to what is regarded as the same culture to behave differently with reference to the norms prevailing in the differentiated groups in which the individual participates—norms which are neither static, absolute, nor isolated from one another.

Psychoanalysis, according to Dr. French, has a contribution to make to the analysis of social phenomena by viewing social conflict as analogous to psychic conflict. By social conflict, however, he means in general the involvement of large numbers of individuals in psychic conflicts. Consequently, he suggests that just as the therapeutic effect of insight into individual neuroses has been demonstrated by psychoanalysis, so a comparable technique may be employed to deal with conflicting social interests. How this technique is to be developed, however, he does not indicate, aside from stating that in a democracy this technique consists in the freest possible public discussion. Although it has frequently been pointed out by sociologists that there is a relationship between mental conflict and culture conflict, the latter is by no means considered merely a repetition in the mass of the former. Indeed, there is considerable sociological evidence to indicate that psychic conflict and personal disorganization may have as their basic cause the culture conflicts operative in the society.[7] Psychoanalytic literature itself has recently admitted the relationships between culture and neurosis. In her volume on *New Ways in Psychoanalysis,* Dr. Karen Horney, after re-examining the Freudian hypotheses concerning the basic instinctual drives, comes to the conclusion that types of response which hitherto had been imputed exclusively to the organism actually have their source in the culture and that an analysis of the social context in which the individual lives makes intelligible not only his personal motives but the possibilities for their gratification, the frustrations, and the mechanisms of wish fulfilment which characterize his personality.[8]

Dr. Harry Stack Sullivan comes to the problem of the individual and society with a rich clinical experience which might be expected to predispose him to a view which emphasizes the primacy of the organism. It is therefore gratifying to note that the universe of interpersonal relations, which constitutes his central field of interest, is almost identical with the modern sociological

7   Thorsten Sellin, *Culture Conflict and Crime* (Social Research Council Bull. 41 [New York, 1938]).

8   See especially chap. x, "Culture and Neuroses" (New York: W. W. Norton & Co., 1939).

approach. Although as a psychiatrist he would begin the study of his patients with an analysis of their psychobiological states, he regards each personality "as an indeterminate entity some significant characteristics of which may be inferred from the processes that occur in the group of persons—real and fantastic—in which the subject-individual participates." Our social matrix, which many naïvely regard as an undifferentiated relationship affecting all of us in much the same way, turns out upon analysis to consist of a highly differentiated set of universes of interpersonal relations in which different persons participate in various degrees. Although the constellation of social situations in which we are placed may exhibit relatively durable integration in fairly restricted social worlds with settled systems of norms and values, it is only by sensing the personal meanings of the situations and norms to the individual that we can arrive at an understanding of maladjusted personalities. Ordinarily the individual participates in differential but more or less compatible roles in the social world which comprise the orbit of his social life. It is only when these roles are incongruent with the individual's psychobiological traits, or when they markedly conflict, that our interpersonal relations are permeated by insecurity, frustration, and personality problems.

Professor Malinowski, although he approaches the problem of the relation between the individual and the group from the field of cultural anthropology, insists that, in order to avoid the fallacy of the "group mind" and the "collective sensorium," the group must be defended as the assemblage of individuals and that we must begin our analysis with a conception of the individual as a biological reality. On the other hand, the individual, the personality, the self, or the mind, cannot be described adequately except in terms of membership in a group "unless we wish to hug the figment of the individual as a self-contained entity." The satisfaction of bodily needs under conditions of culture—which in the case of human life means under all conditions—reveals the complete dependence of the individual upon the group. Personality turns out to be culturally molded instead of an unadulterated product of physiological processes. In the study of the personality, therefore, we need to take account not merely of the organism and of the world of nature but of the man-made product, the tools, and the cultural value which are the products of group life. In attempting to comprehend the wide variations of personal behavior within the matrix of a culture, we must pay heed not merely to the relationship of the individual to *the* group but to the highly variegated associations in which he participates.

These contributions to the understanding of personality and society, coming as they do from research specialists in various aspects of human behavior, indicate unmistakably the trend toward the recognition of the significance of social interaction as the basic process in the formation both of human nature and of the social order. Though it is desirable and necessary to construe the basic units of analysis differently, the really significant questions that we raise about human behavior cannot be answered by any one of the traditional fields of specialization. If we examine the shortcomings of each segmental approach to this problem, we discover that they are in large measure the result of limited perspectives which have led to distorted conceptions of the factors influencing human behavior when pursued without a recognition of the alternative and complementary understandings made available through other disciplines. It is a sign of scientific progress that the first step in the realistic analysis of the relations between the individual and the group—the transcending of the long-established barriers between the various academically departmentalized fields of interest—is now in the process of realization.

2

CONSENSUS AND MASS

COMMUNICATION

ON SUCH an occasion as one's presidential address it is customary to offer a discourse on one's favorite topic, under unusual conditions of freedom bordering on license. If one is so inclined, he is even permitted to preach a sermon, though it is well to remember that the congregation is free to depart before the benediction.

It is tempting to exhort one's fellows in the scientific world to live up to the great responsibilities which the sorry state of the world might be presumed to devolve upon them. The physical knowledge that threatens to destroy us is obviously not matched by social knowledge requisite to save civilization, and insofar as the future of mankind depends upon such knowledge, we must confess that we do not have enough of it to give.

There may be some among us who feel that we already have the knowledge to prevent disaster but that we lack the power to put that knowledge into effect. Such a claim, however, is a confes-

Reprinted from *Community Life and Social Policy*, ed. Elizabeth Wirth Marvick and Albert J. Reiss, Jr. (Chicago: University of Chicago Press, 1956), pp. 368–91, first published in the *American Sociological Review*, XIII (February, 1948), 1–15. Presidential Address read before the annual meeting of the American Sociological Society, New York City, December 28–30, 1947.

sion that we lack perhaps the most important knowledge that we need, namely, the knowledge to unlock the power requisite to put our existing knowledge usefully to work. The many problems of the present-day social world call for a kind of knowledge comparable to the knowledge of the physical world which led to the atomic bomb, on the one hand, and which promises to lead to the harnessing of atomic energy for peaceful purposes, on the other hand. The great task before us is to discover the ways and means of mobilizing human action to prevent the suicide of civilization in the face of the new physical power which has recently been discovered to make that eventuality at least a threatening possibility. After we have tried our best to obtain such knowledge as can be obtained, there is still time to worry about how to put that knowledge to use in the exercise of power.

Perhaps it is a temperamental trait rather than an orthodox tradition of science to turn in a period of turmoil away from the problems of the world to the problems of science, and, as we customarily say, to take the long view and devote one's self to the building up of a body of knowledge which may or may not be relevant to the problems of life but which satisfies one's intellectual curiosity. It is curious that the reputation of a realist goes to one who never thinks about reality and that the reputation of a social scientist goes to one as far away from the actual problems and operations of society as he can get.

Happy are those who can find this refuge. It is easier and safer, to be sure, to withdraw into the study chamber or the laboratory when the world is on fire, provided the insulation from the world is sufficiently fireproof. It is easier, also, for the physical and biological scientist to find such insulation than it is for the social scientist. This is partly due to the nature of the subject matter and partly due to the traditions of science and scholarship in these fields themselves. The scientific study of social phenomena is not yet institutionalized like the study of physical and biological phenomena. The student of society will be plagued by the difficulties of achieving "objectivity," by the existence of social values, by the competition with common-sense knowledge, by the limits of his freedom and capacity to experiment, and by other serious and peculiar handicaps which trouble the natural scientist less or not at all. But the social scientist, whose very subject matter is the social world, can avoid studying the processes and problems of man in society only by pretending to be something he is not, or by lapsing into such a remote degree of abstraction or triviality as to make the resemblance between what he does and what he professes to be doing purely coincidental.

The favorite topic of the present speaker, you will be surprised to discover, happens to be sociology, which, since it is a broad field and will tax the patience if expounded in detail, calls for some selection. I have chosen to discuss the topic of consensus because I believe it provides both an approach to the central problem of sociology and to the problems of the contemporary world. I regard the study of consensus as the central task of sociology, which is to understand the behavior of men insofar as that behavior is influenced by group life. Because the mark of any society is the capacity of its members to understand one another and to act in concert toward common objectives and under common norms, the analysis of consensus rightly constitutes the focus of sociological investigation. But to discuss the nature of consensus in all kinds of human groups in different cultural settings would be a formidable task. Similarly, an analysis of the conditions conducive to consensus under varying circumstances would be a vast undertaking. My observations will therefore be directed to the conditions under which consensus functions in mass societies as distinguished from more compact, intimate groups, such as the family and other primary associations.

Before exploring the nature and conditions of consensus, it seems appropriate to indicate the salient characteristics of mass societies. As we look back upon previous social aggregations, such as those of the ancient kingdoms or the Roman Empire, we wonder how, given the primitive communications that obtained, such impressive numbers and territories could be held together under a common regime over any considerable span of time. If we discover, however, that these aggregations were not truly societies but were little more than administrative areas, creatures of military domination along the main arteries of communication from some center of power, and that the economic base of their cohesion rested on exploitation of the outlying territories and peoples by the rulers at a center through their representatives who were scattered thinly over the territory, the magnitude of these aggregations does not seem too impressive. Mass societies as we find them today, however, show greater marks of integration. They are aggregations of people who participate to a much greater degree in the common life and, at least in democratic parts of the world, comprise people whose attitudes, sentiments, and opinions have some bearing upon the policies pursued by their governments. In this sense mass societies are a creation of the modern age and are the product of the division of labor, of mass communication, and a more or less democratically achieved consensus.

Since we shall speak of our society as a mass society and of the communication that it involves as mass communication, it behooves us to depict the characteristics of the mass. Its most obvious trait is that it involves great numbers, in contradistinction to the smaller aggregates with which we have become familiar through the study of primitive life and earlier historical forms of human association. Second, and again almost by definition, it consists of aggregates of men widely dispersed over the face of the earth, as distinguished from the compact local groups of former periods. Third, the mass is composed of heterogeneous members in that it includes people living under widely different conditions, under widely varying cultures, coming from diverse strata of society, engaging in different occupations, and hence having different interests, standards of life, and degrees of prestige, power, and influence. Fourth, the mass is an aggregate of anonymous individuals, as may be indicated by the fact that though millions of individuals listening to a radio program, reading a newspaper, or seeing a movie are exposed to the same images, they are not aware of who the fellow-members of the audience are, nor are those who transmit these images certain of the composition of their audience. These anonymous persons who constitute the mass may be, and usually are, of course, aware of their part in a mass, and they make some assumptions as to who their fellow-members are and how many of them there are. They are likewise capable of identifying themselves with their anonymous fellows, who are exposed to the same images, and may even gain some support from the knowledge of their existence. They may even act as if they had their unanimous support, as is illustrated by the slogan "Fifty million Frenchmen can't be wrong" or by the much disputed bandwagon effect resulting from the publication of the results of public opinion polls. Fifth, the mass does not constitute an organized group. It is without recognized leadership and a well-defined program of action. If it acts collectively at all, it does so only as a crowd or as a mob; but since it is dispersed in space, it cannot even move as these elementary social bodies are capable of action, although it may be far from constituting, as Carlyle thought, "an inert lump." Sixth, the mass has no common customs or traditions, no institutions, and no rules governing the action of the individuals. Hence it is open to suggestions, and its behavior, to a greater degree than that of organized bodies, is capricious and unpredictable. Finally, the mass consists of unattached individuals or, at best, individuals who for the time being behave not as members of a group, playing specific roles representative of their position in that group, but rather as discrete entities. In modern urban industrial society our membership in each of the multiple organizations to which we belong represents our interests only in some limited aspect of our total personal life. There is no group which even remotely professes to speak for us in our total capacity as men or in all the roles that we play. Although through our membership in these organized groups we become articulate, contribute to the molding of public opinion, and participate more or less actively in the determination of social policies, there remains for all of us a quite considerable range of ideas and ideals which are subject to manipulation from the outside and in reference to which there is no appreciable reciprocal interaction between ourselves and others similarly situated. It is this area of life which furnishes the opportunity for others to entrap us or to lead us toward goals with the formulation of which we have had little or nothing whatever to do. All of us are in some respects characterized in our conduct by mass behavior.

The fragmentation of human interests in heterogeneous, complex modern societies is so far advanced that, as Robert E. Park put it, "What a man belongs to constitutes most of his life career and all of his obituary." The trend in group organization is not merely toward the multiplication and diversification of organizations but also toward bodies of enormously increased size. We have witnessed in recent decades the development of numerous giant organizations in business and industry, in labor, in the professions, in religion, in government, and in social life which seem to dominate our existence and to characterize our civilization.

Many of these organizations have become so colossal that they themselves approximate masses. The sense of belonging and of participation which smaller and more compactly organized groups are able to generate is largely frustrated by the very size of the typical organizations of our time. This is perhaps a price we must be willing to pay for living in an interdependent and technologically advanced world. But it should also constitute a major challenge to the analytical skill and the inventive imagination of social scientists, especially sociologists; for it is to a large extent upon the ability to maintain effective contact between the members and two-way communication between the leaders and the membership of these giant structures that the future of democracy rests.

The problem is complicated by the fact that this mass democratic society, enormous in scope and intricate in structure, presents a dynamic equilibrium in which one of the principal conditions of effective collective action is the accuracy and speed with which the shifting interests and attitudes of great masses of men, whether organized or unorganized, can be ascertained and brought to bear upon the determination of policy.

Another significant feature of modern mass society, and especially of mass democracies, is the instability of the interests and motives of the members, with correspondingly frequent changes in leadership and consequent uncertainty as to the locus of decisive power at any one juncture of events. If the spokesmen in any group are to know for whom they are speaking, they must be able to assess how strong or enduring the interests are that they profess to represent and whether, indeed, the groups for which they speak are at all interested in the issue.

Mass societies, furthermore, involve vast concentrations of power and authority and complicated machinery of administration. Perhaps the most urgent need that goes unmet in such a society is the capacity for prompt decisions in the face of recurrent crises. The fact that concerted action in such societies, if they are to remain democratic, must take into consideration the shifting constellation of public opinion imposes upon those who guide its destinies a responsibility which can only be met by the utilization of all the relevant sources of knowledge and the perfection of very much more advanced techniques than we now seem to possess.

When a social philosopher of the previous generation, Herbert Spencer, undertook to compare human society with the biological organism, he thought he had found that the one thing which human society lacked to make it truly comparable to a biological organism was a social sensorium which would serve as the equivalent of the central nervous system and "the mind" in the individual organism. Whatever we may think about such analogies, this alleged lack of a social mind to go with the social body is the deficiency that we must supply if organized social life, on the scale on which we must now live it, is to endure. The only reasonable equivalent of "mind" in the individual organism that we can think of as an essential in the social organism can be supplied through consensus.

A thoughtful student, Edward Sapir, has described society as "a highly intricate network of partial or complete understandings between the members of organizational units." Consensus is the sign that such partial or complete understanding has been reached on a number of issues confronting the members of a group that it is entitled to be called a society. It implies that a measure of agreement has been reached. The agreement, however, is neither imposed by coercion nor fixed by custom so as no longer to be subject to discussion. It is always partial and developing and has constantly to be won. It results from the interpenetration of views based upon mutual consent and upon feeling as well as thinking together.

If men of diverse experiences and interests are to have ideas and ideals in common, they must have the ability to communicate. It is precisely here, however, that we encounter a paradox. In order to communicate effectively with one another we must have common knowledge, but in a mass society it is through communication that we must obtain this common body of knowledge. The resolution of this paradox seems to lie in the possibility that though men of diverse backgrounds, experiences, and interests are incapable of communicating with and understanding one another at first, much less arriving at agreement, they must initially be content to grope haltingly for such elementary understandings as can be supplied on the basis of the scanty and superficial common experiences that even the most casual and superficial contact supplies. They must and do live in the hope that as experience is widened and deepened effective communication will improve apace.

We assume human beings the world over are sufficiently alike in their basic nature and their life careers that even the most alien groups in contact with one another, no matter how indirectly and remotely, will have some elementary capacity to put themselves in the place of the other, that the common understanding that comes through communication will have a cumulative effect, and that every step toward understanding becomes the basis for a still broader and deeper basis of understanding.

Modern society exhibits two major aspects. On the one hand, it consists of organized groups, ranging from informally constituted intimate groups to highly formalized organizations such as the modern corporation, the union, the church, and the state. On the other hand, there are detached masses held together, if at all, by the mass media of communication. The analysis of consensus must necessarily take account of these phases.

On every level of social life calling for concerted action, whether it be that of organized groups or the mass, we need a degree of consensus capable of mobilizing the energies of the members or at least of neutralizing their opposition or apathy. Wherever and whenever we seek to enlist the uncoerced cooperation and participation of numbers of diverse men in the pursuit of a common cause, "We need," as John Dewey has said, "one world of intelligence and understanding, if we are to obtain one world in other forms of human activity."[1]

Society has developed many ways of inducing consent. We may first point to the kind of acquiescence induced by superior force. Power is not equally distributed among the members of most societies, and there probably is no society where it is so equally distributed that all the members are equally capable of exerting their will upon the others. In its extreme form this inequality of power and influence is exemplified by dictatorship. But even in a dictatorship, though the ultimate monopoly of violence rests with the dictator, the members of the society count for something, and the dictator does not enjoy unlimited opportunity to coerce his subjects. Although, for instance, in the case of the present Soviet regime we are convinced of the actuality of its dictatorial character, we recognize that there are certain limits beyond which the dictators cannot go and that if the conditions of life which they can provide for their people and the hopes that they can hold out to them fall below a certain minimum, there will be rebellion and counter-revolution. Similarly, we act, at least with reference to the Voice of America broadcasts to the Soviet people, as if even their public opinion were of some importance.

Though social cohesion in a dictatorship rests ultimately upon force and violence, it need not at all times exercise this force and violence brutally and arbitrarily. It can be held in reserve for occasions when it is absolutely necessary, and indeed the wise dictator knows this principle of prudence in the exercise of his unquestioned power. Suppression may be the first or last stage in the life cycle. It can, for instance, be translated into law, however authoritarian and arbitrary its character, and into a religious control resting upon fear. This attenuated form of the exercise of force has been the practice at least of modern dictators ever since Machiavelli offered his counsel to the dictators of his day. It should be noted, of course, that people may never know

<hr />

[1]   John Dewey, "Liberating the Social Scientist: A Plea To Unshackle the Study of Man," *Commentary*, IV, No. 4 (October, 1947), 382.

that they are exploited and oppressed until they see their own humble status juxtaposed to an actual condition of relative freedom and opportunity that exists in some other society with which they are in contact, or unless they can recall some previous condition of existence in which these forms of oppression did not prevail, or unless, finally, there is held out to them some ideal condition to which they consider themselves entitled. The idea of "natural rights" is an example of injecting into the minds of men an ideology which serves as an ideal against which they can measure their actual condition, and the experience with this ideology in recent times shows that it has made dictatorship of any kind untenable in the long run. The notion of the inalienable rights of man and of the dignity of the human personality is at work in increasing measure over all the world to challenge autocratic rule in every realm of human life.

Closely related to the type of basis of consensus provided by force and authority is the consensus that rests upon a common identification with great heroes or leaders, of which the charismatic leader depicted by Max Weber is perhaps the most suitable example. There are many roads that lead to leadership, although they are not the same roads in all societies. Force and ruthlessness, law and authority, the sacred sanctions of religion or of tradition, the wisdom of personality of the leader himself, or even the belief in his wisdom or personal qualities, separately or in combination, may establish a man or a group in a position of leadership which can evoke consensus on the part of the followers. Whatever these original sources are, they may be reinforced by propaganda and education and thus come to have a symbolic significance far out of proportion to the original sources.

Just as leaders can serve as instruments for building consensus, so ideas and ideals and the symbols with which they become identified can create cohesion in the group. The Cross and the Crescent, the Stars and Stripes, and the Hammer and Sickle, the Magna Carta, the Declaration of Independence, and the Four Freedoms, not to speak of the popular stereotypes and the slogans which are the stock-in-trade of so much of our present-day propaganda and public relations, are and will continue to be potential forces for creating and maintaining consensus. The instrumentalities of mass communication lend themselves particularly well to the dissemination of these symbols on a scale hitherto thought impossible. We happen to live in a world in which, despite barriers of technology and of politics, the whole human race becomes potentially exposed to the same symbols. They are weapons of offense and of defense, and they are bonds of union or of discord, depending upon the purposes which those who use them have in mind.

Sociologists have long been accustomed to analyze in particular one of the bases of consensus, namely, the consensus that derives from the social heritage of a people—from a common culture, from a common history and set of traditions, from the mores—which can make anything seem right, true, good, beautiful, and possible. It is this basis of common social life as patterned by these traditions that makes it possible in the last analysis for any group to think of itself and to act as a society, to regard itself as a "we" group and to counterpose this "we" experience to all that is alien. The extent to which force and authority, law, religious sanction and leadership, propaganda and education, and the apparatus of symbols can be used effectively depends in large part upon this substratum of a common basis of knowledge, belief, and standards molded by tradition and reinforced by the ongoing social life which embodies that tradition.

The fact that the instrumentalities of mass communication operate in situations already prepared for them may lead to the mistaken impression that they or the content and symbols which they disseminate do the trick. It is rather the consensual basis that already exists in society which lends to mass communication its effectiveness. A number of changes, however, since the days of the primitive local and isolated group life of our ancestors have profoundly affected the force of tradition. The movements of population and the contact between people from the ends of the earth, the opening of world markets, and the spread of modern technology, the growth of cities, the operation of mass media of communication, the increasing literacy of the masses of people over all the world, have combined to disintegrate local cohesion and to bring hitherto disparate and parochial cultures into contact with each other. Out of this ferment has come the disenchantment of absolute faiths which expresses itself in the secular outlook of modern man.

One characteristic of this secularism is the increasing skepticism toward all dogmas and ideologies. Reluctant to accept things on the old authority and often unable to sustain a reasoned belief in its place, the secular man cultivates his personal tastes and elevates his right to choose as a faith in itself.

Another feature of this secularism is the change from naïveté to sophistication. One of the prime virtues on which the modern man prides himself is that he will not be taken in by anybody; that he resists those who offer him a pig-in-a-poke; that he suspects the motives of the salesman of goods or of ideas; that he wishes to see the evidence upon which the appeal rests; and that he claims the right to exercise independent judgment on the validity of that evidence. This has in turn led to a perfection of the means of persuasion through the invention of ways of making the irrational appear rational and of subtle means for making people interested in things that may not be to their interest. It has led to an enormous interest in discovering through scientific means what the interests, prejudices, and predilections of men are and how they can be manipulated by appropriate appeals.

This secularism carries with it the disintegration of unitary faiths and doctrines, on the one hand, and their blending into new syncretisms which seek to combine a variety of hitherto incongruous elements in such a way as to attract the greatest number of followers. The symbols and slogans that formerly were characteristic of one party are mingled with those of others in order to woo more effectively the greatest number of adherents. Ideas and ideals that formerly stood for one set of objectives come to be perverted and diluted until they can comprise objectives which formerly seemed incongruous and until it seems that the unambiguous labels under which men formerly united not only no longer differentiate parties but actually can come to have the most contradictory content in order to appeal to all parties.

In addition to force and authority, leadership and personal prestige, ideas, ideals and the symbols into which they are incorporated, and social traditions, we must consider an aspect of the basis of consensus which, though it overlaps with others, is nevertheless so distinctive of our society as to require separate treatment. I refer to public opinion. This, of course, is not an independent force but is an aspect of every ongoing society.

Public opinion is formed in the course of living, acting, and making decisions on issues. It is precipitated through the clash of representative ideas reflecting more or less faithfully the positions confronting the respective groups that compose the society. Our society and others comparable to it are composed of varieties of constituent groups, occupational and economic, racial and ethnic and religious. Each of these groups articulates its own interests, has its own powers, leadership, creed, political and corporate organization.

Not all members of each group have an equal share of influence, nor is the strength of each group determined solely by the size of its membership. These groups are not loose aggregations of men, and it is not necessary for all members of each group to share the official view of the group to which they give their adherence. There will be some who are indifferent or even hostile to what the group stands for, but that they do not rebel can clearly be seen in our present-day political parties or major economic or religious organizations. The role which individuals play is not determined alone by their age, sex, race, occupation, economic or educational status, although these may significantly influence the character and policies of the groups to which the individuals belong. What counts, rather, is their power, prestige, strategic position, their resources, their articulateness, the effectiveness of their organization and leadership. Within the group those who make the decisions and who exercise the dominant influence are subjected to pressures from all sides and radiate influence upon their group. The old saying, "I am your leader;

therefore I must follow you," suggests the extent to which independent judgment is limited even among the leaders. The decisive part of public opinion, then, is the organization of views on issues that exercise an impact upon those who are in a position to make decisions.

The characteristic feature of public opinion in our society lies both in the fact that so many human beings are affiliated with a variety of organized groups, each of which represents only a segment of their interest, and that another large proportion of our fellow men is unattached to any stable group, in that sense constituting unorganized masses, and thereby leave the decision-making to those who are organized and can exercise their corporate power.

In modern democracies, and to some extent in all inclusive societies on the scale of modern states, men exercise their influence and voice their aspirations through delegated powers, operating through functionaries and leaders, through lobbies, party organizations, religious denominations, and a variety of other organized groups. This seems to be the characteristic way of representative democratic government. In the course of the flow of communication the interests and grievances, the sentiments, attitudes, and opinions of the people at the bottom may become grossly distorted, and the people at the top may find themselves so remote from their constituents that they may either be ignorant of their actual feelings or may seriously misinterpret the fragmentary knowledge that they do have. It is at this point that public opinion studies may prove significant. We have already witnessed in the United States the rise of what might be called "government by Western Union," which reminds one of the story of the lady who went to the telegraph office and said, "I should like to send a telegram to my Congressman to use his own judgment."

The various bases upon which consensus rests are, of course, not unrelated to the ways in which consensus is reached. Of these only some of the principal channels may be alluded to here: persuasion, discussion, debate, education, negotiation, parliamentary procedure, diplomacy, bargaining, adjudication, contractual relations, and compromise are all means for arriving at a sufficient degree of agreement to make the ongoing life of society, despite differences in interests, possible. Ultimately, consent in the face of differences comes down to a contrast between force and fraud, on the one hand, and persuasion and rational agreement, on the other hand. In some cases, however, the march of events may bring agreement where previously none was possible. If consent does not precede action, there is still a chance to obtain consent in the course of action itself. The submission that comes with coercion, it should be noted, does not truly give us consensus. It results rather in what the Nazis called *Gleichschaltung.*

As over against the use of violence and fraud to obtain pseudo-consensus, which even in authoritarian regimes is a precarious basis of power and social solidarity, democracies must resort to the art of compromise which results in agreements more or less rationally arrived at—agreements the terms of which neither party wants but at the same time cannot refuse to accept. Whereas authoritarianism gives us a seeming unanimity, which has been described as the unanimity of the graveyard, democracies rest upon the ultimate agreement to disagree, which is tolerance of a divergent view. Even democracies, when they are in a hurry or when they are threatened by imminent danger, may sometimes have to resort to the shortcut of coercion, as is typical of the military interludes in democratic history; whereas autocracies may be able to afford at times to allow freedom in considerable areas of living which do not threaten the basis of autocratic power. In general, however, we may say that where consensus exists, coercion is unnecessary and where continuous coercion must be resorted to, it is a sign that the regime is either in its initial stages or nearing its end. If might is not right, then might has at any rate to cloak itself in the mantle of rightness to persist, for no authoritarian government can ultimately determine the thinking of people, including what the people think of those who govern them.

The more intelligent and earnest people are, the less likely it is that they will agree on all subjects. Coercion can achieve spurious agreement on all issues, but consent can be obtained only provisionally and perhaps only on those issues which do not threaten too deeply the interests, the ideas, and ideals of the heterodox. We seem to have worked out quite pragmatically in our democratic society the limits beyond which we are reluctant to push the struggle for agreement. We have agreed that uniformity is undesirable. We have, for instance, through the Bill of Rights, exempted religion from the sphere of necessary agreement, and we have enlarged the area of political freedom up to a "clear and present danger" line.

We have recognized moreover that it is not necessary to obtain agreement on everything in order to operate as an effectively functioning society. There is embodied in our sense of good taste a sensitiveness to our differences, some of which it is not correct to translate into issues for public debate and discussion. We are willing, frequently, to let our silence count as consent on a good many issues which we think are either too trivial or too delicate to push the point. And above all, we have developed patience to endure heresies and sufferance to endure transitory annoyance in the hope that minorities can, under freedom, develop themselves into majorities; we have come to believe that for most purposes of life it is more economical, though perhaps less interesting, to count noses than to break heads.

But modern societies, whether they are autocratic or democratic, have learned in the face of their size and complexity and their internal heterogeneity that the engineering of public consent is one of the great arts to be cultivated. Democracies, as distinguished from autocracies, seem to have taken the longer view by recognizing, as did Machiavelli, that pseudo-consensus achieved by force cannot long endure. He said: "It cannot be called talent to slay fellow citizens, to deceive friends, to be without faith, without mercy, without religion; such methods may gain empire but not glory." Democracies proceed on the assumption that even if the contending parties fight it out violently there is no assurance that the problem over which they fought won't remain after the stronger has suppressed the weaker. Even military conquest uses the technique of undermining the will of the enemy, and nowadays after enemies have surrendered, we send public opinion pollsters among them to learn how best to govern them. The believers in the democratic principle have learned not to be impatient in the process of reaching agreement; they have learned that society can go on as long as we agree not to settle our disagreements by resort to force. They have had to learn that society can remain democratic only as long as we recognize and respect that essential residue, the freedom and dignity of every personality, which is no less important than it was before merely because it seems to have become a cliché. They have come to know also, as a contemporary philosopher has put it, that "lacking the consensus a legal crime may be a social virtue and religious heresy a moral duty."

Consensus in mass democracies, therefore, is not so much agreement on all issues or even on the most essential substantive issues among all the members of society as it is the established habit of intercommunication, of discussion, debate, negotiation and compromise, and the toleration of heresies, or even of indifference, up to the point of "clear and present danger" which threatens the life of the society itself. Rather than resting upon unanimity, it rests upon a sense of group identification and participation in the life of a society, upon the willingness to allow our representatives to speak for us even though they do not always faithfully represent our views, if indeed we have any views at all on many of the issues under discussion, and upon our disposition to fit ourselves into a program that our group has adopted and to acquiesce in group decisions unless the matter is fundamentally incompatible with our interests and integrity.

Consensus is supported and maintained not merely by the ties of interdependence and by a common cultural base, by a set of institutions embodying the settled traditions of the people, and the norms and standards that they imply and impose—not merely by the living together and dealing with one another—but also, and not least important, by the continuing currents of mass communication, which in turn rest for their meaningfulness and effectiveness upon the pre-existence of some sort of society, which hold that society together and mobilize it for continuous concerted action.

To the traditional ways of communication—rumor, gossip, personal contact, pulpit, school, and forum—we have added in our generation the mass media of communication, consisting of the radio, the motion picture, and the press. These new media represent giant enterprises dependent upon, and designed to reach, a mass audience. By virtue of the fact that they are dependent upon mass patronage, these media transcend the peculiar interests and preoccupations of the special and segmental organized groups and direct their appeal to the mass. To reach their mass audiences they are constantly tempted to reduce their content, whether it be that of entertainment, enlightenment, or appeal to action, to the lowest common denominator, to what is believed will interest the greatest number, if not everybody. Since these mass media are so often tied to a mass market for their sustenance, they tend furthermore to be as near everything to everybody and hence nothing to anybody as it is possible to be.

Those who manage the mass communication enterprises have, of course, also some incentives to counteract this leveling influence of the mass audience by appeals to the tastes and interests of special groups. The "third program" of the British Broadcasting Corporation is an experiment in bringing high cultural values to a selected audience and in educating a wider audience to them.

It is these mass media, however, upon which the human race depends to hold it together. Mass communication is rapidly becoming, if it is not already, the main framework of the web of social life. In retrospect we can see how shrewd Hitler and his cohorts were in recognizing that in these instrumentalities they controlled the principal means for moving great masses of men into at least temporary adherence to their objectives and in using them for their own purpose. That they almost succeeded and that the rest of the world had to pay a terrible price in blood and treasure at the last moment to avert their domination might serve as a warning to those who minimize the importance of mass communication. It might remind them that we live in an era when the control over these media constitutes perhaps the most important source of power in the social universe. It is interesting to note that modern dictators who espouse the doctrine of the elite and who profess to hold the masses in great contempt have shown themselves frequently to be more sensitive to the whims of the mass than have some leaders of democratic societies. Mass media can be used to manipulate and exploit existing situations and opportunities.

Recent investigations by polling and interview techniques have revealed that despite the dense blanketing of our country with informal educational and propaganda appeals, despite the enormous ramification of organized groups which discuss and disseminate knowledge on issues of current importance, there are vast areas of ignorance on some of the most important issues confronting our society. The National Opinion Research Center recently found that less than half of the people polled had any reasonably clear meaning of what a tariff is. Other investigations have shown that on even the most central public issues of our time only a small fraction of our people have sufficient understanding to act intelligently. This suggests that the state of public opinion as an aspect of consensus in a society such as ours calls for an unrelenting effort for popular education and for access to reliable sources of information. This does not mean that everybody must be equally well informed on such questions as the tariff, but it does suggest the need for general education to enable the citizen to participate more intelligently and critically in general public discussion as well as to equip him to act with greater knowledge and responsibility in the special interest groups with which he is identified.

If we consider, in addition to the vast areas of ignorance, the astonishing degree of apathy and indifference that prevails concerning even the issues of transcendent importance, it becomes clear why mass democracies so often appear incapable of competing effectually with authoritarian societies. Here, again, the price we must pay for the survival of a way of life that we cherish calls for the expenditure of an immensely greater share of our resources than thus far we have been willing to devote to information and education. This calls for continual effort to dispel areas of ignorance and areas of indifference which may in part be based upon ignorance. The content of what is to be communicated must therefore be adapted to the audience to which it is addressed, and there must be awareness that we may be speaking over the heads of people or that the symbols that we use may mean entirely different things to others than they do to us. The predominance of the entertainment feature, particularly in such media as radio and motion picture, does not preclude the appeal to intelligence. It suggests rather that information and education services to be effective must also be interesting.

Communication, as it is carried on largely through verbal intercourse, can be fortified by a body of common experiences shared by the many and can be dramatized through art and literature and other means for vivifying ideas and ideals, in order to achieve a sounder basis of common understanding. In the world of science we come about as near to a world society as in any phase of human life, and this world-wide scope of communication which science exemplifies might well serve as a model to be approximated in other realms of human experience; for science, including perhaps even social science and philosophic scholarship, has proved its power to surmount local, national, sectarian, and class barriers and even to infiltrate through the obstacles of official censorship. The same appears to be true of art.

There has been much discussion recently, more with reference to the radio and motion picture than to the older medium of the press, concerning the concentration of control over these mass media of communication. The fact that the media of communication tend toward monopolistic control, as is evidenced by the building up of industrial empires in this field of enterprise, has serious implications for mass democracy. The concentration of such power in a few hands—whether through press associations, newspaper columns, syndicates, radio networks, or motion-picture combines—may create great imbalance in the presentation of divergent, especially minority, views. It may result in censorship no less real for being unofficial and may threaten the free and universal access to the factual knowledge and balanced interpretation which underlie intelligent decision.

In a society dominated by centers of unquestioned power and authority reinforced by sacred traditions and rituals and capable of eliciting unquestioning loyalty to its norms and purposes, such mass communication devices would not constitute a serious problem. They would reinforce but would not greatly alter the social structure. But in a society where all men irrespective of race, creed, origin, and status claim and are to be granted an increasing share of participation in the common life and in the making of common decisions, the control of these media of mass communication constitutes a central problem. If it is consensus that makes an aggregate of men into a society, and if consensus is increasingly at the mercy of the functioning of the mass communication agencies as it is in a democratic world, then the control over these instrumentalities becomes one of the principal sources of political, economic, and social power. The harnessing of this power is an infinitely more complex and vital problem than any previous challenge that the human race has had to meet.

In mass communication we have unlocked a new social force of as yet incalculable magnitude. In comparison with all previous social means for building or destroying the world this new force looms as a gigantic instrument of infinite possibilities for good or evil. It has the power to build loyalties, to undermine them, and thus by furthering or hindering consensus to affect all other sources of power. By giving people access to alternative views mass communication does of course open the door to the disintegration of all existing social solidarities, while it creates new ones. It is of the first importance, therefore, that we understand its nature, its possibilities, its limits, and the means of harnessing it to human purposes.

I should like to allude to the problems of consensus as they arise in some of the more crucial spheres of human interaction in contemporary society. The first of these is the sphere of racial and cultural relations, the second is the field of industrial relations, and the third is the area of international relations. I do not mean to suggest that these are the only areas where we face the problems of consensus. I use them merely for illustrative purposes, recognizing that the same problems are also found in family relations, in informal associations, in local community life, and in the operations of government. These three, however, seem to reflect the most characteristic features of mass communication as it impinges upon consensus in modern mass democracies such as our own.

The spread of industrialism and of capitalism with its world markets and its free workers has given rise among other institutions to giant corporations and giant unions involving great concentrations of power. The competition and conflicting interests within and between these organizations affect every aspect of social life and determine the level of living and the utilization of the resources of all society. Management and unions, aware of the crucial influence of public opinion upon their relative positions, have not been slow to utilize the instruments of mass communication, both internally and in relation to one another, and in the effort to mold the attitudes and to affect the decisions of society. Insofar as these decisions involve national policies, the effort of each side has been directed to rallying support for itself by molding the attitudes and opinions of the larger public.

The relationship between conflicting groups such as these illustrates the significance of consensus within the group for the capacity of each to deal with its opponent. From the standpoint of the larger society the need for a more inclusive consensus involving both of these constellations is indispensable for the maintenance of industrial peace. Propaganda appeals directed toward the larger public, toward government, and toward organized bodies in society are among the indispensable elements in the strategy of collective bargaining, arbitration, labor legislation, and the conduct of strikes. The means of mass communication play no less significant a role in the maintenance of mass production and mass markets.

The rise of self-conscious racial and cultural minorities, which has proceeded parallel to the spread of the ideal of equality and the institutions of mass democracy through ever larger areas of the world, has accentuated the problems of racial and cultural relations. The contrast between contemporary society and primitive and earlier historical societies with respect to the contact between diverse racial and cultural groups is startling. Whereas everyone in a primitive, ancient, and medieval society had a more or less fixed place in the social structure, depending to a large extent upon the character and position of his ancestors, today all of us are men on the move and on the make, and all of us by transcending the cultural bounds of our narrower society become to some extent marginal men. More and more the relations of life that were formerly settled by sacred tradition and custom become subjects of discussion, debate, negotiation, and overt conflict. Many of the problems affecting our national solidarity through our loyalties rest for their orderly adjustment upon the achievement of consensus across the lines of the diverse races and cultures of which America is comprised. The great obstacles encountered by those who attempted to achieve in the face of prejudice and discrimination a national solidarity sufficient to see our nation through the recent war should recall to all of us the reality of the existence of minorities in our midst. If the experiment of America shows anything, it shows that, despite the many setbacks which the democratic ideal and practice have suffered, we are determined to achieve consensus and have found the road toward it through the idea of cultural pluralism, which is another expression for the toleration of differences.

Nowhere do the problems of racial and cultural relations present themselves more dramatically than they do in our great cities, where the people of varying stocks and cultures live in dense physical concentration. Whereas in an earlier society it was unusual to meet a stranger, under the conditions of life in great cities it is an equal rarity to meet someone who is familiar. Although our faces may still light up when in the crowds of the great cities we see a friend, we have nevertheless learned to live with people of diverse background and character to a degree sufficient at least to achieve the requirements of a fairly orderly, productive, and peaceful society.

What is true of self-conscious minorities, impelled by the ideal of the equality of man in our own communities and in our own nation, is increasingly true of the world at large. The so-called backward peoples are being brought within the orbit of a world society resting upon a world consensus. The numerous organized groups and movements among dominant and minority groups alike, using the instruments of mass communication to bring their ideas before a world public, are increasingly evident.

People who are not versed in the language of sociologists and in the serious subjects with which they are preoccupied must ask why it is that sociologists who claim as their vocation the study of social interaction have paid so little attention to interaction on the grandest scale of all, namely, the interaction between national states and what we call international relations, for in this sphere is exemplified the operation of consensus upon which the future of mankind depends.

We have been making some progress in the building of world consensus. We do have a fairly general recognition of economic interdependence on a world scale. We have a great deal more of traffic across the bounds of nations and of continents than the world has ever seen before. We have even some incipient international institutions whose strength is being tested by the increasing tensions of an emerging single world in which we have contacts and conflicts of interest and of ideas with people of whom we were formerly oblivious. We even can see some semblance of emerging world loyalties which makes the expression "world citizenship" sound less utopian than it did before. The instruments of mass communication, particularly the radio and, it seems soon, television combining the faithful transmission of the voice with that of the visual image of the human face and gesture, are particularly well suited to supply the means for the furtherance of understanding across the borders of sovereign states.

As long as we do not have a monopoly of power to coerce all the other nations and peoples of the earth into our way of life, the only road we can travel is that of continued negotiation, persuasion, and compromise. We should probably, even if we had the power of coercion, not be able to use it on others without destroying the very values we sought to strengthen.

If our ways of thought and conception of freedom and democracy, our system of economy, and our political and social ideals seem to be, as I am sure they seem to many, irreconcilable with those of the only other remaining power constellation in the world, it is well to recall that there was a time when Catholics and

Protestants felt very passionately that they could not live in peace in the same state. Time has fortunately proved them wrong. There have been other conflicts in the history of man which seemed at the time equally irresolvable. The uncomfortable but at the same time reassuring fact, however, is that today in this shrunken world there are more effective ways of interfering with the internal life of any society by those without through the instrumentalities of mass communication, which are no respecters of boundaries and which find ways of surmounting all barriers. What is more, these products of mass communication have a way of reaching the great inert masses of the world, for making them restless and mobilizing them for action, or at least for making the dominant groups in their respective societies more responsive to their pressure.

Mass communication will not, of course, by itself produce the minimum of world consensus requisite for peace and world society. But it does not operate by itself. It operates through, and in conjunction with, existing and emerging institutions in a climate of opinion and ultimately through, and upon, human beings. There are other things in the world besides mass communication, but these other things, some of which I have indicated, are tied increasingly to mass communication and through this tie give it its strategic significance.

The media of mass communication, like all the technological instruments that man has invented, are themselves neutral. They can be used to instil a fighting faith or the will to reconciliation. At any rate, the relationship that will allow the fullest use of the world's resources to meet human needs under freedom, order, and peace calls today for nothing less than the building of a world consensus, for a social-psychological integration of the human race commensurate with the interdependent far-flung and rich material resources and human energies of the world.

In mobilizing the instrumentalities of mass communication for the building of that consensus, we cannot fail to remind ourselves that along with the perfection of these means of human intercourse science has also perfected unprecedented means of mass destruction. But in the case of the instruments of mass communication and of atomic energy, the inventors of the instruments do not dictate the uses to which they shall be put. As a contemporary historian recently put it: "If our characteristic Western gift [by which he refers to technology] proves to have been a blessing for mankind, it will be a great blessing; and, if a curse, a great curse. If things go well, the epitaph of history on the Franks [by which he means us] may run: 'Here lie the technicians, who united mankind'; and if things go badly: 'Here lie the technicians, who exterminated the human race.' "[2] The author of these remarks fails to point out that there may not be anybody left to carve that epitaph.

If we are uneasy today, it is not because of these products of science but because of what men may do with these products of human ingenuity. There is a frightful peril in delay, and the realization of this peril is rapidly leading to intellectual paralysis instead of greater intellectual exertion. The atomic bomb will not, we are told, yield to a physical defense or a counter-weapon. The only defense we have is social—the creation of world consensus. Since the mass media of communications are capable of providing the picture of social reality, the symbolic framework of thought and fantasy, and the incentives for human action on an enormous scale, the knowledge of their effective use should become the most important quest of social science, particularly of sociology. The circumstances under which we live do not any longer allow the saints to sit in their ivory tower while burly sinners rule the world.

I hereby extend a cordial invitation to my fellow sociologists, and such other social scientists, including the statisticians, who care to join us, to return to the subject matter for the cultivation of which society sustains us, though let it be admitted, on a none too luxurious level. That subject matter is the life of man in society, and the heart of that subject matter today is the understanding of the processes through which consensus on a world scale is created. Unless we solve that problem, and solve it in a reasonably satisfactory way soon, there will be no opportunity to work at any of the others on which our minds or our hearts are set.

2   Arnold Toynbee, "Technology: Distinguishing Mark of the West," *Listener* (November 20, 1947), p. 895.

3

IDEOLOGICAL ASPECTS OF SOCIAL

DISORGANIZATION

The Ideological Element in Social Problems

THE NOTION that ideologies play an important part in contemporary social life seems to have penetrated into the sphere of popular discourse. Today even the newspapers occasionally refer to "ideologies" when they wish to allude to a complex of ideas, a body of doctrines, the programs of movements, the platforms of parties—in fact, to any creed or theory that takes on an intellectual and rationalized form. It would be difficult to imagine a single social problem of which the analysis and proposed solution did not reckon ideological factors. They are an elusive but significant part of our contemporary social landscape. They serve as landmarks which help us to find our way in what otherwise would be a chaotic social world by providing us with guidance in defining and evaluating situations. Ideologies enable us to identify ourselves with social movements and groups which offer interpretations and solutions of problems that could rarely be undertaken by each individual independently. They aid us in

Reprinted from *Community Life and Social Policy*, ed. Elizabeth Wirth Marvick and Albert J. Reiss, Jr. (Chicago: University of Chicago Press, 1956), pp. 192–205, first published in the *American Sociological Review*, V (August, 1910), 472–82.

reducing excessive individuation and indifference in respect to social problems by furnishing us with goals by which more or less articulate groups become integrated.

While they help us to get our bearings and to sustain our capacity for collective action, it must be recognized that much of our confusion and indecision is in part attributable to the wide variety of ideologies to which we are exposed and to the intermixture of conflicting ideological elements that direct the attention and court the loyalties of the several members of the society. A further confusion is introduced by the fact that the beliefs and creeds which men profess do not always correspond to the principles—if any—which find expression in their actual conduct. Consequently, in the world of action as well as in social science, ideologies are often referred to as *mere* ideologies, as if they were irrelevant epiphenomena having no substantial roots in and relations to the realities of existence. It is the object of this paper to elaborate the proposition that our contemporary social problems cannot be adequately treated and that the situations to which they refer cannot be understood unless one takes due account of the role of ideological involvements.

There is a widespread belief that the problems of maladjustment of men to one another and to the world in which they live arise out of the nature of men or of things. Despite the work of a long line of social scientists who have indicated that the situations we call social problems are problematical only because they represent deviations from socially accepted norms and expectations, there is substantial evidence to indicate that even some contemporary sociologists continue to deal with social problems as if they did not involve evaluational elements.

Value Systems and Social Disorganization

Reference to a society as "disorganized" implies some criteria of disorganization and conversely some marks by which an organized society may be identified. There is no society without an ethos, i.e., without shared values, objectives, preferences, and the well-founded anticipation of the members that all the others recognize the rules of the society and will abide by them.

The concept of social disorganization thus has a normative basis. A shrewd observer, De Tocqueville, wrote a century ago: "A society can exist only when a great number of men consider a great number of things in the same point of view; when they hold the same opinions upon many subjects, and when the same occurrences suggest the same thoughts and impressions to their minds."[1] Some one or another version of this theme has been an essential part of every acceptable definition of society long before Tocqueville so formulated it and ever since.[2] If a society is a set of common understandings, a system of reciprocally acknowledged claims and expectations expressed in action, it follows that a human aggregation cannot be regarded as a society until it achieves this capacity for collective action, although it may manifest a high degree of symbiotic or functional interdependence between the individuals composing it. Such an aggregate may constitute a community without being a society. It follows further that the degree to which the members of a society lose their common understandings, i.e., the extent to which consensus is undermined, is the measure of that society's state of disorganization. The degree to which there is agreement as to the values and norms of a society expressed in its explicit rules and in the preferences its members manifest with reference to these rules furnishes us with criteria of the degree to which a society may be said to be disorganized.

But not all deviations from norms are to be regarded as *prima facie* evidence of social disorganization. It is possible to have a wide range of individual differentiation and deviation from norms in a society without approaching a state of social disorganization. Not all conduct we call crime is to be interpreted as social disorganization; nor is the incidence of divorce to be taken at face value as a measure of family disorganization.[3]

1   *Democracy in America*, tr. Henry Reeve (New York, 1899), I, 398.

2   W. I. Thomas and F. Znaniecki, *The Polish Peasant in Europe and America* (New York, 1927), I, 32–33; II, 1128–29.

3   "In other words, social organization is not coextensive with individual morality, nor does social disorganization correspond to individual

Types of Social Disorganization

A major type of social disorganization is that characterized by conflicts between norms. Such conflicts are rare in stable,
compact, and homogeneous societies, as an abundance of literature from primitive and folk societies indicates,[4] but in societies
in rapid or sudden change either through migration, change in
technology, or basis of subsistence, subjected to contact with alien
groups, or brought within the influence of modern civilization,
there may appear wide chasms between the old and the new, the
indigenous and the imported, the traditional and the deliberately
imposed systems of values and codes of conduct. Colonization,
conquest, immigration, the invasion of industry, and the impact
of whatever content the modern mass-communication devices
carry to the ends of the earth may bring about cleavages in the
systems of values of a formerly integrated society. In such cases,
disorganization may be the product of the tensions arising out of
the attempt to conform to mutually contradictory norms coexist-
ing within a single system and calling for incompatible responses
to a given situation. In any ongoing social order, we must recognize the operation of what Sumner called "the strain of improvement and consistency." The demands for the resolution of conflicts may be more frequent and insistent in a society whose value
system and institutional framework are subjected to the stresses
induced by changes due to internal trends or to contacts with
alien cultures.

Disorganization may also result, however, from the coexistence within a society of two or more independent systems of

---

demoralization," *ibid.*, p. 1129. There may be cases of behavior involving
deviation from the norms of the society without substantial disbelief in the
validity of the violated norms. As Healy says: "We constantly find the delinquent fully able to express his conscious belief that delinquency represents wrong conduct, but evidently his feeling about its wrongfulness has
not been sufficiently strong to function as a preventive," William Healy
and Augusta F. Bronner, *New Light on Delinquency and Its Treatment*
(New Haven, 1936), p. 11.

4   See, for instance, Thorsten Sellin, "Culture Conflict and Crime"
(Social Science Research Council Bulletin No. 41 [1938]), pp. 58 ff.

norms, each of which claims the allegiance of a segment of society which in other respects is interdependent with the rest. If in such instances we speak of social disorganization, we should be clear that the condition is not necessarily the consequence of new norms suddenly injected into the society but rather is likely to be the product of a mode of life which does not permit a universal consensus or single set of norms to develop.

It should further be noted that ecological interdependence does not automatically generate consensus. Especially in our modern great cities, where primary group relations are minimal and secondary relations are segmental and usually amoral, we tend to treat aggregations of men who are merely spatially contiguous and functionally interdependent as if they were true societies. Under such circumstances, what we are disposed to call social disorganization is rather a situation in which organization in the sense of a common set of norms was never able to develop to any appreciable degree. What we have is an unorganized rather than a disorganized society.

The impression of the absence of a common value system that one gains by viewing the urban community as a whole can be interpreted as a relative state of disorganization only when one contrasts the city with the more or less integrated communities from which its inhabitants typically are recruited and with the relatively organized character of social life that obtains in the smaller constituent segments of the urban community itself. The interpenetration of diverse ethnic and cultural groups in the urban world has resulted in the enormous multiplication of value systems, each one of which is binding only upon a segment of the population and upon individuals in specific segments of their round of life. The mere multiplication of norms, together with the tendency toward segmentalization of life, increases the chances that the norms impinging upon the individuals will provoke conflicts and tensions.

Disorganization may result not alone from overt conflict between these systems of norms and from the segmental nature of these norms but also from the ambiguities of definition, which increase as wider and more heterogeneous aggregates of men are expected to share the goals and standards of the same society. Obviously, as Sellin points out, "All culture conflicts are conflicts of *meanings:* social values, interests, norms. There can be no clashes between the material objects of culture."[5] It is therefore in the divergence and ambiguity of meanings that we must seek the source of much of our social disorganization.

Ideologies and Social Solidarity

From time immemorial one of the central problems of society has been how consensus may be achieved. In relatively simple and static societies this problem is not a serious one, since consensus rests upon tradition and authority and is reinforced by sacred sanctions and, if need be, by force the legitimacy of which is unquestioned. In societies where such customs have not as yet emerged, where the activities are so ramified and involve such narrow segments of the individual's career that generally binding customary rules have no opportunity to develop, or where such rules have fallen into decay, other less spontaneous measures have to be resorted to. Of these, laws and ordinances are the classic illustration, but we know of no society in which laws, with the accompanying sanctions of punishment, achieve so perfect a consensus as folk societies can achieve through custom and a common form of life. In addition to laws and customs we have a body of conventions, of rules of the game, which, although they may occasionally be disregarded, are generally respected even though their violation does not entail serious sanctions. Increasingly, however, as societies lose their kinship base, we come to rely upon more formal and rational bases for achieving a unity which formerly could be relied upon to emanate from less deliberate means. Formal education and propaganda are the typical devices invoked.

As the belief in the intrinsic validity of our norms is undermined, supporting ideologies come into play with reference to the institutions and values that are threatened. These ideologies sanctify actions and institutions to which the customary norms do not extend and act, so to speak, as a surrogate for custom and tradition. The ideologies which we develop, however, are not arbitrar-

5   *Ibid.*, p. 58.

ily superimposed upon our practices and institutions. To cite
Professor Park:

> There is, as Sumner says, implicit in every institution a concept and
> a philosophy. In the efforts of men acting together to pursue a consist-
> ent course of action in a changing world this concept emerges and the
> philosophy which was implicit becomes explicit. It may take the form
> of a rationalization or a justification for the institution's existence—
> what might be described as the institution's *apologia pro vita sua*.
> Although there may be implicit in the practices of every institution
> an idea and a philosophy, it is only in a changing society where it
> becomes necessary to defend or redefine its functions that this phi-
> losophy is likely to achieve a formal and dogmatic statement; and
> even then the body of sentiment and ideas which support these prin-
> ciples may remain, like an iceberg, more or less completely submerged
> in the "collective unconscious," whatever that is. It is furthermore
> only in a political society, in which a public exists that permits dis-
> cussion, rather than in a society organized on a familial and author-
> itative basis that rational principles tend to supersede tradition and
> custom as a basis of organization and control. Besides, mankind has
> never been as completely rational in either its behavior or its thinking
> as was once supposed. As Sumner remarks, "property, marriage, and
> religion are still almost entirely in the mores." It is, however, in the
> nature of political society that every class, caste, institution, or other
> functional unit should have its own dogma and its individual life-
> program. In a familial society, dogma and ideology may perhaps be
> said to exist potentially and in the egg. They are not so likely to be
> stated formally as a rule or principle of action.[6]

Whereas the lawyer and the theologian, since ideologies are
their main stock in trade, have dealt with them as solid realities,
some sociologists have been inclined to consider them as irrelevant or as only of secondary importance. They have dismissed
them as rationalizations of the reasons and have looked instead
for the "real" motives of action which were supposed to be hidden behind the professed motives or pretexts. As a result they
have perhaps failed to see that the ideologies may sometimes ac-

[6]   Robert E. Park, "Symbiosis and Socialization: A Frame of Reference for the Study of Society," *American Journal of Sociology* (July,
1939), pp. 8–9.

tually state the basic determining factors correctly, or at least that through the rationalizations the causes of conduct might be discovered. As Kant succinctly put it, "One should not believe everything people say, nor should one believe that they say it without reason."

An analysis of the ideologies of the society in question aids us not only in discovering the conflict of norms but also conversely in discovering the factors contributing to the social solidarity of the group. The belief in the intrinsic validity of norms may, according to Max Weber's classification, rest upon a charismatic, traditional, or rational basis.[7] The undermining of these bases of our beliefs would presumably lead to disorganization. Another basis of social solidarity to which secondary societies have increasingly resorted to encourage conformity is the fear of sanctions, which in a highly complex secular society tends to be increasingly ineffective. There may be said to be a third source of conformity with norms, namely, expediency, i.e., the tendency of each individual to act in accordance with what he conceives to be his own self-interest—a procedure characteristic of individualistic, competitive societies. Even sheer opportunism tends to be converted into a principle of action. We have become so accustomed to the acceptance of rationality as a norm of conduct that we find ourselves under pressure, if we want our program accepted, to convince others we are acting rationally and to fortify our action by invoking a principle. As a student of contemporary political ideologies puts it:

We live in an age of self-conscious communities. Even the crudest of the regimes of contemporary Europe, the regime which, admittedly, owes least to a systematically thought-out doctrine, the Fascist regime in Italy, appears to value self-righteousness enough to join with the others in claiming a doctrine of its own. Opportunism has suffered the emasculation of being converted into a principle; we have lost not only the candour of Machiavelli but also even the candour of the *Anti Machiavel*. But it is a loss not to be regretted without qualification. It is evidence, at least, that nobody now expects a hearing who does not

[7]   Max Weber, *Wirtschaft und Gesellschaft* (2d ed.; Tübingen, 1925).

exhibit some anxiety to act on principle, who is not prepared to explain his conduct in some terms other than those of mere personal inclination.[8]

Ideologies and Collective Action

The most important thing to know about a society, whether it be a family, a city, a nation, a class, a church, or a political party, is to know what it takes for granted and what values it holds sacred and inviolable. In the measure in which these values are regarded as ultimate imperatives, they are neither discussed nor debated. Often they are not even explicitly stated. You will seldom find them unequivocally formulated in constitutions or in party platforms or in theological creeds. They are revealed in collective action rather than in verbal utterances. They are to be inferred from what people do. They are often crystallized into and hidden behind symbols, slogans, and stereotypes which, if they are seen in the light of concrete behavior, can aid us in ascertaining the motives that prompt men's actions and the values which constitute the ends of such actions. The real facts to which these symbols and verbal utterances vaguely and ambiguously refer, and the norms which they presuppose, are often much less clearcut and capable of pigeon-holing than the slogans and creeds themselves would indicate. Are Christianity and capitalism mutually exclusive or compatible? Are socialism and equalitarianism mutually contradictory? The proponents of freedom and security, who may naïvely assume that their respective programs are in harmony with one another, find in the implementation of their policies that they almost certainly are at war with each other. The same applies to those who at one and the same time profess to be advocates of progress and order. We want them both, but if we try to achieve either, will we not in some measure lose the other? Is naziism, which was nursed into being by the enemies of socialism, not as great an enemy of capitalism as is communism? The vestiges of liberalistic capitalism in Germany today are believed by experts to be not much, if any, greater than they are in the Soviet Union.

8   Michael Oakeshott, *The Social and Political Doctrines of Contemporary Europe* (Cambridge, 1939), p. xi.

Before we can discover why and in what ways individuals deviate from the norms most of which those who adhere to them take for granted, we must discover what norms people are expected to meet, what same meaning they have for the various participants and spectators in the society or social world in question. A cursory survey reveals that such consensus as does exist in modern Western society when it is not at war is extremely limited, in the sense that those who participate in the consensus constitute only a small proportion of the total society. Moreover, due to the voluntary selection of the members of interest groups in our society into more or less homogeneous units such as political and religious sects, the probability of intragroup consensus in the small intimate aggregates is considerably greater than inclusive intergroup consensus in the larger society. Similarly, we may have segmental consensus without total or integral consensus, in the sense that we may understand each other on a limited number of subjects but not on all the crucial issues with reference to which we are expected to collaborate.[9] The present state of the labor movement in the United States furnishes an example of lack of organization, if not disorganization, that follows from the failure to develop such total or integral consensus; for while the CIO and the AF of L may well be agreed on the need for the effective organization of labor to carry out collective bargaining, the differential interests and the common interests of craft unions representing skilled workers as distinguished from industrial unions representing workers in the mass industries have not found expression in corresponding ideologies or unambiguously formulated programs. Similarly, the failure to develop a program which would reconcile the immediate as distinguished from the long-run objectives has long been a source of ineffectiveness in the socialist movement.

Aside from the failure to develop an integrated ideology reflecting the consensus of a group on those values on which there might well be consensus and on which there must be consensus if the group is to act effectively as a unit, we must also consider

9   It is, of course, conceivable that there should be inclusive segmental consensus in the sense of universal agreement within the society on a limited number of issues. This is an essential supposition of liberalism.

types of situations in which groups with a marked degree of functional interdependence fail to develop an adequate ideology because in some respects they are in conflict with one another. Thus
within the labor movement, groups have often failed to achieve
effective unity because racial or religious ideologies have divided
them and set them against one another, although their economic
and political interests and ideologies were largly congruent with
one another. The demoralization of the German labor movement
before Hitler and the deleterious effect on labor solidarity in the
United States because of prejudice against admitting Negro workers into the trade unions are instances in point.

Since consensus conditions and results from the participation
of persons in a common life, the limits of consensus are marked
by the range of effective communication. Consensus may disintegrate because communication between the individuals and groups
who are expected to act collectively is reduced to a minimum. As
John Dewey has pointed out, "Everything which bars freedom
and fullness of communication sets up barriers which divide human beings into sets and cliques, into antagonistic sects and factions, and the democratic way of life is undermined."[10]

There are many typical instances in which we find that the
consensus which exists is purely verbal; it does not manifest itself
in concerted action. In such cases, we are dealing with what might
be called mere lip service to the prevailing ideologies. It is almost
certain that a person who would literally follow the ideology of
the Christian religion as set forth in any of its denominational versions for even as short a period as twenty-four hours would find
himself in conflict with his fellow Christians, who ostensibly profess the same doctrines and creeds but interpret them less literally. The more denotative and precise the definition of our values
becomes, the more likely it is that fewer individuals will share
them. A united front movement must obviously employ an ideology which will appeal not only to the working classes but to the
middle classes and professional groups as well. The more it does
this, the less distinguishable it will be from other groups in the
political arena with which it is at war. As its slogans are designed

[10]   *John Dewey and the Promise of America* (New York, 1939), p. 15.

to attract the largest possible number, it cannot well expect to enlist the complete and unqualified loyalty of any one of the groups which have only temporarily compromised their sectarian position for the sake of union. The fact that our ideologies have become widely disseminated through propaganda fostered by interest groups makes us regard them with less naïve fervor than our ancient faiths whose source was attributed to a prophet's revelation or whose origin was obscured by timeless tradition.

Before considering the extent to which a multiplicity of ideologies may be taken as a symptom of impending or actual disorganization of the ethos of a society and of its specific institutions around which they develop, it is well to consider their normal functions. Ideologies develop in the course of ordinary group life when it becomes necessary to make the premises, values, and ends of the collectivity explicit and to provide the social movements that emerge in societies with a body of doctrines, beliefs, and myths. As Park says:

. . . the ideology of a society or of a social group is, like its customs and its folkways, an integral part of its social structure. . . . The ideology of a class, caste, or social group seems to perform the same role in the functioning of a collective unit that the individual's conception of himself performs in the function of his personality. As the individual's conception of himself projects his acts into the future and in that fashion serves to control and direct the course of his career, so in the case of a society its ideology may be said to direct control, and give consistency, in the vicissitudes of a changing world, as to its collective acts.[11]

In the actual struggle, however, of the divergent interest groups to gain recognition and power, and in the attempt of a society to maintain itself intact against the currents of social change, it happens that the ideologies that come to be formulated do not always directly and fully reveal the common objectives of the group in an unambiguous fashion. They may be used to conceal as well as to reveal the true interests of those interested in propagating them. The ideology may be designed to serve as a weapon of attack against inner and outer enemies and to formu-

[11]   Park, *loc. cit.*

late the criticisms of whatever contrary interpretation of the world the group finds it necessary to attack and condemn. Conversely, the ideology constitutes a body of defensive arguments to sanctify the group's program, aspirations, and the means for achieving them. It is used as an instrument to justify the group's purpose both to the members and outsiders. Since it is not merely a statement of ends but an instrument for achieving these ends, the ideology must function to gain and hold adherents; hence it must not merely articulate policies but also guide the tactics and practical operations. It must not only furnish direction but offer attraction, inspiration, hope, and maintain discipline and morale. It must be ambiguous enough to enlist widespread support and yet definitive enough to attract attention, to be distinctive, and to induce active identification. If we seek to establish consensus in contemporary society, even on a few fundamental issues, it cannot obviously be attained by pursuing a laissez faire policy.

Ideologies as Instruments in Social Reorganization

In a world such as that of Europe in the Middle Ages, before the advent of mass literacy and mass democracy, the discussion of ideas was the exclusive preoccupation of a very small, delimited section of society, but since then the authoritarian sanctions of church and state have been undermined. Today, with mass communication, the newspaper, the radio, and motion picture, and with the political power resident in the masses of men who have to be persuaded or moved, the dissemination of ideas has become an art and a big business. Propaganda has become the price we pay for our literacy and our suffrage. We have become the victims of the mouthpieces and loudspeakers of those who have acquired the power to make decisions and those who seek to wrest it from them. Propaganda has become the chief means for enlarging the scope of consensus and the number of persons sharing it, and the consensus that we get as a result is often an unstable and spurious one. In the effort of every ideology to gain worldwide circulation and acceptance and to universalize itself, it must obviously be simplified and debased. It must appear to be internally consistent. Its internal contradictions and its logical weak spots must be obscured, and the events which might test it must never occur. While strengthening solidarity among its adherents, it must necessarily sharpen and exaggerate the differences in extragroup relations.

While ideologies tend to build up consensus, they also undermine consensus. In gaining force and acceptability they often become rigid and ossified and thus reduce their elasticity in the face of changing situations. An existing ideology also prevents the emergence of a new ideology which might be more congruent with an emerging situation requiring a new orientation and adjustment. Ideologies, like other products of cultural life, tend to continue to exist for reasons other than those that brought them into existence. Like the interest groups and the functionaries that have a stake in other institutions, so the pressure groups and their functionaries—in this case the intellectuals—have a proprietary interest in the maintenance of the ideologies which they sponsor.

When the philosophy of a group is made explicit and becomes conscious, it tends to be deprived of the spontaneous loyalty and adherence of the group and must seek support through contrived persuasion and studied means of propaganda. From the standpoint of social solidarity the difference between contemporary society and a less segmentalized social order is essentially the difference between unreflective social cohesion brought about by tradition as distinguished from reflective co-operation induced by rational selection of common ends and means. Particularly in an urban world, where a wide variety of schemes of conduct representing divergent social worlds meet, clash, and interpenetrate, the chances of any one set of norms surviving or emerging as sacred for all are slender. Here, if anywhere, we should find doctrines and principles losing force and faith decaying as sophistication progresses. The disillusionment of their respective sympathizers that has followed in the wake of the tactical twists and turns of Communist and Nazi policies toward one another's program has been a startling event. It has left the supporters of the respective ideologies in a state of confusion and demoralization.

We are inclined to call a person naïve who takes at face value what he reads in the papers or hears over the radio, or who embraces the planks in a party platform as a faith and a correct chart of what the party will do when it comes into power. Cynicism with reference to the alleged values of contending groups and skepticism with reference to the alleged truths have become characteristic of the modern sophisticated man. We seek to protect ourselves against alluring ideologies by the systematic development of detachment, distrust, and suspicion, and a more or less elaborate armamentarium of counterarguments and rationalization. The force of these ideologies has consequently been dulled. Every faith is suspect, no prophet is regarded as infallible, no leader sincere, no mission inspired, and no conviction unshakable. We cultivate a lack of confidence toward those who are our partners and our leaders, and we privatize our existence. Frequently, our incorporation in a movement or a society consists in nothing more than the mere verbal utterance that we accept a creed or doctrine without professing to understand it or to take it seriously. When the symbols representing the values of a society fall into such a state of decay, we approach the condition of *anomie* which Durkheim describes as a state of social void or normlessness in which certain types of suicide, crime, family and community disorganization, and social disorder flourish.

Through the analysis of our ideologies we may be able to discover the clues that indicate the disintegration of our social structure and to spot the areas of life where disorganization threatens to occur. The ambiguities of systems of values and the contradictions between them reflect not merely the segmentalization of society but its effort to discover a deliberate and consciously contrived basis for conformity when these spontaneous acceptances of the norms can no longer be relied upon. In the course of reconstructing a literate and democratic society upon this new basis, the ideologies of the segmental groups within societies and of the larger social aggregates which comprise them vie with one another, with the result that no single system of values can expect universal acceptance, and the conduct of the large masses of individuals is increasingly privatized.

Until we can specify these norms and describe their content

and meaning, their relation to one another, and their congruence with the problems of daily living, the study of both personal and social disorganization and our attempts to treat them cannot be adequate. In the study of social disorganization, therefore, as in the study of human social life generally, while it is desirable to concentrate on overt action—of which, of course, language itself is one form—it is not so irrelevant as some have thought to take account of what people say. For despite the deflections, distortion, and concealment of their verbal utterances, men do betray, even if they do not always accurately and completely reveal in them, their motives and their values; and if we do not have an understanding of these motives and values, we do not know men as social beings.

4

URBANISM AS A WAY OF LIFE

The City and Contemporary Civilization

JUST AS the beginning of Western civilization is marked by the permanent settlement of formerly nomadic peoples in the Mediterranean basin, so the beginning of what is distinctively modern in our civilization is best signalized by the growth of great cities. Nowhere has mankind been farther removed from organic nature than under the conditions of life characteristic of these cities. The contemporary world no longer presents a picture of small isolated groups of human beings scattered over a vast territory, as Sumner described primitive society.[1] The distinctive feature of man's mode of living in the modern age is his concentration into gigantic aggregations around which cluster lesser centers and from which radiate the ideas and practices that we call civilization.

The degree to which the contemporary world may be said to be "urban" is not fully or accurately measured by the proportion of the total population living in cities. The influences which cities exert upon the social life of man are greater than the ratio of the urban population would indicate; for the city is not only increas-

Reprinted from *Community Life and Social Policy*, ed. Elizabeth Wirth Marvick and Albert J. Reiss, Jr. (Chicago: University of Chicago Press, 1956), pp. 110–32, first published in the *American Journal of Sociology*, XLIV (July, 1938), 1–24.

[1] William Graham Sumner, *Folkways* (Boston, 1906), p. 12.

ingly the dwelling-place and the workshop of modern man, but it is the initiating and controlling center of economic, political, and cultural life that has drawn the most remote communities of the world into its orbit and woven diverse areas, peoples, and activities into a cosmos.

The growth of cities and the urbanization of the world comprise one of the most impressive facts of modern times. Although it is impossible to state precisely what proportion of the estimated total world population of approximately 1,800,000,000 is urban, 69.2 per cent of the total population of those countries that do distinguish between urban and rural areas is urban.[2] Because the world's population is very unevenly distributed and because the growth of cities is not very far advanced in some of the countries that have only recently been touched by industrialism, this average understates the extent to which urban concentration has proceeded in those countries where the impact of the industrial revolution has been more forceful and of less recent date. This shift from a rural to a predominantly urban society, which has taken place within the span of a single generation in such industrialized areas as the United States and Japan, has been accompanied by profound changes in virtually every phase of social life. It is these changes and their ramifications that invite the attention of the sociologist to the study of the differences between the rural and the urban mode of living. The pursuit of this interest is an indispensable prerequisite for the comprehension and possible mastery of some of the most crucial contemporary problems of social life since it is likely to furnish one of the most revealing perspectives for the understanding of the ongoing changes in human nature and the social order.[3]

[2]   S. V. Pearson, *The Growth and Distribution of Population* (New York, 1935), p. 211.

[3]   Whereas rural life in the United States has for a long time been a subject of considerable interest on the part of governmental bureaus, the most notable case of a comprehensive report being that submitted by the Country Life Commission to President Theodore Roosevelt in 1909, no equally comprehensive official inquiry into urban life was undertaken until the establishment of a Research Committee on Urbanism of the National Resources Committee. (Cf. *Our Cities: Their Role in the National Economy* [Washington: Government Printing Office, 1937].)

Because the city is the product of growth rather than of instantaneous creation, it is to be expected that the influences which it exerts upon the modes of life should not be able to wipe out completely the previously dominant modes of human association. To a greater or lesser degree, therefore, our social life bares the imprint of an earlier folk society, the characteristic modes of settlement of which were the farm, the manor, and the village. This historic influence is reinforced by the circumstances that the population of the city itself is in large measure recruited from the countryside, where a mode of life reminiscent of this earlier form of existence persists. Hence we should not expect to find abrupt and discontinuous variation between urban and rural types of personality. The city and the country may be regarded as two poles in reference to one or the other of which all human settlements tend to arrange themselves. In viewing urban-industrial and rural-folk society as ideal types of communities, we may obtain a perspective for the analysis of the basic models of human association as they appear in contemporary civilization.

A Sociological Definition of the City

Despite the preponderant significance of the city in our civilization, our knowledge of the nature of urbanism and the process of urbanization is meager, notwithstanding many attempts to isolate the distinguishing characteristics of urban life. Geographers, historians, economists, and political scientists have incorporated the points of view of their respective disciplines into diverse definitions of the city. While in no sense intended to supersede these, the formulation of a sociological approach to the city may incidentally serve to call attention to the interrelations between them by emphasizing the peculiar characteristics of the city as a particular form of human association. A sociologically significant definition of the city seeks to select those elements of urbanism which mark it as a distinctive mode of human group life.

The characterization of a community as urban on the basis of size alone is obviously arbitrary. It is difficult to defend the present census definition which designates a community of 2,500 and above as urban and all others as rural. The situation would be the same if the criterion were 4,000, 8,000, 10,000, 25,000, or 100,-000 population, for although in the latter case we might feel that we were more nearly dealing with an urban aggregate than would be the case in communities of lesser size, no definition of urbanism can hope to be completely satisfying as long as numbers are regarded as the sole criterion. Moreover, it is not difficult to demonstrate that communities of less than the arbitrarily set number of inhabitants, lying within the range of influence of metropolitan centers, have greater claim to recognition as urban communities than do larger ones leading a more isolated existence in a predominantly rural area. Finally, it should be recognized that census definitions are unduly influenced by the fact that the city, statistically speaking, is always an administrative concept in that the corporate limits play a decisive role in delineating the urban area. Nowhere is this more clearly apparent than in the concentrations on the peripheries of great metropolitan centers of people who cross arbitrary administrative boundaries of city, county, state, and nation.

As long as we identify urbanism with the physical entity of the city, viewing it merely as rigidly delimited in space, and proceed as if urban attributes abruptly ceased to be manifested beyond an arbitrary boundary line, we are not likely to arrive at any adequate conception of urbanism as a mode of life. The technological developments in transportation and communication which virtually mark a new epoch in human history have accentuated the role of cities as dominant elements in our civilization and have enormously extended the urban mode of living beyond the confines of the city itself. The dominance of the city, especially of the great city, may be regarded as a consequence of the concentration in cities of industrial, commercial, financial, and administrative facilities and actvities, transportation and communication lines, and cultural and recreational equipment such as the press, radio stations, theaters, libraries, museums, concert halls, operas, hospitals, colleges, research and publishing centers, professional organizations, and religious and welfare institutions. Were it not for the attraction and suggestions that the city exerts

through these instrumentalities upon the rural population, the
differences between the rural and the urban modes of life would
be even greater than they are. Urbanization no longer denotes
merely the process by which persons are attracted to a place
called the city and incorporated into its system of life. It refers
also to that cumulative accentuation of the characteristics distinctive of the mode of life which is associated with the growth of
cities, and finally to the changes in the direction of modes of life
recognized as urban which are apparent among people, wherever
they may be, who have come under the spell of the influences
which the city exerts by virtue of the power of its institutions and
personalities operating through the means of communication and
transportation.

The shortcomings which attach to number of inhabitants as a
criterion of urbanism apply for the most part to density of population as well. Whether we accept the density of 10,000 persons
per square mile as Mark Jefferson[4] proposed, or 1,000, which
Willcox[5] preferred to regard as the criterion of urban settlements,
it is clear that unless density is correlated with significant social
characteristics it can furnish only an arbitrary basis for differentiating urban from rural communities. Since our census enumer-
ates the night rather than the day population of an area, the locale
of the most intensive urban life—the city center—generally has
low population density, and the industrial and commercial areas of
the city, which contain the most characteristic economic activities
underlying urban society, would scarcely anywhere be truly urban
if density were literally interpreted as a mark of urbanism. The
fact that the urban community is distinguished by a large aggregation and relatively dense concentration of population can
scarcely be left out of account in a definition of the city; nevertheless these criteria must be seen as relative to the general
cultural context in which cities arise and exist. They are sociologically relevant only in so far as they operate as conditioning
factors in social life.

4   "The Anthropogeography of Some Great Cities," *Bulletin of the
American Geographical Society*, XLI (1909), 537–66.

5   Walter F. Willcox, "A Definition of 'City' in Terms of Density,"
in E. W. Burgess, *The Urban Community* (Chicago, 1926), p. 119.

The same criticisms apply to such criteria as the occupation of the inhabitants, the existence of certain physical facilities, institutions, and forms of political organization. The question is not whether cities in our civilization or in others do exhibit these distinctive traits, but how potent they are in molding the character of social life into its specifically urban form. Nor in formulating a fertile definition can we afford to overlook the great variations between cities. By means of a typology of cities based upon size, location, age, and function, such as we have undertaken to establish in our recent report to the National Resources Committee,[6] we have found it feasible to array and classify urban communities ranging from struggling small towns to thriving world centers, from isolated trading-centers in the midst of agricultural regions to thriving world ports and commercial and industrial conurbations. Such differences as these appear crucial because the social characteristics and influences of these different "cities" vary widely.

A serviceable definition of urbanism should not only denote the essential characteristics which all cities—at least those in our culture—have in common, but should lend itself to the discovery of their variations. An industrial city will differ significantly in social respects from a commercial, mining, fishing, resort, university, or capital city. A one-industry city will present sets of social characteristics different from those of a multi-industry city, as will an industrially balanced from an imbalanced city, a suburb from a satellite, a residential suburb from an industrial suburb, a city within a metropolitan region from one lying outside, an old city from a new one, a southern city from a New England one, a middle western from a Pacific Coast city, a growing from a stable and from a dying city.

A sociological definition must obviously be inclusive enough to comprise whatever essential characteristics these different types of cities have in common as social entities, but it obviously cannot be so detailed as to take account of all the variations implicit in the manifold classes sketched above. Presumably some of the characteristics of cities are more significant in conditioning the

[6] *Op. cit.*, p. 8.

nature of urban life than others, and we may expect the outstanding features of the urban-social scene to vary in accordance with size, density, and differences in the functional type of cities. Moreover, we may infer that rural life will bear the imprint of urbanism in the measure that through contact and communication it comes under the influence of cities. It may contribute to the clarity of subsequent statements to repeat that while the locus of urbanism as a mode of life is, of course, to be found characteristically in places which fulfil the requirements we shall set up as a definition of the city, urbanism is not confined to such localities but is manifest in varying degrees wherever the influences of the city reach.

While urbanism, or that complex of traits which makes up the characteristic mode of life in cities, and urbanization, which denotes the development and extensions of these factors, are thus not exclusively found in settlements which are cities in the physical and demographic sense, they do, nevertheless, find their most pronounced expression in such areas, especially in metropolitan cities. In formulating a definition of the city it is necessary to exercise caution in order to avoid identifying urbanism as a way of life with any specific locally or historically conditioned cultural influences which, though they may significantly affect the specific character of the community, are not the essential determinants of its character as a city.

It is particularly important to call attention to the danger of confusing urbanism with industrialism and modern capitalism. The rise of cities in the modern world is undoubtedly not independent of the emergence of modern power-driven machine technology, mass production, and capitalistic enterprise; but different as the cities of earlier epochs may have been by virtue of their development in a preindustrial and precapitalistic order from the great cities of today, they were also cities.

For sociological purposes a city may be defined as a relatively large, dense, and permanent settlement of socially heterogeneous individuals. On the basis of the postulates which this minimal definition suggests, a theory of urbanism may be formulated in the light of existing knowledge concerning social groups.

A Theory of Urbanism

In the rich literature on the city we look in vain for a theory systematizing the available knowledge concerning the city as a social entity. We do indeed have excellent formulations of theories on such special problems as the growth of the city viewed as a historical trend and as a recurrent process,[7] and we have a wealth of literature presenting insights of sociological relevance and empirical studies offering detailed information on a variety of particular aspects of urban life. But despite the multiplication of research and textbooks on the city, we do not as yet have a comprehensive body of compendent hypotheses which may be derived from a set of postulates implicitly contained in a sociological definition of the city. Neither have we abstracted such hypotheses from our general sociological knowledge which may be substantiated through empirical research. The closest approximations to a systematic theory of urbanism are to be found in a penetrating essay, "Die Stadt," by Max Weber[8] and in a memorable paper by Robert E. Park on "The City: Suggestions for the Investigation of Human Behavior in the Urban Environment."[9] But even these excellent contributions are far from constituting an ordered and coherent framework of theory upon which research might profitably proceed.

Given a limited number of identifying characteristics of the city, I can better assay the consequences or further characteristics of them in the light of general sociological theory and empirical research. I hope in this manner to arrive at the essential propositions comprising a theory of urbanism. Some of these propositions can be supported by a considerable body of already available research materials; others may be accepted as hypotheses for

[7]   See Robert E. Park, Ernest W. Burgess, *et al., The City* (Chicago, 1925), esp. chaps. ii and iii; Werner Sombart, "Städtische Siedlung, Stadt," *Handwörterbuch der Soziologie*, ed. Alfred Vierkandt (Stuttgart, 1931).

[8]   *Wirtschaft und Gesellschaft* (Tübingen, 1925), Part I, chap. viii, pp. 514–601.

[9]   Park, Burgess, *et al., op. cit.*, chap. i.

which a certain amount of presumptive evidence exists, but for which more ample and exact verification would be required. At least such a procedure will, it is hoped, show what in the way of systematic knowledge of the city we now have and what are the crucial and fruitful hypotheses for future research.

The central problem of the sociologist of the city is to discover the forms of social action and organization that typically emerge in relatively permanent, compact settlements of large numbers of heterogeneous individuals. We must also infer that urbanism will assume its most characteristic and extreme form in the measure in which the conditions with which it is congruent are present. Thus the larger, the more densely populated, and the more heterogeneous a community, the more accentuated the characteristics associated with urbanism will be. It should be recognized, however, that social institutions and practices may be accepted and continued for reasons other than those that originally brought them into existence, and that accordingly the urban mode of life may be perpetuated under conditions quite foreign to those necessary for its origin.

Some justification may be in order for the choice of the principal terms comprising our definition of the city, a definition which ought to be as inclusive and at the same time as denotative as possible without unnecessary assumptions. To say that large numbers are necessary to constitute a city means, of course, large numbers in relation to a restricted area or high density of settlement. There are, nevertheless, good reasons for treating large numbers and density as separate factors, because each may be connected with significantly different social consequences. Similarly the need for adding heterogeneity to numbers of population as a necessary and distinct criterion of urbanism might be questioned, since we should expect the range of differences to increase with numbers. In defense, it may be said that the city shows a kind and degree of heterogeneity of population which cannot be wholly accounted for by the law of large numbers or adequately represented by means of a normal distribution curve. Because the population of the city does not reproduce itself, it must recruit its migrants from other cities, the countryside, and—in the United

States until recently—from other countries. The city has thus historically been the melting-pot of races, peoples, and cultures, and a most favorable breeding-ground of new biological and cultural hybrids. It has not only tolerated but rewarded individual differences. It has brought together people from the ends of the earth *because* they are different and thus useful to one another, rather than because they are homogeneous and like-minded.[10]

A number of sociological propositions concerning the relationship between (*a*) numbers of population, (*b*) density of settlement, (*c*) heterogeneity of inhabitants and group life can be formulated on the basis of observation and research.

SIZE OF THE POPULATION AGGREGATE Ever since Aristotle's *Politics*,[11] it has been recognized that increasing the num-

[10] The justification for including the term "permanent" in the definition may appear necessary. Our failure to give an extensive justification for this qualifying mark of the urban rests on the obvious fact that unless human settlements take a fairly permanent root in a locality the characteristics of urban life cannot arise, and conversely the living together of large numbers of heterogeneous individuals under dense conditions is not possible without the development of a more or less technological structure.

[11] See esp. vii. 4. 4–14, trans. B. Jowett, from which the following may be quoted:

"To the size of states there is a limit, as there is to other things, plants, animals, implements; for none of these retain their natural power when they are too large or too small, but they either wholly lose their nature, or are spoiled. . . . [A] state when composed of too few is not as a state ought to be, self-sufficing; when of too many, though self-sufficing in all mere necessaries, it is a nation and not a state, being almost incapable of constitutional government. For who can be the general of such a vast multitude, or who the herald, unless he have the voice of a Stentor?

"A state then only begins to exist when it has attained a population sufficient for a good life in the political community; it may indeed somewhat exceed this number. But, as I was saying, there must be a limit. What should be the limit will be easily ascertained by experience. For both governors and governed have duties to perform; the special functions of a governor are to command and to judge. But if the citizens of a state are to judge and to distribute offices according to merit, then they must know each other's characters; where they do not possess this knowledge, both the election to offices and the decision of lawsuits will go wrong. When the population is very large they are manifestly settled at haphazard, which clearly ought not to be. Besides, in an overpopulous state foreigners

ber of inhabitants in a settlement beyond a certain limit will affect the relationships between them and the character of the city. Large numbers involve, as has been pointed out, a greater range of individual variation. Furthermore, the greater the number of individuals participating in a process of interaction, the greater is the *potential* differentiation between them. The personal traits, the occupations, the cultural life, and the ideas of the members of an urban community may, therefore, be expected to range between more widely separated poles than those of rural inhabitants.

That such variations should give rise to the spatial segregation of individuals according to color, ethnic heritage, economic and social status, tastes and preferences, may readily be inferred. The bonds of kinship, of neighborliness, and the sentiments arising out of living together for generations under a common folk tradition are likely to be absent or, at best, relatively weak in an aggregate the members of which have such diverse origins and backgrounds. Under such circumstances competition and formal control mechanisms furnish the substitutes for the bonds of solidarity that are relied upon to hold a folk society together.

Increase in the number of inhabitants of a community beyond a few hundred is bound to limit the possibility of each member of the community knowing all the others personally. Max Weber, in recognizing the social significance of this fact, explained that from a sociological point of view large numbers of inhabitants and density of settlement mean a lack of that mutual acquaintanceship which ordinarily inheres between the inhabitants in a neighborhood.[12] The increase in numbers thus involves a changed character of the social relationships. As Georg Simmel points out: "[If] the unceasing external contact of numbers of persons in the city should be met by the same number of inner reactions as in the small town, in which one knows almost every person he meets

---

and metics will readily acquire the rights of citizens, for who will find them out? Clearly, then, the best limit of the population of a state is the largest number which suffices for the purposes of life, and can be taken in at a single view. Enough concerning the size of a city."

12   *Op. cit.*, p. 514.

and to each of whom he has a positive relationship, one would be completely atomized internally and would fall into an unthinkable mental condition."[13] The multiplication of persons in a state of interaction under conditions which make their contact as full personalities impossible produces that segmentalization of human relationships which has sometimes been seized upon by students of the mental life of the cities as an explanation for the "schizoid" character of urban personality. This is not to say that the urban inhabitants have fewer acquaintances than rural inhabitants, for the reverse may actually be true; it means rather that in relation to the number of people whom they see and with whom they rub elbows in the course of daily life, they know a smaller proportion, and of these they have less intensive knowledge.

Characteristically, urbanites meet one another in highly segmental roles. They are, to be sure, dependent upon more people for the satisfactions of their life-needs than are rural people and thus are associated with a greater number of organized groups, but they are less dependent upon particular persons, and their dependence upon others is confined to a highly fractionalized aspect of the other's round of activity. This is essentially what is meant by saying that the city is characterized by secondary rather than primary contacts. The contacts of the city may indeed be face to face, but they are nevertheless impersonal, superficial, transitory, and segmental. The reserve, the indifference, and the blasé outlook which urbanites manifest in their relationships may thus be regarded as devices for immunizing themselves against the personal claims and expectations of others.

The superficiality, the anonymity, and the transitory character of urban social relations make intelligible, also, the sophistication and the rationality generally ascribed to city-dwellers. Our acquaintances tend to stand in a relationship of utility to us in the sense that the role which each one plays in our life is overwhelmingly regarded as a means for the achievement of our own ends. Whereas the individual gains, on the one hand, a certain degree of emancipation or freedom from the personal and emotional con-

---

13 "Die Grossstädte und das Geistesleben," *Die Grossstadt,* ed. Theodor Petermann (Dresden, 1903), pp. 187–206.

trols of intimate groups, he loses, on the other hand, the spontaneous self-expression, the morale, and the sense of participation that comes with living in an integrated society. This constitutes essentially the state of *anomie,* or the social void, to which Durkheim alludes in attempting to account for the various forms of social disorganization in technological society.

The segmental character and utilitarian accent of interpersonal relations in the city find their institutional expression in the proliferation of specialized tasks which we see in their most developed form in the professions. The operations of the pecuniary nexus lead to predatory relationships, which tend to obstruct the efficient functioning of the social order unless checked by professional codes and occupational etiquette. The premium put upon utility and efficiency suggests the adaptability of the corporate device for the organization of enterprises in which individuals can engage only in groups. The advantage that the corporation has over the individual entrepreneur and the partnership in the urban-industrial world derives not only from the possibility it affords of centralizing the resources of thousands of individuals or from the legal privilege of limited liability and perpetual succession, but from the fact that the corporation has no soul.

The specialization of individuals, particularly in their occupations, can proceed only, as Adam Smith pointed out, upon the basis of an enlarged market, which in turn accentuates the division of labor. This enlarged market is only in part supplied by the city's hinterland; in large measure it is found among the large numbers that the city itself contains. The dominance of the city over the surrounding hinterland becomes explicable in terms of the division of labor which urban life occasions and promotes. The extreme degree of interdependence and the unstable equilibrium of urban life are closely associated with the division of labor and the specialization of occupations. This interdependence and this instability are increased by the tendency of each city to specialize in those functions in which it has the greatest advantage.

In a community composed of a larger number of individuals than can know one another intimately and can be assembled in one spot, it becomes necessary to communicate through indirect media and to articulate individual interests by a process of delegation. Typically in the city, interests are made effective through representation. The individual counts for little, but the voice of the representative is heard with a deference roughly proportional to the numbers for whom he speaks.

While this characterization of urbanism, in so far as it derives from large numbers, does not by any means exhaust the sociological inferences that might be drawn from our knowledge of the relationship of the size of a group to the characteristic behavior of the members, for the sake of brevity the assertions made may serve to exemplify the sort of propositions that might be developed.

DENSITY   As in the case of numbers, so in the case of concentration in limited space certain consequences of relevance in sociological analysis of the city emerge. Of these only a few can be indicated.

As Darwin pointed out for flora and fauna and as Durkheim noted in the case of human societies,[14] an increase in numbers when area is held constant (i.e., an increase in density) tends to produce differentiation and specialization, since only in this way can the area support increased numbers. Density thus reinforces the effect of numbers in diversifying men and their activities and in increasing the complexity of the social structure.

On the subjective side, as Simmel has suggested, the close physical contact of numerous individuals necessarily produces a shift in the media through which we orient ourselves to the urban milieu, especially to our fellow-men. Typically, our physical contacts are close but our social contacts are distant. The urban world puts a premium on visual recognition. We see the uniform which denotes the role of the functionaries, and are oblivious to the personal eccentricities hidden behind the uniform. We tend to acquire and develop a sensitivity to a world of artifacts, and become progressively farther removed from the world of nature.

We are exposed to glaring contrasts between splendor and squalor, between riches and poverty, intelligence and ignorance, order and chaos. The competition for space is great, so that each

14   É. Durkheim, *De la division du travail social* (Paris, 1932), p. 248.

area generally tends to be put to the use which yields the greatest economic return. Place of work tends to become dissociated from place of residence, for the proximity of industrial and commercial establishments makes an area both economically and socially undesirable for residential purposes.

Density, land values, rentals, accessibility, healthfulness, prestige, aesthetic consideration, absence of nuisances such as noise, smoke, and dirt determine the desirability of various areas of the city as places of settlement for different sections of the population. Place and nature of work, income, racial and ethnic characteristics, social status, custom, habit, taste, preference, and prejudice are among the significant factors in accordance with which the urban population is selected and distributed into more or less distinct settlements. Diverse population elements inhabiting a compact settlement thus become segregated from one another in the degree in which their requirements and modes of life are incompatible and in the measure in which they are antagonistic. Similarly, persons of homogeneous status and needs unwittingly drift into, consciously select, or are forced by circumstances into the same area. The different parts of the city acquire specialized functions, and the city consequently comes to resemble a mosaic of social worlds in which the transition from one to the other is abrupt. The juxtaposition of divergent personalities and modes of life tends to produce a relativistic perspective and a sense of toleration of differences which may be regarded as prerequisites for rationality and which lead toward the secularization of life.[15]

The close living together and working together of individuals who have no sentimental and emotional ties foster a spirit of competition, aggrandizement, and mutual exploitation. Formal controls are instituted to counteract irresponsibility and potential disorder. Without rigid adherence to predictable routines a large compact society would scarcely be able to maintain itself. The

[15]   The extent to which the segregation of the population into distinct ecological and cultural areas and the resulting social attitude of tolerance, rationality, and secular mentality are functions of density as distinguished from heterogeneity is difficult to determine. Most likely we are dealing here with phenomena which are consequences of the simultaneous operation of both factors.

clock and the traffic signal are symbolic of the basis of our social order in the urban world. Frequent close physical contact, coupled with great social distance, accentuates the reserve of unattached individuals toward one another and, unless compensated by other opportunities for response, gives rise to loneliness. The necessary frequent movement of great numbers of individuals in a congested habitat causes friction and irritation. Nervous tensions which derive from such personal frustrations are increased by the rapid tempo and the complicated technology under which life in dense areas must be lived.

HETEROGENEITY The social interaction among such a variety of personality types in the urban milieu tends to break down the rigidity of caste lines and to complicate the class structure; it thus induces a more ramified and differentiated framework of social stratification than is found in more integrated societies. The heightened mobility of the individual, which brings him within the range of stimulation by a great number of diverse individuals and subjects him to fluctuating status in the differentiated social groups that compose the social structure of the city, brings him toward the acceptance of instability and insecurity in the world at large as a norm. This fact helps to account too, for the sophistication and cosmopolitanism of the urbanite. No single group has the undivided allegiance of the individual. The groups with which he is affiliated do not lend themselves readily to a simple hierarchical arrangement. By virtue of his different interests arising out of different aspects of social life, the individual acquires membership in widely divergent groups, each of which functions only with reference to a single segment of his personality. Nor do these groups easily permit of a concentric arrangement so that the narrower ones fall within the circumference of the more inclusive ones, as is more likely to be the case in the rural community or in primitive societies. Rather the groups with which the person typically is affiliated are tangential to each other or intersect in highly variable fashion.

Partly as a result of the physical footlooseness of the population and partly as a result of their social mobility, the turnover in group membership generally is rapid. Place of residence, place and character of employment, income, and interests fluctuate, and the task of holding organizations together and maintaining and promoting intimate and lasting acquaintanceship between the members is difficult. This applies strikingly to the local areas within the city into which persons become segregated more by virtue of differences in race, language, income, and social status than through choice or positive attraction to people like themselves. Overwhelmingly the city-dweller is not a home-owner, and since a transitory habitat does not generate binding traditions and sentiments, only rarely is he a true neighbor. There is little opportunity for the individual to obtain a conception of the city as a whole or to survey his place in the total scheme. Consequently he finds it difficult to determine what is to his own "best interests" and to decide between the issues and leaders presented to him by the agencies of mass suggestion. Individuals who are thus detached from the organized bodies which integrate society comprise the fluid masses that make collective behavior in the urban community so unpredictable and hence so problematical.

Although the city, through the recruitment of variant types to perform its diverse tasks and the accentuation of their uniqueness through competition and the premium upon eccentricity, novelty, efficient performance, and inventiveness, produces a highly differentiated population, it also exercises a leveling influence. Wherever large numbers of differently constituted individuals congregate, the process of depersonalization also enters. This leveling tendency inheres in part in the economic basis of the city. The development of large cities, at least in the modern age, was largely dependent upon the concentrative force of steam. The rise of the factory made possible mass production for an impersonal market. The fullest exploitation of the possibilities of the division of labor and mass production, however, is possible only with standardization of processes and products. A money economy goes hand in hand with such a system of production. Progressively as cities have developed upon a background of this system of production, the pecuniary nexus which implies the purchasability of services and things has displaced personal relations as the basis of association. Individuality under these circumstances must be replaced by categories. When large numbers have to make common use of facilities and institutions, those facilities and institutions must serve the needs of the average person rather than those of particular individuals. The services of the public utilities, of the recreational, educational, and cultural institutions, must be adjusted to mass requirements. Similarly, the cultural institutions, such as the schools, the movies, the radio, and the newspapers, by virtue of their mass clientele, must necessarily operate as leveling influences. The political process as it appears in urban life could not be understood unless one examined the mass appeals made through modern propaganda techniques. If the individual would participate at all in the social, political, and economic life of the city, he must subordinate some of his individuality to the demands of the larger community and in that measure immerse himself in mass movements.

The Relation between a Theory of Urbanism and Sociological Research

By means of a body of theory such as that illustratively sketched above, the complicated and many-sided phenomena of urbanism may be analyzed in terms of a limited number of basic categories. The sociological approach to the city thus acquires an essential unity and coherence enabling the empirical investigator not merely to focus more distinctly upon the problems and processes that properly fall in his province but also to treat his subject matter in a more integrated and systematic fashion. A few typical findings of empirical research in the field of urbanism, with special reference to the United States, may be indicated to substantiate the theoretical propositions set forth in the preceding pages, and some of the crucial problems for further study may be outlined.

On the basis of the three variables, number, density of settlement, and degree of heterogenity, of the urban population, it appears possible to explain the characteristics of urban life and to account for the differences between cities of various sizes and types.

Urbanism as a characteristic mode of life may be approached

empirically from three interrelated perspectives: (1) as a physical structure comprising a population base, a technology, and an ecological order; (2) as a system of social organization involving a characteristic social structure, a series of social institutions, and a typical pattern of social relationships; and (3) as a set of attitudes and ideas, and a constellation of personalities engaging in typical forms of collective behavior and subject to characteristic mechanisms of social control.

URBANISM IN ECOLOGICAL PERSPECTIVE   Since in the case of physical structure and ecological processes we are able to operate with fairly objective indices, it becomes possible to arrive at quite precise and generally quantitative results. The dominance of the city over its hinterland becomes explicable through the functional characteristics of the city which derive in large measure from the effect of numbers and density. Many of the technical facilities and the skills and organizations to which urban life gives rise can grow and prosper only in cities where the demand is sufficiently great. The nature and scope of the services rendered by these organizations and institutions and the advantage which they enjoy over the less developed facilities of smaller towns enhance the dominance of the city, making ever wider regions dependent upon the central metropolis.

The composition of an urban population shows the operation of selective and differentiating factors. Cities contain a larger proportion of persons in the prime of life than rural areas, which contain more old and very young people. In this, as in so many other respects, the larger the city the more this specific characteristic of urbanism is apparent. With the exception of the largest cities, which have attracted the bulk of the foreign-born males, and a few other special types of cities, women predominate numerically over men. The heterogeneity of the urban population is further indicated along racial and ethnic lines. The foreign-born and their children constitute nearly two-thirds of all the inhabitants of cities of one million and over. Their proportion in the urban population declines as the size of the city decreases, until in the rural areas they comprise only about one-sixth of the total population. The larger cities similarly have attracted more Negroes and other racial groups than have the smaller communities. Considering that age, sex, race, and ethnic origin are associated with other factors such as occupation and interest, one sees that a major characteristic of the urban-dweller is his dissimilarity from his fellows. Never before have such large masses of people of diverse traits as we find in our cities been thrown together into such close physical contact as in the great cities of America. Cities generally, and American cities in particular, comprise a motley of peoples and cultures of highly differentiated modes of life between which there often is only the faintest communication, the greatest indifference, the broadest tolerance, occasionally bitter strife, but always the sharpest contrast.

The failure of the urban population to reproduce itself appears to be a biological consequence of a combination of factors in the complex of urban life, and the decline in the birth rate generally may be regarded as one of the most significant signs of the urbanization of the Western world. Though the proportion of deaths in cities is slightly greater than in the country, the outstanding difference between the failure of present-day cities to maintain their population and that of cities of the past is that in former times it was due to the exceedingly high death rates in cities, whereas today, since cities have become more livable from a health standpoint, it is due to low birth rates. These biological characteristics of the urban population are significant sociologically, not merely because they reflect the urban mode of existence but also because they condition the growth and future dominance of cities and their basic social organization. Since cities are the consumers rather than the producers of men, the value of human life and the social estimation of the personality will not be unaffected by the balance between births and deaths. The pattern of land use, of land values, rentals, and ownership, the nature and functioning of the physical structures, of housing, of transportation and communication facilities, of public utilities—these and many other phases of the physical mechanism of the city are not isolated phenomena unrelated to the city as a social entity but are affected by and affect the urban mode of life.

URBANISM AS A FORM OF SOCIAL ORGANIZATION   The distinctive features of the urban mode of life have often been described sociologically as consisting of the substitution of secondary for primary contacts, the weakening of bonds of kinship, and the declining social significance of the family, the disappearance of the neighborhood, and the undermining of the traditional basis of social solidarity. All these phenomena can be substantially verified through objective indices. Thus, for instance, the low and declining urban-reproduction rates suggest that the city is not conducive to the traditional type of family life, including the rearing of children and the maintenance of the home as the locus of a whole round of vital activities. The transfer of industrial, educational, and recreational activities to specialized institutions outside the home has deprived the family of some of its most characteristic historical functions. In cities mothers are more likely to be employed, lodgers are more frequently part of the household, marriage tends to be postponed, and the proportion of single and unattached people is greater. Families are smaller and more frequently without children than in the country. The family as a unit of social life is emancipated from the larger kinship group characteristic of the country, and the individual members pursue their own diverging interests in their vocational, educational, religious, recreational, and political life.

Such functions as the maintenance of health, the methods of alleviating the hardships associated with personal and social insecurity, the provisions for education, recreation, and cultural advancement have given rise to highly specialized institutions on a community-wide, statewide, or even national basis. The same factors which have brought about greater personal insecurity also underlie the wider contrasts between individuals to be found in the urban world. While the city has broken down the rigid caste lines of pre-industrial society, it has sharpened and differentiated income and status groups. Generally, a larger proportion of the adult-urban population is gainfully employed than is the case with the adult-rural population. The white-collar class, comprising those employed in trade, in clerical, and in professional work, are proportionately more numerous in large cities and in metropolitan centers and in smaller towns than in the country.

On the whole, the city discourages an economic life in which the individual in time of crisis has a basis of subsistence to fall back upon, and it discourages self-employment. While incomes of city people are on the average higher than those of country people, the cost of living seems to be higher in the larger cities. Home-ownership involves greater burdens and is rarer. Rents are higher and absorb a larger proportion of the income. Although the urban-dweller has the benefit of many communal services, he spends a large proportion of his income for such items as recreation and advancement and a smaller proportion for food. What the communal services do not furnish, the urbanite must purchase, and there is virtually no human need which has remained unexploited by commercialism. Catering to thrills and furnishing means of escape from drudgery, monotony, and routine thus become one of the major functions of urban recreation, which at its best furnishes means for creative self-expression and spontaneous group association, but which more typically in the urban world results in passive spectatorism, on the one hand, or sensational record-smashing feats, on the other.

Reduced to a stage of virtual impotence as an individual, the urbanite is bound to exert himself by joining with others of similar interest into groups organized to obtain his ends. This results in the enormous multiplication of voluntary organizations directed toward as great a variety of objectives as there are human needs and interests. While, on the one hand, the traditional ties of human association are weakened, urban existence involves a much greater degree of interdependence between man and man and a more complicated, fragile, and volatile form of mutual interrelations over many phases of which the individual as such can exert scarcely any control. Frequently there is only the most tenuous relationship between the economic position or other basic factors that determine the individual's existence in the urban world and the voluntary groups with which he is affiliated. In a primitive and in a rural society it is generally possible to predict on the basis of a few known factors who will belong to what and who will associate with whom in almost every relationship of life, but in the city we can only project the general pattern of group for-

mation and affiliation, and this pattern will display many incongruities and contradictions.

URBAN PERSONALITY AND COLLECTIVE BEHAVIOR   It is
largely through the activities of the voluntary groups, be their
objectives economic, political, educational, religious, recreational,
or cultural, that the urbanite expresses and develops his personality, acquires status, and is able to carry on the round of activities that constitute his life career. It may easily be inferred,
however, that the organizational framework which these highly
differentiated functions call into being does not of itself insure the
consistency and integrity of the personalities whose interests it en-
lists. Personal disorganization, mental breakdown, suicide, delinquency, crime, corruption, and disorder might be expected under
these circumstances to be more prevalent in the urban than in the
rural community. This has been confirmed in so far as comparable
indexes are available, but the mechanisms underlying these phenomena require further analysis.

Since for most group purposes it is impossible in the city to
appeal individually to the large number of discrete and differentiated citizens, and since it is only through the organizations to
which men belong that their interests and resources can be enlisted for a collective cause, it may be inferred that social control
in the city should typically proceed through formally organized
groups. It follows, too, that the masses of men in the city are subject to manipulation by symbols and stereotypes managed by individuals working from afar or operating invisibly behind the
scenes through their control of the instruments of communication.
Self-government either in the economic, or political, or the cultural realm is under these circumstances reduced to a mere figure
of speech, or, at best, is subject to the unstable equilibrium of
pressure groups. In view of the ineffectiveness of actual kinship
ties, we create fictional kinship groups. In the face of the disappearance of the territorial unit as a basis of social solidarity, we
create interest units. Meanwhile the city as a community resolves
itself into a series of tenuous segmental relationships superimposed upon a territorial base with a definite center but without a
definite periphery, and upon a division of labor which far tran-

scends the immediate locality and is world-wide in scope. The larger the number of persons in a state of interaction with another, the lower is the level of communication and the greater is the tendency for communication to proceed on an elementary level, i.e., on the basis of those things which are assumed to be common or to be of interest to all.

It is obviously, therefore, to the emerging trends in the communication system and to the production and distribution technology that has come into existence with modern civilization that we must look for the symptoms which will indicate the probable development of urbanism as a mode of social life. The direction of the ongoing changes in urbanism will for good or ill transform not only the city but the world.

It is only in so far as the sociologist, with a workable theory of urbanism, has a clear conception of the city as a social entity that he can hope to develop a unified body of reliable knowledge—which what passes as "urban sociology" is certainly not at the present time. By taking his point of departure from a theory of urbanism such as that sketched in the foregoing pages, a theory to be elaborated, tested, and revised in the light of further analysis and empirical research, the sociologist can hope to determine the criteria of relevance and validity of factual data. The miscellaneous assortment of disconnected information which has hitherto found its way into sociological treatises on the city may thus be sifted and incorporated into a coherent body of knowledge. Incidentally, only by means of some such theory will the sociologist escape the futile practice of voicing in the name of sociological science a variety of often unsupportable judgments about poverty, housing, city-planning, sanitation, municipal administration, policing, marketing, transportation, and other technical issues. Though the sociologist cannot solve any of these practical problems—at least not by himself—he may, if he discovers his proper function, have an important contribution to make to their comprehension and solution. The prospects for doing this are brightest through a general, theoretical, rather than through an *ad hoc* approach.

5

THE GHETTO

FOR THE past five hundred years the Jewish settlements in the Western world have been known as ghettos. The modern ghetto, some evidence of which is found in every city of even moderate size, traces its ancestry back to the medieval European urban institution by means of which the Jews were segregated from the rest of the population. In the East, until recently, the ghetto took the form of the "pale" of settlement, which represents a ghetto within a ghetto. The ghetto is no longer the place of officially regulated settlement of the Jews, but rather a local cultural area which has arisen quite informally. In the American cities the name "ghetto" applies particularly to those areas where the poorest and most backward groups of the Jewish population, usually the recently arrived immigrants, find their home.

From the standpoint of the sociologist the ghetto as an institution is of interest first of all because it represents a prolonged case study in isolation. It may be regarded as a form of accommodation through which a minority has effectually been subordinated to a dominant group. The ghetto exhibits at least one historical form of dealing with a dissenting minority within a larger population, and as such has served as an instrument of control.

Reprinted from *Community Life and Social Policy*, ed. Elizabeth Wirth Marvick and Albert J. Reiss, Jr. (Chicago: University of Chicago Press, 1956), pp. 261–74, first published in the *American Journal of Sociology*, XXXIII (July, 1927), 57–71.

At the same time the ghetto represents a form of toleration through which a *modus vivendi* is established between groups that are in conflict with each other on fundamental issues. Some of these functions are still served by the modern ghetto, which, in other respects, has a character quite distinct from that of the medieval institution. In western Europe and America, however, it is of primary interest because it shows the actual processes of distribution and grouping of the population in urban communities. It indicates the ways in which cultural groups give expression to their heritages when transplanted to a strange habitat; it evidences the constant sifting and resifting that goes on in a population, the factors that are operative in assigning locations to each section, and the forces through which the community maintains its integrity and continuity. Finally, it demonstrates the subtle ways in which this cultural community is transformed by degrees until it blends with the larger community about it, meanwhile reappearing in various altered guises of its old and unmistakable atmosphere.

This paper concerns itself not with the history of the ghetto but with its natural history. Viewed from this angle the study of the ghetto is likely to throw light on a number of related phenomena, such as the origin of segregated areas and the development of local communities in general; for, while the ghetto is, strictly speaking, a Jewish institution, there are forms of ghettos that contain not merely Jews. Our cities contain Little Sicilies, Little Polands, Chinatowns, and Black Belts. There are Bohemias and Hobohemias, slums and Gold Coasts, vice areas and Rialtos in every metropolitan community. The forces that underlie the formation and development of these areas bear a close resemblance to those at work in the ghetto. These forms of community life are likely to become more intelligible if we know something of the Jewish ghetto.

The concentration of the Jews into segregated local areas in the medieval cities did not originate with any formal edict of church or state. The ghetto was not, as is sometimes mistakenly believed, the arbitrary creation of the authorities, designed to deal with an alien people. The ghetto was not the product of de-

sign on the part of anyone, but rather the unwitting crystallization of needs and practices rooted in the customs and heritages,
religious and secular, of the Jews themselves. Long before it was
made compulsory, the Jews lived in separate parts of the cities in
Western lands of their own accord. The Jews drifted into separate
cultural areas, not by external pressure or by deliberate design.
The factors that operated toward the founding of locally separated
communities by the Jews are to be sought in the character of Jewish traditions, in the habits and customs, not only of the Jews
themselves, but of the medieval town-dweller in general. To the
Jews the spatially separated and socially isolated community
seemed to offer the best opportunity for following their religious
precepts, their established ritual and diet, and the numerous functions which tied the individual to familial and communal institutions. In some instances it was the fear of the remainder of the
population, no doubt, which induced them to seek each other's
company, or the ruler under whose protection they stood found it
desirable, for purposes of revenue and control, to grant them a
separate quarter. The general tenor of medieval life no doubt
played an important role, for it was customary for members of the
same occupational group to live in the same locality, and the
Jews, forming as a whole a separate vocational class and having
a distinct economic status, were merely falling in line, therefore,
with the framework of medieval society, in which everyone was
tied to some locality. In addition, there were the numerous ties of
kinship and acquaintanceship which developed an *esprit de corps*
as a significant factor in community life. There was the item of a
common language, of community of ideas and interest, and the
mere congeniality that arises even between strangers who, coming
from the same locality, meet in a strange place. Finally, the segregation of the Jews in ghettos is identical in many respects with
the development of segregated areas in general. The tolerance that
strange modes of life need and find in immigrant settlements, in
Latin quarters, in vice districts, and in racial colonies is a powerful factor in the sifting of the urban population and its allocation
in separate local areas where inhabitants obtain freedom from
hostile criticism and the backing of a group of kindred spirits.

Corresponding to the local separateness of the Jew from his Christian neighbors there is to be noted the functional separation of the two groups. Just as the world beyond the ghetto wall was external to the life within the ghetto, so the personal relationships between Jews and non-Jews were those of externality and utility. The Jews supplemented the economic complex of medieval European life. They served a number of functions which the inhabitants of the town were incapable of exercising. The Jews were allowed to trade and engage in exchange, occupations which the church did not permit Christians to engage in. Besides, the Jews were valuable taxable property and could be relied on to furnish much needed revenue. On the other hand, the Jews, too, regarded the Christian population as a means to an end, as a utility. The Christians could perform functions such as eating the hind quarter of beef and could purchase the commodities that the Jews had for sale; they could borrow money from the Jew and pay interest; they could perform innumerable services for him which he could not perform himself. In the rigid structure of medieval life the Jews found a strategic place. The attitude of the medieval church had coupled trade and finance with sin. The Jews were free from this taboo, which made the occupation of merchant and banker seem undesirable to the Christian population. The Christian churchmen were not troubled about the "perils of the Jewish soul," for, so far as they knew, he had no soul to be saved. What made the trade relation possible, however, was not merely the fact that it was mutually advantageous, but the fact that trade relationships are possible when no other form of contact between two peoples can take place. The Jew, being a stranger, and belonging as he did to a separate and distinct class, was admirably fitted to become the merchant and banker. He drifted to the towns and cities where trade was possible and profitable. Here he could utilize all the distant contacts that he had developed in the course of his wandering. His attachment to the community at large was slight, and when necessity demanded it he could migrate to a locality where opportunities were greater. He owned no real property to which he was tied, nor was he the serf of a feudal lord. His mobility in turn developed versatility. He saw opportunities in places where no native could see them. While the ghetto was never more than a temporary stopping-place, the Jew was never a hobo, for he had an aim, a destination, and his community went with him in his migrations.

While the Jew's contacts with the outside world were categorical and abstract, within his own community he was at home. Here he could relax from etiquette and formalism. His contacts with his fellow Jews were warm, intimate, and free. Especially was this true of his family life, within the inner circle of which he received that appreciation and sympathetic understanding which the larger world could not offer. In his own community, which was based upon the solidarity of the families that composed it, he was a person with status. Whenever he returned from a journey to a distant market or from his daily work, he came back to the family fold, there to be recreated and reaffirmed as a man and as a Jew. Even when he was far removed from his kin, he lived his real inner life in his dreams and hopes with them. He could converse with his own kind in that familiar tongue which the rest of the world could not understand. He was bound by common troubles, by numerous ceremonies and sentiments to his small group that lived its own life oblivious of the world beyond the confines of the ghetto. Without the backing of his group, without the security that he enjoyed in his inner circle of friends and countrymen, life would have been intolerable.

Through the instrumentality of the ghetto there gradually developed that social distance which effectually isolated the Jew from the remainder of the population. These barriers did not completely inhibit contact, but they reduced it to the type of relationships which were of a secondary and formal nature. As these barriers crystallized and his life was lived more and more removed from the rest of the world, the solidarity of his own little community was enhanced until it became strictly divorced from the larger world without.

The forms of community life that had arisen naturally and spontaneously in the course of the attempt of the Jews to adapt themselves to their surroundings gradually became formalized in custom and precedent, and finally crystallized into legal enactment. What the Jews had sought as a privilege was soon to be imposed upon them by law. As the Jews had come to occupy a more important position in medieval economy, and as the church at about the time of the Crusades became more militant, there set in a period of active regulation. The ghetto became compulsory. But the institution of the ghetto had by this time become firmly rooted in the habits and attitudes of the Jews. The historians of the ghetto are usually inclined to overemphasize the confining effect of the barriers that were set up around the Jew, and the provincial and stagnant character of ghetto existence. They forget that there was nevertheless a teeming life within the ghetto which was probably more active than life outside.

The laws that came to regulate the conduct of the Jews and Christians were merely the formal expressions of social distances that had already been ingrained in the people. While on the one hand the Jew was coming to be more and more a member of a class—an abstraction—on the other hand there persisted the tendency to react to him as a human being. The ghetto made the Jew self-conscious. Life in the ghetto was bearable only because there was a larger world outside, of which many Jews often got more than a passing glimpse. As a result they often lived on the fringe of two worlds. There was always some movement to get out of the ghetto on the part of those who were attracted by the wide world that lay beyond the horizon of the ghetto walls and who were cramped by the seemingly narrow life within. Sometimes a Jew would leave the ghetto and become converted; and sometimes these converts, broken and humiliated, would return to the ghetto to taste again of the warm, intimate, tribal life that was to be found nowhere but among their people. On such occasions the romance of the renegade would be told in the ghetto streets, and the whole community would thereby be welded into a solid mass amid the solemn ceremonies by which the stray member was reincorporated into the community.

The inner solidarity of the ghetto community always lay in the ties of family life, and through the organization in the synagogue these families gained status within a community. Confined as the province of the ghetto was, there was ample opportunity for the display of capacity for leadership. The ghetto community was minutely specialized and highly integrated. There were probably more distinct types of personality and institutions within the narrow ghetto streets than in the larger world outside.

The typical ghetto is a densely populated, walled-in-area usually found near the arteries of commerce or in the vicinity of a market. The Jewish quarter, even before the days of the compulsory ghetto, seems to have grown up round the synagogue, which was the center of Jewish life locally as well as religiously. A common feature of all ghettos was the cemetery, a communal responsibility to which unusual sentimental interest was attached. There were a number of educational, recreational, and hygienic institutions, such as a school for the young, a bath, a slaughter house, a bakehouse, and a dance hall. In the close life within the ghetto walls almost nothing was left to the devices of the individual. Life was well organized, and custom and ritual played an institutionalizing role which still accounts for the high degree of organization of Jewish communities, often verging on overorganization. These institutions did not arise ready made. They represent what life always is, an adaptation to the physical and social needs of a people. In this case particularly, those institutions that had to deal with the conflict and disorder within the group and the pressure from without were the characteristic form of accommodation to the isolation which the ghetto symbolized and enforced. This holds good not merely for the institutions of the ghetto, but for the functionaries and personalities that center around them. The Jews as we know them today are themselves a product of the ghetto.

The ghetto, from the standpoint of biology, was a closely inbreeding, self-perpetuating group to such an extent that it may properly be called a closed community. Not that there was no intermarriage, but these mixed marriages as a rule were lost to the ghetto. The Jews have frequently and rightly been pointed out as the classic example of the great force of religious and racial prejudices, of segregation and isolation, in giving rise to distinct physical and social types. Those types persist roughly to the extent that ghetto life and its effects have continued relatively unchanged, which is most true of eastern Europe and the Orient. The difference in community life accounts in large part for the differences between various local groupings within the Jewish population.

The Russian, Polish, and in part the Roumanian Jews differ from those of western Europe—the German, French, Dutch, and English Jews—in several fundamental respects. For a long period the Jews of the east were merely a cultural dependency—an outpost—of western Jewry. When an independent cultural life did develop in Russia, Poland, and Lithuania, it was self-sufficient and self-contained, set apart from the larger world. Not so with the Jews of western Europe. They were never quite impervious to the currents of thought and the social changes that characterized the life of Europe after the Renaissance. While the Jews of the east lived in large part in rural communities, in a village world, those of the west were predominantly a city people in touch with the centers of trade and finance near and far and in touch at least for some time with the pulsating intellectual life of the world. While the Jews of the Rhine cities were associating with men of thought and of affairs, their brethren in Russia were dealing with peasants and an uncultured, decadent, feudal nobility. When the Jewries of the west were already seething with modernist religious, political, and social movements, those of the east were still steeped in mysticism and medieval ritual. While the western Jews were moving along with the tide of progress, those of the east were still sharing the backwardness and isolation of the gentile world of villagers and peasants. Although until the middle of the last century the Jews of the east were never quite so confined in their physical movements as were the ghetto Jews of the west, the former lived in a smaller world, a world characterized by rigidity and and stability; and when they were herded into cities, in which they constituted the preponderant bulk of the total population, they merely turned these cities into large villages that had little in common with the urban centers of the west. Many features of local life in the modern Jewish community bear the imprint of the successive waves of immigrants first from the west and then from the east.

The formal enactments that made the ghetto the legal dwelling-place of the Jews were abolished toward the middle of the last century in most of the countries of the world. Strangely enough, the abolition of the legal ghetto was opposed by a great portion of Jews as late as a hundred years ago, for they had a premonition that the leveling of the ghetto walls would mean the wiping out of separate community life, which the formal ghetto rules merely symbolized. Those who saw in the new freedom the waning influence of the Jewish religion and the ultimate dissolution of Jewish life in separate communities had two things left to console them: (1) the formal equality decreed by law did not at once gain for the Jew ready acceptance and a parallel social status among his fellow-citizens; and (2) although western Jewry seemed to be crumbling, there were approximately six millions of Jews left on the other side of the Vistula who were still clinging to the old bonds that exclusion and oppression had fashioned. But since that time even Russia has been revolutionized, and the so-called "last bulwark" of Judaism threatens to disappear.

Just as the ghetto arose before formal decrees forced the Jews into segregated areas, so the ghetto persists after these decrees have been annulled. Israel Zangwill has said: "People who have been living in a ghetto for a couple of centuries are not able to step outside merely because the gates are thrown down, nor to efface the brands on their souls by putting off their yellow badges. The isolation from without will have come to seem the law of their being."[1] The formal abolition of the ghetto and the granting of citizenship did for the Jews about what the Emancipation Proclamation did for the Negro. Slavery was more than a mere legal relationship, and the ghetto was more than a statute. It had become an institution. Though the physical walls of the ghetto have been torn down, an invisible wall of isolation still maintains the distance between the Jew and his neighbors.

Even in towns containing only a handful of Jews, there will be found in all parts of the world some more or less definitely organized community. The ecological factors that enter into its development are essentially those of the medieval ghetto. There

[1]   *Children of the Ghetto*, p. 6.

are several items besides the continuity of tradition from within and prejudice from without that account for the persistence of the modern ghetto, particularly in American cities. One of these is the colonization movement among the Jews, by which Old World communities are sometimes kept intact in the New World. But even where no such organized effort exists, it is remarkable to what extent the Jewish community tends to perpetuate its old surroundings.

To a large extent the modern ghetto is necessitated by the precepts and practices of orthodox Judaism, by the need of dwelling within easy reach of the synagogue, the schoolroom, and the ritual bath, the kosher butcher shop and the kosher dairy. But even for those who are indifferent to religious observances and ritual practices, residence in the ghetto is necessitated by social and economic circumstances. Ignorance of the language of the new country, of its labour conditions, and of its general habits and ways of thought, as well as the natural timidity of a fugitive from a land of persecution, compels the immigrant Jew to settle in the colony of his co-religionists. Among them he is perfectly at home; he finds the path of employment comparatively smooth, and if his efforts to attain it be delayed, he is helped in the interval by charity from a dozen hands.[2]

In countries where the contact between Jew and non-Jew has been continued for a few generations, and where no new immigration from other countries in which the Jews retained their old status has taken place, the ghetto has to a large extent disintegrated. Under these circumstances, not only does the ghetto tend to disappear, but the race tends to disappear with it. Contact with the world through education, commerce, and the arts tends to bring about a substitution of the cultural values of the world at large for those of the ghetto. This contact, moreover, frequently brings about intermarriage, which is most frequent in those localities where intercourse between Jew and Gentile is least restricted. It is safe to say that the present fifteen and a half million Jews in the world constitute only a small proportion of the living descendants of the original Jewish settlers in the Western world at the beginning of the Christian era. They are merely the residue

[2]   Israel Cohen, *Jewish Life in Modern Times*, pp. 37–38.

of a much larger group whose Jewish identity has been lost in the general stream of population. What has happened in the case of the Jews is essentially what has happened in all minority groups in recent times. As the barriers of isolation have receded, social intercourse and interbreeding have decimated the size of the group and leveled its distinguishing characteristics to those of the milieu.

A Jewish community may in some respects be said to exist after the obstacles to ready intercourse with the world outside have been removed, but it tends to become a nondescript community. Where, however, as is the case in most large cities of western Europe and especially the United States, a steady influx of new immigrants has replenished the disintegrating community, there a ghetto, with all the characteristic local color, has grown up and maintains itself. Such a community is the Chicago ghetto.

Western ghettos differ from those of eastern Europe and the Orient in that the former comprise at least two sections, the native and the foreign. The native section lives in some sort of concentration within convenient distance from the communal institutions. A rise in material prosperity is generally followed by a removal to a better district where a new Jewish area is created, but one less distinguished from its environment by external tokens. The foreign section, however, lives in a state of dense concentration. Their poverty makes them settle in the poor quarter of the town, where they reproduce the social conditions in which they have been born and bred, so far as the new environment will allow. The ghetto in the east may be a symbol of political bondage; but in the west the only bondage that it typifies is that exercised by economic status, by sentiment and tradition.[3]

If you would know what kind of Jew a man is, ask him where he lives; for no single factor indicates as much about the character of the Jew as the area in which he lives. It is an index not only to his economic status, his occupation, his religion, but to his politics and his outlook on life and the stage in the assimilative process that he has reached.

West of the Chicago River, in the shadow of the central busi-

3   *Ibid.*, p. 37.

ness district, lies a densely populated rectangle of crowded tenements representing the greater part of Chicago's immigrant colonies, among them the ghetto. It contains the most varied assortment of people to be found in any similar area of the world. This area has been the stamping ground of virtually every immigrant group that has come to Chicago. The occupation of this area by the Jews is, it seems, merely a passing phase of a long process of succession in which one population group has been crowded out by another. There is, however, an unmistakable regularity in this process. In the course of the growth of the city and the invasion of the slums by new groups of immigrants there has resulted a constancy of association between Jews and other ethnic groups. Each racial and cultural group tends to settle in that part of the city which, from the point of view of rents, standards of living, accessibility, and tolerance, makes the reproduction of the Old World life easiest. In the course of the invasion of these tides of immigrants the ghetto has become converted from the outskirts of an overgrown village to the slum of a great city in little more than one generation. The Jews have successively displaced the Germans, the Irish, and the Bohemians, and have themselves been displaced by the Poles and Lithuanians, the Italians, the Greeks, and Turks, and finally the Negroes. The Poles and Jews detest each other thoroughly, but they can trade with each other very successfully. They have transferred the accommodation to each other from the Old World to the New. The latest invasion of the ghetto by the Negro is of more than passing interest. The Negro, like the immigrant, is segregated in the city into a racial colony; economic factors, race prejudice, and cultural differences combine to set him apart. The Negro has drifted to the abandoned sections of the ghetto for precisely the same reasons that the Jews and the Italians came there. Unlike the white landlords and residents of former days and in other parts of the city, the Jews have offered no appreciable resistance to the invasion of the Negroes. The Negroes pay good rent and spend their money readily. Many of the immigrants of the ghetto have not as yet discovered the color line.

The transition and deterioration of the ghetto has been proceeding at such speed that the complexion of the area changes from day to day. Dilapidated structures that a decade ago were Lutheran and Catholic churches have since become synagogues, and have now been turned into African M. E. churches. Under the latest coat of paint of a store-front colored mission there are vestiges of signs reading "Kosher Butchershop" and "Deutsche Apotheke."

True to the ancient pattern, the most colorful and active section of the ghetto is the street market, which resembles a medieval fair more than the shopping district of a modern city. But this institution, together with the rest of the ghetto culture, is fast declining. The life of the immigrants in the ghetto is so circumscribed and they are so integrally a part of it that they are unaware of its existence. It is the children of the immigrant who discover the ghetto and then . . . flee. What a few years ago was a steady but slow outward movement has now developed into a veritable stampede to get out of the ghetto; for, with all its varied activities and its colorful atmosphere, the ghetto nevertheless is a small world. It throbs with a life which is provincial and sectarian. Its successes are measured on a small scale, and its range of expression is limited.

Not until the immigrant leaves the ghetto does he become fully conscious of himself and his status. He feels a sense of personal freedom and expansion as he takes up his residence in the more modern and less Jewish area of second settlement. As late as twenty years ago, when the first Jewish fugitives from the ghetto invaded Lawndale, an area about two miles west, which in Chicago represents the area of second settlement, they came into collision with the Irish and the Germans, who had turned what was recently a prairie into something like a park. It took the Jews about ten years to convert it into a densely settled apartment-house area. At first they could not rent. Experience in the ghetto from which the Irish and Germans had been displaced had given these residents a vision of what was in store for their homes. But this time the Jews could afford to buy, and they bought in blocks. By 1910, Lawndale had become a second ghetto. Its synagogues were a little more modern than those of Maxwell Street; the beards of the Lawndale Jews were a little trimmer, and their coats a little shorter, than in the original ghetto; but Lawndale had become Jewish. Those residents of the ghetto who stayed behind derisively called Lawndale "Deutschland" and its inhabitants "Deitchuks," because they were affecting German ways.

But the Lawndale Jews found little rest and satisfaction. Their erstwhile neighbors, impelled by identical motives—to flee from their fellow Jews, and be less Jewish—had given Lawndale a new complexion, unmistakably Jewish, though not quite as genuine as that of the ghetto itself.

In their attempt to flee from the ghetto, the partially assimilated Jews have found that the ghetto has followed them, and a new exodus sets in. The plans of those who fled from the ghetto in order to obtain status as human beings—as successful business or professional men, rather than as Jews—have been frustrated by the similar plans of others. So it is with the third settlement in the fashionable apartment hotels and the suburbs. As the area becomes predominantly Jewish, the non-Jewish settlers move, and the Jews begin the pursuit anew. Scarcely does the Jew get a glimpse of the freer world that looms beyond the ghetto when he becomes irritated by the presence of his fellow Jews, more Jewish than himself; he is bored, disgusted, and resumes his flight.

In the process he changes his character and his institutions. But what has held the community together in spite of all disintegrating forces from within and without is not only the replenishment of the ghetto by new immigrants—for this is a waning factor—but rather the return to the ghetto of those who have fled but have been disappointed and disillusioned about the results of their flight. They have found the outside world cold and unresponsive to their claims, and return to the warmth and the intimacy of the ghetto. Finally, the Jewish community has been kept intact by the fact that the outside world has treated it as an entity. The Jewish problem, if there be one, lies in the fact that the ghetto persists in spite of the attempt of so many to flee. As long as the nucleus remains, it will serve as a symbol of community life to which even those who are far removed in space and in sympathies belong and by which they are identified.

The Jews as individuals do not always find the way to assimilation blocked. They make friends as well as enemies. The contacts between cultural and racial groups inevitably produce harmony as well as friction; and the one cannot be promoted nor the other prevented by nostrums and ready-made programs and administrative devices. Interaction is life, and life is a growth which defies attempts at control and direction, however rational they may be, that do not take account of this dynamic process. In the struggle for status, personality arises. The Jew, like every other human being, owes his unique character to this struggle, and that character will change and perhaps disappear as the struggle changes or subsides.

What makes the Jewish community—composed as it is of heterogeneous cultural elements and distributed in separate areas of our cities—a community is its capacity to act corporately. It is a cultural community and constitutes as near an approach to communal life as the modern city has to offer. The ghetto, be it Chinese, Negro, Sicilian, or Jewish, can be completely understood only if it is viewed as a sociopsychological, as well as an ecological, phenomenon; for it is not merely a physical fact, but also a state of mind.

6

SOME JEWISH TYPES

OF PERSONALITY

THE SOCIOLOGIST, in transforming the unique or individual experience into a representative or typical one, arrives at the social type, which consists of a set of attitudes on the part of the person toward himself and the group and a corresponding set of attitudes of the group toward him, which together determine the role of the person in his social milieu. The extent to which social types may be depicted depends upon the definiteness of the organization of the attitudes and their characteristic cohesion about a core of significant social traits. The range of the personality types in a given social group is indicative of the culture of that group.

The Jew as a Social Type

Although there is probably no people that has furnished the basis for more contradictory conclusions regarding racial and cultural traits than the Jews, the elementary question as to whether the Jews are a race, a nationality, or a cultural group

Reprinted from *Community Life and Social Policy*, ed. Elizabeth Wirth Marvick and Albert J. Reiss, Jr. (Chicago: University of Chicago Press, 1956), pp. 275–80, first published in *Publications of the American Sociological Society*, XXXII (1926), 90–96.

remains unsettled. There are those who, with Chamberlain, believe that the Jew constitutes a clear racial type whose characteristics are unmistakable.[1] Hilaire Belloc prefers to think of the
Jews not as a race but primarily as a nationality. In fact he
points out that the Jews themselves have called their people a
race when it suited them, a nationality when necessity demanded
it, a religious group, and finally a cultural body, by virtue of the
historic process, when their situation made such a status desirable.[2]

Fishberg sees in the Jew a social type. He writes:

What is that "Jewish type," that Jewish physiognomy, which char-
acterizes the Jew? It is the opinion of the present author that it is less
than skin deep. Primarily it is dependent on dress and deportment
of the Jews in countries where they live in strict isolation from their
Christian or Moslem neighbors. It is not the body which marks the
Jew; it is his soul. In other words, the type is not anthropological or
physical; it is social or psychic. Centuries of confinement in the ghetto,
social ostracism, ceaseless suffering under the ban of abuse and persecution have been instrumental in producing a characteristic psychic
type which manifests itself in his cast of countenance which is considered peculiarly "Jewish." . . . The ghetto face is purely psychic, just
like the actor's, the soldier's, the minister's face.[3]

What is typical of the Jews as a group is their characteristic
"run of attention," or the direction of their habits and interests—
which have become fixed through centuries of communal life in
segregated areas—and the persistence of a set of cultural traits,
most significant of which were, perhaps, those relating to their
religious ritualism, which was fairly uniform throughout the
world and which pervaded every sphere of life.

Jewish Types

Striking as the differences between Jew and non-Jew may
be, the individual and sectional differences within the Jewish

[1]   Houston Stewart Chamberlain, *Foundations of the Nineteenth
Century*, II, 537.

[2]   Hilaire Belloc, *The Jews* (Boston and New York, 1923).

[3]   Maurice Fishberg, *The Jews: A Study of Race and Environment*,
p. 162.

group are even greater. The Jews of Asia, North Africa, and eastern Europe differ profoundly from those to the west.

The Jews of any particular country, althought exposed to the same general influences, are not molded into a uniform pattern. Having settled in the land at different periods, and having brought from their previous homes different modes of life and different degrees of conservatism, they resist the surrounding influences with unequal will and strength and exhibit varying grades of assimilation to the general population. In each individual country, therefore, there is a series of classes or types of Jews, shaded off from one another, and thus the multiplicity of types in the world forms an almost endless series.[4]

While the Jews of the west have, in varying measure, had the opportunity to taste the life outside the ghetto walls, the Jews of the east have only gradually and recently come to share some of the cultural heritages of their neighbors. The diversity of the sources of Jewish immigration to the United States accounts for the corresponding multiplicity of Jewish types that are met with in every Jewish community in our large cities. These social differentiations are reflected in the religious, the vocational, and the cultural aspects of the lives of the people, and result in diverse organizations of attitudes and habits which are clearly recognizable, not only by the observer, but by the members of the group itself. They can be detected in the folklore and the literature, in the theater and the marketplace; they give rise to many problems of social organization and control; they are as complete an index as any at present obtainable of the culture traits and the culture pattern of the group.

In this discussion it is scarcely possible to do more than enumerate some of the most characteristic and picturesque personalities that are met with in the average community. From the standpoint of worldly success, especially in the vocational sphere, we meet with a personality known as *Mensch,* or, the "allrightnick." Both types represent persons of superior economic status, but while the former has achieved his success without sacrificing his identity as a Jew, the latter in his opportunism has thrown overboard most of the cultural baggage of his group, and as a consequence is treated with a certain attitude of disdain. The "allright-

4   Israel Cohen, *Jewish Life in Modern Times,* p. 15.

nick" offends the group because he is no respecter of its values. The Jews have been so well known as businessmen ever since the Middle Ages that we should be indeed surprised to find that this vocational type lacked status, but the "allrightnick" represents the reprehensible type of businessman to whom success is everything and in whose life-organization there is no place for any of the other forms of achievement that the culture offers.

Social types seem to run in pairs and may be conceived of as opposite poles in a range of attitudes and values. At one end of the scale we find the *Mensch* and the "allrightnick"; or at the other, the *Schlemiel:* "Although the Jew has acquired the reputation of being the personification of the commercial spirit, he is sometimes quite shiftless and helpless, failing miserably in everything he undertakes, as though pursued by some mocking sprite, and good-humoredly nicknamed by his brethren a *Schlemiel.*"[5]

The facility with which the Jew can adapt himself vocationally to a changing, and sometimes to a hostile, environment has often been pointed out: "If a Jew cannot succeed in one calling he promptly adopts another, and he is a veritable 'quick-change artist' in the variety of his vocations. He is a peddler, teacher, commission agent, precentor, and marriage broker by turns, regularly consoling himself with the thought that 'God will help,' and invariably ready to help his neighbor. It is in regard to existences such as these that Dr. Max Nordau coined the expression *Luftmenschen,* people whose only apparent means of subsistence is the air they breathe."[6]

This *Luftmensch,* who in America, by virtue of his getting-by philosophy, is identified with the hobo, constitutes the bulk of the homeless men's problem with which Jewish social agencies have to deal in increasing numbers, probably because in America he can find support for his habits and attitudes, not only in the traditional tolerance and sympathy of his own cultural group, but also in the larger group about him.

There is a type of Jew referred to by the group itself as *Schacherjude,* more familiarly known as a huckster or peddler. Here we find an illustration of the competitive process by which

[5]   *Ibid.,* p. 186.   [6]   *Ibid.,* p. 210.

an alien or immigrant group is relegated to the occupations which to the native seem degrading and undesirable, but which to the immigrant represent merely the opportunity to eke out an existence. A number of vocational types center about that Jewish institution, the synagogue. The rabbi, the teacher, the *Chazan* or cantor, the *Shochet* or slaughterer, the *Shamus* or sexton (whose place was once important and honored but has recently lost its status)—all these survive to the present day. There are still some survivors of that unique vocational type known as the *Schadchen,* or marriage broker, once an honorable and most useful occupation. These occupations, arising out of the needs of the group and centering around its institutions, tend to assume the character of professions. Even the occupation of the *Schnorrer,* or beggar, is so organized. The philanthropist and the beggar furnish a striking instance of the polarity of social types. The insolence of the Jewish beggar, growing out of the theory that the recipient of a gift was enabling the donor to perform a religious duty and was, in a sense, the benefactor of the donor, made the *Schnorrer* a most persistent and troublesome figure in modern Jewish society.[7]

The ideal of intellectuality which, in the ghetto of the Old World, produced the type of student known as the *Yeshiba Bochar,* or talmudical student, and the *Melammed,* or rabbinical teacher, persists, though it may be in secular form. In the olden days when religious learning was the highest virtue, a prosperous merchant would prefer a poor but learned student as the future husband for his daughter; in the modern ghetto a lawyer, a doctor, an artist, or a writer are the prizes that the rich businessman will seek as his sons-in-law.

The social type of the intellectual demonstrates that for the persistence of a social type there is needed a favorable set of attitudes and habits in the cultural group. There can be intellectuals only in a community that prizes them, supports them by means of its wealth, admiration, and status. If the community consists only of ignoramuses, the intellectuals leave it and seek those freer and more cosmopolitan centers, usually in the

[7]   Israel Abrahams, *Jewish Life in the Middle Ages,* pp. 310–11.

largest cities, where intellectuality is rewarded and can find a favorable habitat. As economic success and social status become more and more the highest ideals of the group, intellectuality ceases to serve as a means for obtaining prestige, and the intellectual as a social type is transformed and ultimately becomes extinct.

At the opposite extreme in the scale of values in the Jewish community stands the *Groberjung,* or the uncouth, uneducated individual who has no appreciation for intellectuality. Be he rich or poor, his place in the social scale is a humble and obscure one.

There is scarcely a ghetto community that does not support and attract to its midst a pious, patriarchal personage known as the *Zaddik* whose exemplary conduct is pointed to as an example worthy of emulation on the part of the young. He is held in high esteem and sometimes is lavishly rewarded with gifts of the material sort. At the opposite pole we find the apostate, or *Meshumad,* who is scorned and frequently ostracized from the community. There is also a type known as the *Kleikodeshnik,* the person who makes piousness his profession and who, behind a mask of conformity to the ritual, lives upon and exploits a credulous public until discovered. Other types arising out of the religious complex of the group are the *Schönerjüd,* the conservative, learned, though idle, person; the *Staatsbalabos,* or the patriarchal leader; the *Kolboinik,* or the personification of all wickedness; and the *Gottskossak,* or the self-appointed judge of the piety of the members of the community.

Other well-defined types are the *Lodgenik,* or the joiner; the *Genosse,* who preaches socialism in and out of season; the *Kibitzer,* or the genial, idle joker; the *Leptcheche,* or the gossip; the "society-lady"; the *Radikalke,* or the young lady from the ghetto, of the garrulous kind and emancipated ways, quoting from authors she has not read, very free, unmarried, and ugly.

From the point of view of the assimilative process there are several well-known types, who, arranged in a series, mark the transition from the ghetto Jew to the one who has definitely left the ghetto walls behind him and to whose children the social heritages of the ghetto will appear stranger than fiction. The

Deitchuk, or the person affecting German background and German ways, and the *Ototot,* or the person who is almost emancipated but clings to a little beard, are typical of these intermediate stages.

These social types, ranging themselves in clusters or constellations, each with his little patronage or audience that calls him forth and perpetuates him, each changing as the attitudes and habits of the group undergo transformation and being lost as he passes from one group to another, constitute the social topography of the Jewish community. Through the sifting and allocation that goes on in the city they find their location in the different areas of settlement that make up the immigrant colony. Together they constitute the personal nuclei around which the fabric of the culture of the group is woven. A detailed analysis of the crucial personality types in any given area or cultural group shows that they depend upon a set of habits and attitudes in the group for their existence and are the direct expressions of the values of the group. As the life of the group changes, there appears a host of new social types, mainly outgrowths and transformations of previous patterns which have become fixed through experience.

7

TYPES OF NATIONALISM

A NATIONALITY may be conceived of as a people who, because of the belief in their common descent and their mission in the world, by virtue of their common cultural heritage and historical career aspire to sovereignty over a territory or seek to maintain or enlarge their political or cultural influence in the face of opposition. Nationalism refers to the social movements, attitudes, and ideologies which characterize the behavior of nationalities engaged in the struggle to achieve, maintain, or enhance their position in the world.

Because of the significant role played by nationalism in current world affairs, its study has attracted a great body of scholars and produced an enormous literature.[1] This literature, aside from that portion of it which is patently propagandistic, consists largely of historical treatments of nationalism in specific countries and epochs. This is as it should be, for the more general scientific study of nationalism obviously presupposes the accumulation of a large, ordered body of reliable historical data. The subject of

Reprinted from *Community Life and Social Policy*, ed. Elizabeth Wirth Marvick and Albert J. Reiss, Jr. (Chicago: University of Chicago Press, 1956), pp. 354–67, first published in the *American Journal of Sociology*, XLI (May, 1936), 723–37.

1   For a comprehensive, classified, and annotated bibliography cf. Koppel S. Pinson, *A Bibliographical Introduction to Nationalism* (New York, 1935).

nationalism has such wide ramifications and comprises such a variety and complexity of phenomena that its scientific study has appeared forbidding. There are, indeed, a large number of treatises that have dealt with one or another phase of nationalism in a non-historical manner. Nationalism has been studied in its connection with race,[2] language, religion, politics, economics, education, and psychology. But despite the occasional allusions to sociology in the titles of books on nationalism, and despite the direct bearing of nationalistic phenomena upon important theoretical problems in sociology, no general sociological study of nationalism exists. The literature of nationalism has recently been considerably enriched by such general and fundamental studies as Professor Carleton J. H. Hayes's *Essays on Nationalism*.[3] As long, however, as we continue to confine ourselves to a particularistic analysis of the nationalisms of different countries and epochs, on the one hand, and treating nationalism as a single undifferentiated phenomenon, on the other hand, there is little prospect of scientific advance on this subject.

This paper proposes a provisional set of types of nationalism as they are found in contemporary Europe. While these forms of nationalism have been identified primarily in Europe, it may be safely assumed that they have a very much wider application. This is not, of course, the first attempt to set forth types of nationalism. Professor Hayes has distinguished between original and derived nationalism.[4] Professor Handman has distinguished four types of nationalism: oppression-nationalism, irredentism,

2   Cf., for instance, Sir Arthur Keith, *Nationality and Race from an Anthropologist's Point of View* (London, 1919) ; John Oakesmith, *Race and Nationality* (London, 1918) ; Erich Koch-Weser, *Deutschlands Aussenpolitik in der Nachkriegszeit, 1919–1929* (Berlin, 1929) ; Louis Wirth, "Race and Nationalism," *Introductory General Course in the Study of Contemporary Society* (Chicago, 1934), pp. 395–413; Pinson, *op. cit.*, items 67–73.

3   New York, 1926.

4   "Two Varieties of Nationalism: Original and Derived," in Association of History Teachers of the Middle States and Maryland, *Proceedings*, No. 26 (1928), pp. 71–83.

precaution-nationalism, and prestige-nationalism.[5] In some respects the types here suggested coincide with those delineated by Handman. The basic assumption underlying our typology, however, is that a typology of nationalism must correspond to the types of relations of opposition and of conflict which characterize the relations between the groups. Sociologically a nationality is a conflict group. The self- and group-consciousness generated by nationalistic movements corresponds to the nature of the intergroup relationship that exists between one nationality and another. To some extent the types of nationalism here set forth represent various stages in the same nationalistic movement. The discrimination between these types, however, is intended to reveal the fundamental differences in motivation and in meaning which in spite of a seeming similarity of goal give each, from a sociological point of view, a distinctive character.

Hegemony Nationalism

What gave the nineteenth century the label "the epoch of nationalism" was a series of movements of national unification which we might identify as "hegemony nationalism," and of which the movements resulting in the unification of Italy and the formation of the German Empire are representative specimens. Among the factors that played an animating role in these movements were contiguity of territory, similarity of language, and kinship of culture. These movements which had been nourished by the memory of previous dynastic unions of separate states, by a more or less common history, language, and culture, eventually became defined in political terms with an integrated state and national sovereignty as their goal. The question of racial unity seems not to have played a decisive role, but in the literary movements preceding the political stage, mystical references to race generally used for hortatory purposes, are occasionally found. The decisive factors seem to have been the economic, political, and military advantage to be derived from consolidating smaller principalities into larger and more dynamic units. The internal

[5]   Max Sylvius Handman, "The Sentiment of Nationalism," *Political Science Quarterly*, XXXVI (March, 1921), 104–21.

weakness of such an organization may result from mere arbitrary agglomeration of territory and peoples without regard to cultural and political homogeneity and compatibility, as is demonstrated by the disintegration of the Austro-Hungarian Empire at the conclusion of World War I. On the other hand, a unitary state may arise even in the presence of diversity of language, culture, and historical experience, as is demonstrated by Switzerland, which, as Wieser has put it, is "a state without being a nation,"[6] but which, unlike most other states, virtually has no foreign politics.[7] Switzerland occupies a unique geographical position, and, as so often happens, has been cemented into unity by external pressure.[8]

The personal feeling of expansion with which nationalism infuses a citizenry and the collective force which such a movement generates are not likely to halt abruptly after the formal goals of the movement have been attained. After a nationality has achieved political autonomy, it sometimes redefines its aims in terms of empire or degenerates into a state of national chauvinism.

Nationalism not infrequently has that sinister meaning which we are inclined to recognize in the suffix "ism." This is a nationalism in which the national feeling of power transcends the actual capacity of the nation, it is the nationalism of avaricious aggressiveness and the nationalism that plays with phrases, in short, national chauvinism. Quite a number of the smaller European nations have been infected with this nationalism. They have taken up the national idea which was to be found among the stronger nations whose successes gave the idea general circulation, so that the smaller nations began to assume the haughty demeanor of the great, without having the latter's accomplishments to their credit. Today we find nationalism even where there is no evidence of the existence of a nation, such as Egypt, in India, and in China, where the masses have not even been touched by enlightenment.[9]

6   Friedrich Wieser, *Das Gesetz der Macht* (Vienna, 1926), p. 363.

7   Adolf Günther, *Die alpenländische Gesellschaft* (Jena, 1930), p. 309.

8   H. M. Long, "Imperial Politics of Great Britain," *Foreign Affairs* (January, 1928), p. 265.

9   Wieser, *op. cit.*, p. 399.

The pan-Germanism of the old German Empire and the pan-Slavism of Czarist Russia are perhaps the most striking examples of the excesses of national ideals. The historian Hans Delbrück, who was one of the bitterest opponents of German imperial chauvinism, said:

The high ideal of our fathers was that the German national state should come into existence without our degenerating, however, to the hatefulness and exclusiveness, which we are in the habit of branding, when we find it in other nations, as chauvinism, Jingoism and Muscovitism. . . . This ideal is threatening to be lost among us. The nobler spirits are beginning to look with horror upon the forms in which the national feelings are expressing themselves today and upon the sort of men who make bold to assume leadership in national affairs.[10]

When the saber-rattling party got the upper hand in Germany, in 1906, he wrote:

What we must take into the bargain is the renunciation of the continuous increase in our external splendor and satiation of our thirst for power, which caused the ruin of France and Russia. This tendency toward national vanity is, unfortunately, altogether too strong among us, and the super-Germans, who, after we have knocked it out of the French, would like to make a *grande nation* out of us, will therefore always find fault with German politics.[11]

The German chancellor, finding himself gradually overwhelmed by extremist nationalistic elements, warned as late as 1913: "Nationalism is the worst enemy of our whole politics, and every measure which has as its aim to make it more difficult for this nationalism to thrive, promotes the welfare of our country."[12] Even today, long before Europe has recovered from the most disastrous war of history, the pan-German nationalists and imperialists are clamoring for a large army and navy, the return of lost territory and colonies, and the restoration of national prestige. One way in which it has been thought that the power of the defeated Central

[10]   *Preussische Jahrbücher* (1899), p. 1678.

[11]   *Ibid.*, CXXVI (1906), 192–93.

[12]   Quoted by Martin Hobohm, "Hans Delbrücks Kampf gegen die Hugenberg Front," *Tagebuch* (October 12, 1929), p. 1680.

Powers could be restored is by a union between Austria and Germany. This union, besides the obvious economies that might result from it, has much to commend it, for it would not create new minorities and would at least eliminate one frontier; but it has been prevented by the aspirations of other European powers who saw in this union a disturbance of the "balance of power" and a threat to the peace of Europe.

That a nationalistic movement in the course of its development may fundamentally change its character and aims is evidenced by the history of the so-called Irredenta. "Originally the effort confined itself to stamping out foreign rule in Italy itself; under Garibaldi, Mazzini, and Cavour this aim was accomplished," but the ambition grew until Gabriele d'Annunzio, under the pretext of "freeing co-nationals who were subjected to foreign rule beyond the borders of Italy," could even cross the Adriatic in the name of Italia Irredenta.[13] As the name indicates, irredentism is a form of nationalism which has many of the characteristics of a holy war. It is not confined to Italy, but was obvious in France between 1871 and 1914 in regard to the "lost provinces" and is developing in Germany today on an even grander scale.

There are two other forms in which the type of nationalism that has thus far been described may appear when charged with unusual vigor: one is imperialism and the other fascism. Of the two the latter is today of greatest interest in Europe. There are many forms of fascism; or, to be more accurate, after the success of the Italian adventure other movements in Europe, which had little similarity to the Italian, appropriated the name. In Spain, for instance, under Primo de Rivera fascism consisted merely of a military dictatorship. Mussolini himself refused to regard the fascistic movements in Germany, Spain, and elsewhere in Europe as the genuine product. "Fascism is a political pseudo-renaissance of post-war Europe," where governments were so thoroughly paralyzed by internal class struggles, by external pressure, and by general discontent that faith in the existing machinery of government was easily dispelled by the emotional appeal to the glories of the

13   Wieser, *op. cit.*, p. 405.

distant past and the even greater prospective glories of the immediate future, if the nation would only awake and put its trust in
its elite.[14] Fascism represents a reaction against parliamentarism
and democracy. For more than two years in Italy fascism maintained that it was an "antiparty" (*antipartito*), but at the cele-
bration of the fifth anniversary of the march on Rome Mussolini
himself admitted that the Fascisti were a party after all, although
a party, which unlike other parties, existed only for the greater
glory of the state. The tremendous emotional enthusiasm generated by the fascistic movement in Italy, and the "irresistible current of national will which fascism attempted to instill in the 'folk-
soul,' "[15] was unable to find adequate expression in the rather
prosaic tasks of domestic reconstruction. Inevitably it acquired
imperialistic ambitions. But Italy was not strong enough as a military and naval power to make any but the most limited imperialistic hopes come true away from home, and became, therefore,
very troublesome to its neighbors. The surplus population of Italy
must seek work outside its borders, and since the nationalistic
movement is confined largely to the bourgeoisie and the youth of
the educated classes, the fascist state attempts artificially to bind
these waves of emigrating workers to the mother-country by
claims of citizenship. "Thus fascism, by making greater claims
than its actual power justified, degenerates to a form of national
chauvinism."[16] Other countries, especially Germany since she lost
her naval power and her colonies, have been attempting to weld
the emigrating citizens to the mother-country through cultural ties
in order to use them to advance political or colonial interests.[17]

[14]   See Hermann Heller, *Europa und der Faschismus* (Berlin and
Leipzig, 1929).

[15]   *Ibid.*; see also Robert Michels, "Analyse des nationalen Elitegedankens," *Jahrbuch für Soziologie*, Vol. III, and *Der Patriotismus: Pro-
legomena zu seiner soziologischen Analyse* (München, 1929).

[16]   Wieser, *op. cit.*, p. 405.

[17]   The activities of the Deutsche im Ausland clubs are representative. One reason why the nationalistic movements of Europe turn out so
frequently to be at the same time anti-Semitic movements is perhaps the
belief that the international affiliations and loyalties of the Jews make that
people appear as doubtful bearers of the nationalistic mission.

What the fascism of Italy has in common with the other fascistic movements of Europe besides the contempt for parliamentary and democratic government is the romantic cult of the aristocracy of race and of talent. These fascistic groups characteristically employ the label *Volk* to refer to their racial or cultural homogeneity in their propaganda.[18]

The tendency of hegemony nationalism to develop ever more aggressive imperialistic claims and aspirations is exemplified by the most recent trends in foreign policy of the fascist dictatorships of Europe. Fascist Italy has defied the rest of the world by its Ethiopian adventure, while in Germany the extreme accentuation of nationalist sentiment as a result of the stimulation of the National-Socialist regime has led to an open denunciation of the Versailles Treaty, to remilitarization of Germany, and even threatens to engulf the world in another war of major proportions.

Particularistic Nationalism

A second major type of nationalism may be referred to as particularistic nationalism. This form of nationalism is based upon the secessionist demand of national autonomy. Such movements characteristically begin with a striving for cultural autonomy or toleration, which when the movement makes headway takes on political significance and finally develops into the demand for political sovereignty. This has been the case in Norway, where the movement was successful, and in Ireland, where it was unsuccessful. In an incipient and utopian form it is to be found among the Jews and the Negroes. The most characteristic expression of this type of nationalism is to be found in such countries as Poland, Czechoslovakia, Finland, Latvia, and Lithuania. Michels has characterized the motives underlying this nationalistic movement as follows:

A people that has become conscious of its national characteristics and the peculiarities of its own culture has the natural desire to con-

18   The movement is known in Germany as the "Völkische Bewegung" (see Richard Benz, *Völkische Erneuerung* [München, 1925], for a sample of the literature of this movement). Cf. Frederick L. Schuman, *The Nazi Dictatorship* (New York, 1935).

serve them in their integrity. In the maintenance of this cultural integrity of the people is to be found the only ethically legitimate form of patriotism. Consequently the national emancipation from a foreign yoke signifies the elimination of a cultural obstacle in the road to humanity. National unity and freedom is the indispensable prerequisite to social freedom and free human existence, for every people that frees itself from foreign rule constitutes one source less for war and revolution.

Thus, besides the patriotism based on profit, on fantasy and on megalomania, we have the patriotism based on cultural needs, which aims to secure and maintain a people's right to its own territory and its own human resources.[19]

But, as has already been suggested, a social movement may often depart from its original goals. Poland furnishes an interesting, though by no means unique, example of the development of a nationalistic movement from a romantic to a realistic stage:

Even the great romantic poets of Poland, who proclaimed a unique form of nationalism, according to which Poland was to be the "Christ of the Nations," i.e., just as Christ redeemed mankind through his martyrdom, so Poland was to redeem the peoples of Europe, even these poets were no longer satisfied with the ethnographically homogeneous Poland. . . . This mystical and romantic nationalism, however, was soon displaced by a quite sober and prosaic variety. The Poles declined the crown of martyrdom and let other nations assume it. The prophet of the new nationalism was Roman Dmowski, the Polish intermediary at the peace conferences in Versailles, who in many books and articles preached . . . the gruffest and most uncompromising nationalism. Even when Poland was still under Russian and Prussian rule fighting for its national existence, he denounced the nationalistic tendencies of the Lithuanians and the Ruthenians as presumptious, and labelled the Jewish strivings for emancipation a disintegrating movement. He disavows the romantic patriotism and displaces it with the modern patriotism, or strictly speaking nationalism, whose object it is not to acquire a certain number of privileges or forms of freedom but to establish the nation as a living, social organism, which has its own spiritual existence based on race and history, its own mentality, its own culture, and needs and interests. . . . To this he added the claim that Poland had a great cultural mission in the East. . . . Even at the

[19]   "Analyse des nationalen Elitegedankens," *op. cit.*, p. 188.

peace conference the official Polish demand was for a territory of 50,000 square kilometers with 38 million inhabitants, which, had it been granted, would have made the Poles a minority in their own state.[20]

The numerous potential nationalities which the Austrian, the German, the Russian, and the Turkish empires had conquered or incorporated in the past became revivified by the developments in Europe resulting in the collapse of these empires. Some of these peoples had at one time had an independent state and a fairly distinct culture, and a few of them had retained a large measure of this consciousness. But the rising national idea which tied itself up to the force of historical heritage not only rekindled the folk spirit but extended and deepened it, because now the masses of the population were in a position to participate in these movements, while formerly they would not have been touched by it. Russia was perhaps most secure of all these empires, for, "with the exception of the Poles, none of the nationalities within her domain had arrived at a point of national consciousness and the immeasurable extent of the empire's dominion had an overpowering effect."[21]

The democratic movement, followed by the collapse of the military and political power of the empires, caused the suppressed national ambitions of the Czechs, the Magyars, the Lithuanians, and others to burst forth with an energy which swung many of the moderate leaders over to the nationalistic cause. "Even Masaryk, a convinced advocate of the compromise with the Germans in Austria, became a decided Czech nationalist."[22] As a result most of these nationalities were able to get recognition for demands which were wholly unjustified by historic and ethnic facts.

While these newly formed states, with arbitrarily drawn boundaries, are still in the throes of nationalistic expansion, other nations, such as Sweden, Denmark, Norway, Holland, and Luxembourg, Spain, Portugal, and others, seem to have arrived at a stage of a relatively stable national equilibrium. As far as they

[20]   Jakob Rappaport, "Die Nationalitätenfrage in Polen," *Jahrb. für Soz.*, III, 237–39.

[21]   Wieser, *op. cit.*, p. 362.   [22]   *Ibid.*, p. 204.

are concerned at least, they seem to have settled on a policy of being content with what they have and living in peace with their neighbors. In this sense the newly formed states seem to be still groping in the nationalistic stage and not to have arrived at the maturity of full national existence. Wieser succinctly describes this state of affairs in the following terms:

A well-known slogan of Lichtenberg, that "human beings would rather fight for their belief than live according to it," might well be adapted to read that "human beings are more ready to fight for their nationality than to fulfill their national ideals in the works of peace." In this respect much remains to be done in the newly created states which came into existence through a peace of force. A state is far from consolidated when it has adapted a constitution, and these states have much more serious problems before them than the states with full national existence, because they are mixed states, with deliberately drawn boundaries and are entering upon the business of government without experience and without guiding traditions of history. . . . These states operate under the illusion that they have dearly fought for their emancipation, but in reality the *entente* powers bought them their freedom, while the nationals of these new states partly stood on the side of the defeated and had no great military leaders to whom they can reverently look as heroes in the national struggle for emancipation. . . .

The Swedes, the Norwegians, the Danes and the Dutch may well feel that they have dearly bought and are entitled to their nationhood, but they represent a modest and moderate nationalism. They live in undisturbed peace with their neighbors, are restricted to and content with their limited homely world and have reconciled themselves to the necessity of losing their surplus population through emigration beyond the sea, with the possible exception of Holland, which through its plantation system is somewhat differently situated. These countries are, for the most part, neutral and peaceful, and their security rests upon the respect of their neighbors and the great powers. To the European these nations must seem like fortunate islands, which rise out of the turbulent sea to whose terrors they were exposed as long as they had not learned to avoid the temptations of external power. . . . Like these northern nations so are Belgium, Spain and Portugal free from world aspirations, and, taken by and large, as far as it lies in their power they have settled on a policy of external peace. . . .

With the new states on the territory of the empires of Austro-Hungary, Turkey and Western Russia it is otherwise. They are artificial creations and are centres of unrest within and without. . . . The Magyars and Bulgarians have not only been deprived of territory and population which rightly belongs to them, but the Poles, the Rumanians and Jugo-Slavians have annexed territory beyond what traditionally was their right. The question is, can they hold it?"[23]

Marginal Nationalism

The third major type of nationalism in Europe is what may be termed "marginal nationalism." It refers to the nationalistic movement characteristic of border territories and populations such as Alsace, Lorraine, Silesia, Schleswig, the Saar and the Rhineland, the Italo-Austrian and Swiss frontier, and similar strategic areas in Europe. The sociological significance of the frontier has recently been recognized.[24] A marginal people—i.e., a population in the frontier region between two states—even more than other peoples, has a mixed culture and a mixed racial makeup. The populations of such territories not only are, as a rule, bilingual or polylingual, but they are also more decidedly nationalistic than the respective hinterland populations with reference to which they are oriented. While through the recent peace treaties a number of particularly dangerous frontiers were remedied, a number of new and vulnerable boundaries were created which are not likely to result in quieting the outraged feelings of local marginal peoples. Every hinterland is likely to give itself the benefit of the doubt in the administration of such territories. There is generally a struggle over the leading positions in the government, the army, and the cultural organs, and school and church questions are always matters of acrimonious controversy. A marginal people is likely to cling to the traditions of its motherland with the utmost tenacity, because the cultural heritage is, under conditions of foreign rule, sometimes the only remaining vestige of unity and

[23]   *Ibid.*, pp. 400–402.

[24]   See Georg Simmel, *Soziologie*, p. 623; Adolf Günther, "Soziologie des Grenzvolkes," *Jahrb. für Soz.*, III, 203 ff.; *Die alpenländische Gesellschaft* (Jena, 1930).

brings the most divergent interests and parties into close co-
operation. The Germans of the border territory are proverbially
more German than those of Berlin. For strategic purposes the
mother-country tends, generally, to accord the border provinces
favored treatment, not merely to bind them more solidly to the
country, but to create the impression in the territory on the other
side of the boundary that it would be desirable to be united with
their brethren. The economic importance of the marginal territory
often intensifies the motives out of which aggression arises. Thus
the existence of important mining resources as is the case in the
Saar, or of navigable streams as is the case along the Vistula, or
of harbors such as Danzig and Trieste, enormously exaggerates
the significance of the marginal area. Often, also, the religious
factor intensifies or minimizes the political tension in the marginal territory. While the Germans of the southern Tyrol are
Catholics, like the Italians of the hinterland, their Catholicism is
more like that of Austria than that of Italy, and the same holds of
the Catholic eastern provinces of Germany which were ceded to
Poland, as well as the Protestant northern Schleswig which was
ceded to Denmark. The attempt which was made during the
French occupation of the Rhineland to create a separatistic movement with ultimate annexation to France failed because of the intense nationalism of that border territory, which is symbolized by
the slogan: "The Rhine—Germany's Stream, Not Germany's
Border."

The Nationalism of Minorities

The fourth type of nationalism that remains to be mentioned is the nationalism of the minorities. The problems to which
the existence of racial, ethnic, cultural, or merely political minorities have given rise in Europe have been made available to
students through a vast and extremely interesting literature.[25]

25   Mention should be made of the following: J. Auerhan, *Die sprach-
lichen Minderheiten in Europa* (1926); M. H. Boehm, *Handbücher des
Ausschusses für Minderheitsrecht* (1926); Mitscherlich, *Nationalismus
Westeuropas* and *Nationalstaat und Nationalwirtschaft und ihre Zukunft*,
1925-7; Volk unter Völkern, ed. K. C. v. Loesch (1925); *Zeitschrift für*

Nothing is perhaps more convincing proof of the racial and cultural interpenetration of the peoples of Europe than the universality and the apparent insolubility of the minorities problem. Every nation of Europe has this problem, and in some it is the question next in importance to the existence of the state itself. Some writers have found it useful to distinguish between nationalities and minorities, referring to the former as "foreign population groups, which, however, do not aspire to independence or union with another state,"[26] while the latter are such groups that are separatistic or hope to be united with their mother-country. The total population that exists in Europe as national minorities has been estimated at thirty million.

The question has sometimes been raised why there is no question of minorities in the United States. While problems similar to those in Europe may be found in the United States, such as the Negro problem, especially in the South and in the large cities of the North, the difference between Europe and America is principally that in Europe the minorities live together in large numbers and are not recent immigrants who have been anxious to, and at least partially successful in, shedding their cultural heritage. If the rise of the nationalistic movement had come a century earlier than it did, it is doubtful if such a nation as Switzerland could have come into existence, consisting as it does of three distinct major nationalities and a number of other minor groups. Similarly, Austria might still exist today were it not for the pull which was exerted upon the constituent ethnic groups from without, be-

---

Politik, ed. Dr. Grabowski, *Nation und Staat, deutsche Zeitschrift für das europäische Minoritätenproblem; Nation und Nationalität,* ed. G. Salomon (Karlsruhe, 1928) ; S. R. Steinmetz, *Soziologie des Krieges* (1928) ; *Die Nationalitäten in Europa* (1927), by the same author, in *Zeitshrift für Erdkunde,* Suppl. 2; for Poland: Jacob Rappaport, *op. cit.;* for Hungary: Zsombor de Szasz, *The Minorities in Rumanian Transylvania* (1927) ; for Switzerland and Italy: Günther, *op. cit.,* and Nicolussi, *Tirol unterm Beil* (1928) ; and for the German minorities in that region: Bartsch, *Das deutsche Leid* (1927) ; for quantitative statements of the minorities question: W. Woytinski, *Die Welt Zahlen* (Berlin, 1925 and 1929) ; Pinson, *op. cit.,* items 116–23.

[26] Steinmetz, *Soziologie des Krieges,* p. 642.

cause there seemed to be a number of economic factors favorable
to its existence. In some countries the minorities question is obscured by the circumstance that there are two principal groups
striving for dominance rather than one dominant group attempting to subordinate a number of relatively weak minorities. Belgium is an illustration of the former, Poland of the latter. In Belgium the conflict between the Dutch element or the Flemish part
of the population and the Walloons or French-speaking group is
drawn along cultural lines, in which language and its use in
schools and universities is a major political question. A similar
conflict existed between Catholic South Germany and Protestant
North Germany which found expression in the *Kulturkampf* under Bismarck, and between Sweden and Norway, which was
peacefully settled through separation into two nations. In countries like Poland, Czechoslovakia, Italy, Yugoslavia, and a number of others the problem is of a much more complex nature:

In Poland there are four national minorities: Germans, Ukrainians,
White-Ruthenians and Jews. These economic, political, cultural, social
and religious peculiarities of these peoples give to the Polish minorities
question a unique expression and enormously impede a peaceful and
desirable solution. The question is first of all a social question which
presents itself in a number of variations: The linguistic problem is
merely the ideational cover which often conceals very complicated
social processes. Among these is the conflict for the soil between the
White-Ruthenian and Ukrainian peasants. The agrarian question is
therefore the focal point of the Ukrainian and White-Ruthenian problem. The fight against the German and Jewish minorities is carried on
under the slogan of the "de-germanization and de-judaization" of the
cities. The Slavic minorities in Poland are struggling for the village,
the German and Jewish for the cities. Not less significant is the fight
of all minorities for the positions as officials in order to provide places
for the intelligentsia of each group and in order to exert a propor-
tionate influence—in accordance with their numerical and economic
strength—upon the governmental and autonomous controlling bodies,
and finally in order to defend their national and cultural values.[27]

It is interesting to note that the Germans at the time of their military occupation of Poland fostered much of this minority feeling

[27]   Rappaport, *op. cit.*, p. 235.

for obvious nationalistic and strategic reasons. Although the Polish constitution provides that "every citizen has the right to maintain his own nationality, to foster his language and customs, and to unfold his national character fully,"[28] these provisions have remained a dead letter, for the autonomy which is granted is not a personal but a territorial autonomy, and can therefore be defeated by the manipulation of the election districts. Unless the actual distribution of the minority population approximately conforms to the election districts, the actual political expression of the minorities can be vitiated. For this reason figures concerning the proportion of minorities to the dominant population as derived from election returns are generally misleading, and for the same reason it is quite easy to defeat the intent of the provisions for plebiscites in so far as it is aimed through them to find a basis for a policy of self-determination.

When one considers the treatment which nationalities that have just won their autonomy grant to their own minorities, one is inclined to believe that a nationality is not complete until it has some minority within its territory whom it can oppress. While undoubtedly in some instances nationalism through a process of consolidation and integration has minimized friction and rivalry, on the whole it has created new conflict situations, internal and external, among the peoples of Europe. Similarly, while in some instances the myth of racial homogeneity has been a unifying factor, on the whole it has inaugurated an epoch of racial and national conceit and chauvinism. Under these circumstances a united Europe, as it has been envisaged by some, even in matters of purely economic co-operation is likely to remain an idle hope for some time to come.

28   *Ibid.*, p. 255.

II. The Sociology of Knowledge

8

PREFACE TO

IDEOLOGY AND UTOPIA

THE ORIGINAL German edition of *Ideology and Utopia* appeared in an atmosphere of acute intellectual tension marked by widespread discussion which subsided only with the exile or enforced silence of those thinkers who sought an honest and tenable solution to the problems raised. Since then the conflicts which in Germany led to the destruction of the liberal Weimar Republic have been felt in countries all over the world, especially in western Europe and the United States. The intellectual problems which at one time were considered the peculiar preoccupation of German writers have enveloped virtually the whole world. What was once regarded as the esoteric concern of a few intellectuals in a single country has become the common plight of modern man.

In response to this situation there has arisen an extensive literature which speaks of the "end," the "decline," the "crisis," the "decay," or the "death" of Western civilization. But despite the alarm which is heralded in such titles, one looks in vain in

Reprinted from *Community Life and Social Policy*, ed. Elizabeth Wirth Marvick and Albert J. Reiss, Jr. (Chicago: University of Chicago Press, 1956), pp. 35–54, first published in, Louis Wirth and Edward A. Shils (trans.), Karl Mannheim's *Ideology and Utopia* (New York: Harcourt, Brace, 1936), pp. xiii–xxxi.

most of this literature for an analysis of the basic factors and processes underlying our social and intellectual chaos. In contrast with these writings, Professor Mannheim's work stands out as a sober, critical, and scholarly analysis of the social currents and situations of our time as they bear upon thought, belief, and action.

It seems to be characteristic of our period that norms and truths which were once believed to be absolute, universal, and eternal, or which were accepted with blissful unawareness of their implications, are being questioned. In the light of modern thought and investigation much of what was once taken for granted is declared to be in need of demonstration and proof. The criteria of proof themselves have become subjects of dispute. We are witnessing not only a general distrust of the validity of ideas but of the motives of those who assert them. This situation is aggravated by a war of each against all in the intellectual arena where personal self-aggrandizement rather than truth has come to be the coveted prize. Increased secularization of life, sharpened social antagonisms, and the accentuation of the spirit of personal competition have permeated regions which were once thought to be wholly under the reign of the disinterested and objective search for truth.

However disquieting this change may appear to be, it has had its wholesome influences as well. Among these might be mentioned the tendency toward a more thoroughgoing self-scrutiny and toward a more comprehensive awareness of the interconnections between ideas and situations than had hitherto been suspected. Although it may seem like grim humor to speak of the beneficent influences arising out of an upheaval that has shaken the foundations of our social and intellectual order, it must be asserted that the spectacle of change and confusion, which confronts social science, presents it at the same time with unprecedented opportunities for fruitful new development. This new development, however, depends on taking full cognizance of the obstacles which beset social thought. This does not imply that self-clarification is the only condition for the further advancement of social science, as will be indicated in what follows, but merely that it is a necessary precondition for further development.

I

The progress of social knowledge is impeded if not paralyzed at present by two fundamental factors, one impinging upon knowledge from without, the other operating within the world of science itself. On the one hand, the powers that have blocked and retarded the advance of knowledge in the past still are not convinced that the advance of social knowledge is compatible with what they regard as their interests, and, on the other hand, the attempt to carry over the tradition and the whole apparatus of scientific work from the physical to the social realm has often resulted in confusion, misunderstanding, and sterility. Scientific thought about social affairs up to now has had to wage war primarily against established intolerance and institutionalized suppression. It has been struggling to establish itself against its external enemies, the authoritarian interest of church, state, and tribe. In the course of the last few centuries, however, what amounts at least to a partial victory against these outside forces has been won, resulting in a measure of toleration of untrammeled inquiry, and even encouragement of free thought. For a brief interlude between the eras of medieval, spiritualized darkness and the rise of modern, secular dictatorships, the Western world gave promise of fulfilling the hope of the enlightened minds of all ages that by the full exercise of intelligence men might triumph over the adversities of nature and the perversities of culture. As so often in the past, however, this hope seems now to be chastened. Whole nations have officially and proudly given themselves up to the cult of irrationality, and even the Anglo-Saxon world which was for so long the haven of freedom and reason has recently provided revivals of intellectual witch hunts.

In the course of the development of the Western mind the pursuit of knowledge about the physical world resulted, after the travail of theological persecution, in the concession to natural science of an autonomous empire of its own. After the sixteenth century, despite some spectacular exceptions, theological dogmatism receded from one domain of inquiry after another until the authority of the natural sciences was generally recognized. In the face of the forward movement of scientific investigation, the church has yielded and time after time readjusted its doctrinal interpretations so that their divergence from scientific discoveries would not be too glaring.

At length the voice of science was heard with a respect approximating the sanctity which formerly was accorded only to authoritarian, religious pronouncements. The revolutions which the theoretical structure of science has undergone in recent decades have left the prestige of the scientific pursuit of truth unshaken. Even though in the last five years the cry has occasionally been raised that science was exerting a disruptive effect upon economic organization and that its output should therefore be restricted, whatever slowing down of the pace of natural science research has taken place during this period is probably more the result of the decreasing economic demand for the products of science than the deliberate attempt to hamper scientific progress in order to stabilize the existing order.

The triumph of natural science over theological and metaphysical dogma is sharply contrasted with the development in the studies of social life. Whereas the empirical procedure had made deep inroads on the dogmas of the ancients concerning nature, the classical social doctrines proved themselves more impervious to the onslaught of the secular and empirical spirit. This may in part have been due to the fact that the knowledge and theorizing about social affairs on the part of the ancients were far in advance of their notions about physics and biology. The opportunity for demonstrating the practical utility of the new natural science had not yet come, and the disutility of existing social doctrines could not be convincingly established. Whereas Aristotle's logic, ethics, aesthetics, politics, and psychology were accepted as authoritative by subsequent periods, his notions of astronomy, physics, and biology were progressively being relegated to the scrap heap of ancient superstitions.

Until early in the eighteenth century political and social theory was still under the dominance of the categories of thought elaborated by the ancient and medieval philosophers and operated largely within a theological framework. That part of social science that had any practical utility was concerned, primarily, with administrative matters. Cameralism and political arithmetic, which represented this current, confined themselves to the homely facts of everyday life and rarely took flights into theory. Consequently that part of social knowledge which was concerned with questions most subject to controversy could scarcely lay claim to the practical value which the natural sciences, after a certain point in their development, had achieved. Nor could those social thinkers from whom alone an advance could come expect the support of the church or the state from which the more orthodox wing derived its financial and moral sustenance. The more secularized social and political theory became and the more thoroughly it dispelled the sanctified myths which legitimized the existing political order, the more precarious became the position of the emerging social science.

A dramatic instance of the difference between the effects of and the attitude toward technological as contrasted with social knowledge is furnished by contemporary Japan. Once that country was opened to the streams of Western influence, the technical products and methods of the latter were eagerly accepted. But social, economic, and political influences from the outside are even today regarded with suspicion and tenaciously resisted.

The enthusiasm with which the results of physical and biological science are embraced in Japan contrasts strikingly with the cautious and guarded cultivation of economic, political, and social investigation. These latter subjects are still, for the most part, subsumed under what the Japanese call *kikenshiso* or "dangerous thoughts." The authorities regard discussion of democracy, constitutionalism, the emperor, socialism, and a host of other subjects as dangerous because knowledge on these topics might subvert the sanctioned beliefs and undermine the existing order.

But lest we think that this condition is peculiar to Japan, it should be emphasized that many of the topics that come under the rubric of "dangerous thought" in Japan were until recently taboo in Western society as well. Even today open, frank, and "objective" inquiry into the most sacred and cherished institutions and beliefs is more or less seriously restricted in every country of the world. It is virtually impossible, for instance, even in England and America, to inquire into the actual facts regarding communism, no matter how disinterestedly, without running the risk of being labeled a communist.

That there is an area of "dangerous thought" in every society is, therefore, scarcely debatable. While we recognize that what it is dangerous to think about may differ from country to country and from epoch to epoch, on the whole the subjects marked with the danger signal are those which the society or the controlling elements in it believe to be so vital and hence so sacred that they will not tolerate their profanation by discussion. But what is not so easily recognized is the fact that thought, even in the absence of official censorship, is disturbing, and, under certain conditions, dangerous and subversive. For thought is a catalytic agent that is capable of unsettling routines, disorganizing habits, breaking up customs, undermining faiths, and generating skepticism.

The distinctive character of social science discourse is to be sought in the fact that every assertion, no matter how objective it may be, has ramifications extending beyond the limits of science itself. Since every assertion of a "fact" about the social world touches the interests of some individual or group, one cannot even call attention to the existence of certain "facts" without courting the objections of those whose very *raison d'être* in society rests upon a divergent interpretation of the "factual" situation.

II

The discussion centering around this issue has traditionally been known as the problem of objectivity in science. In the language of the Anglo-Saxon world to be objective has meant to be impartial, to have no preferences, predilections or prejudices, no biases, no preconceived values or judgments in the presence of the facts. This view was an expression of the older conception of natural law in accord with which the contemplation of the facts of nature, instead of being colored by the norms of conduct of the contemplator, automatically supplied these norms.[1] After the nat-

1   It is precisely to that current of thought which subsequently developed into the sociology of knowledge and which constitutes the main

ural law approach to the problem of objectivity subsided, this non-personal way of looking at the facts themselves again found support for a time through the vogue of positivism. Nineteenth-century social science abounds in warnings against the distorting influences of passion, political interest, nationalism, and class feeling and in appeals for self-purification.

Indeed a good share of the history of modern philosophy and science may be viewed as a trend, if not a concerted drive, toward this type of objectivity. This, it has been assumed, involves the search for valid knowledge through the elimination of biased perception and faulty reasoning on the negative side and the formulation of a critically self-conscious point of view and the development of sound methods of observation and analysis, on the positive side. If it may appear, at first glance, that in the logical and methodological writings on science the thinkers of other nations have been more active than the English and Americans, this notion might well be corrected by calling attention to the long line of thinkers in the English-speaking world who have been preoccupied with these very same problems without specifically labeling them methodology. Certainly the concern with the problems and pitfalls involved in the search for valid knowledge has constituted more than a negligible portion of the works of a long line of brilliant thinkers from Locke through Hume, Bentham, Mill, and Spencer to writers of our own time. We do not always recognize these treatments of the processes of knowing as serious attempts to formulate the epistemological, logical, and psychological premises of a sociology of knowledge, because they do not bear the explicit label and were not deliberately intended as such. Nonetheless, wherever scientific activity has been carried on in an organized and self-conscious fashion, these problems have always received a considerable amount of attention. In fact, in such works as J. S. Mill's *System of Logic* and Herbert Spencer's bril-

---

theme of this book that we owe the insight that political-ethical norms not only cannot be derived from the direct contemplation of the facts, but themselves exert a molding influence upon the very modes of perceiving the facts. Cf. among others the works of Thorstein Veblen, John Dewey, Otto Bauer, and Maurice Halbwachs.

liant and much neglected *Study of Sociology,* the problem of objective social knowledge has received forthright and comprehensive treatment. In the period that followed Spencer this interest in the objectivity of social knowledge was somewhat deflected by the ascendancy of statistical techniques as represented by Francis Galton and Karl Pearson. But in our own day the works of Graham Wallas and John A. Hobson, among others, signalize a return to this interest.

America, despite the barren picture of its intellectual landscape that we so generally find in the writings of Europeans, has produced a number of thinkers who have concerned themselves with this issue. Outstanding in this respect is the work of William Graham Sumner, who, although he approached the problem somewhat obliquely through the analysis of the influence of the folkways and mores upon social norms rather than directly through epistemological criticism, by the vigorous way in which he directed attention to the distorting influence of ethnocentrism upon knowledge, placed the problem of objectivity into a distinctively concrete sociological setting. Unfortunately his disciples have failed to explore further the rich potentialities of his approach and have largely interested themselves in elaborating other phases of his thought. Somewhat similar in his treatment of this problem is Thorstein Veblen who, in a series of brilliant and penetrating essays, has explored the intricate relationships between cultural values and intellectual activities. Further discussion of the same question along realistic lines is found in James Harvey Robinson's *The Mind in the Making,* in which this distinguished historian touches on many of the points which the present volume analyzes in detail. More recently Professor Charles A. Beard's *The Nature of the Social Sciences* has dealt with the possibilities of objective social knowledge from a pedagogical point of view in a manner revealing traces of the influence of Professor Mannheim's work.

Necessary and wholesome as the emphasis on the distorting influence of cultural values and interests upon knowledge was, this negative aspect of the cultural critique of knowledge has arrived at a juncture where the positive and constructive significance of the evaluative elements in thought had to be recognized.

If the earlier discussion of objectivity laid stress upon the elimination of personal and collective bias, the more modern approach calls attention to the positive cognitive importance of this bias. Whereas the former quest for objectivity tended to posit an "object" which was distinct from the "subject," the latter sees an intimate relationship between the object and the perceiving subject. In fact, the most recent view maintains that the object emerges for the subject when, in the course of experience, the interest of the subject is focused upon that particular aspect of the world. Objectivity thus appears in a twofold aspect: one, in which object and subject are discrete and separate entities, the other in which the interplay between them is emphasized. Whereas objectivity in the first sense refers to the reliability of our data and the validity of our conclusions, objectivity in the second sense is concerned with relevance to our interests. In the realm of the social, particularly, truth is not merely a matter of a simple correspondence between thought and existence, but is tinged with the investigator's interest in his subject matter, his standpoint, his evaluations, in short the definition of his object of attention. This conception of objectivity, however, does not imply that henceforth no distinction between truth and error is ascertainable. It does not mean that whatever people imagine to be their perceptions, attitudes, and ideas, or what they want others to believe them to be, corresponds to the facts. Even in this conception of objectivity we must reckon with the distortion produced not merely by inadequate perception or incorrect knowledge of one's self, but also by the inability or unwillingness under certain circumstances to report perceptions and ideas honestly.

This conception of the problem of objectivity which underlies Professor Mannheim's work will not be found totally strange by those who are familiar with that current of American philosophy represented by James, Peirce, Mead, and Dewey. Though Professor Mannheim's approach is the product of a different intellectual heritage, in which Kant, Marx, and Max Weber have played the leading roles, his conclusions on many pivotal issues are identical with those of the American pragmatists. This convergence runs, however, only as far as the limits of the field of social psychology.

Among American sociologists this point of view has been explicitly expressed by the late Charles H. Cooley, and R. M. MacIver, and implicitly by W. I. Thomas and Robert E. Park. One reason why we do not immediately connect the works of these writers with the problem complex of the present volume is that in America the sociology of knowledge deals systematically and explicitly with what has been touched on only incidentally within the framework of the special discipline of social psychology or has been an unexploited by-product of empirical research.

The quest for objectivity gives rise to peculiarly difficult problems in the attempt to establish a rigorous scientific method in the study of social life. Whereas in dealing with the objects in the physical world the scientist may very well confine himself to the external uniformities and regularities that are there presented without seeking to penetrate into the inner meaning of the phenomena, in the social world the search is primarily for an understanding of these inner meanings and connections.

It may be true that there are some social phenomena and, perhaps, some aspects of all social events that can be viewed externally as if they were things. But this should not lead to the inference that only those manifestations of social life which find expression in material things are real. It would be a very narrow conception of social science to limit it to those concrete things which are externally perceivable and measurable.

The literature of social science amply demonstrates that there are large and very definite spheres of social existence in which it is possible to obtain scientific knowledge which is not only reliable but which has significant bearings on social policy and action. It does not follow from the fact that human beings are different from other objects in nature that there is nothing determinate about them. Despite the fact that human beings in their actions show a kind of causation which does not apply to any other objects in nature, namely motivation, it must still be recognized that determinate causal sequences must be assumed to apply to the realm of the social as they do to the physical. It might of course be argued that the precise knowledge we have of causal sequences in other realms has not as yet been established in the social realm.

But if there is to be any knowledge at all beyond the sensing of the unique and transitory events of the moment, the possibility of discovering general trends and predictable series of events analogous to those to be found in the physical world must be posited for the social world as well. The determinism which social science presupposes, however, and of which Professor Mannheim treats so understandingly in this volume, is of a different sort from that involved in the Newtonian celestial mechanics.

There are, to be sure, some social scientists who claim that science must restrict itself to the causation of actual phenomena, that science is not concerned with what should be done, not with what ought to be done, but rather with what can be done and the manner of doing it. According to this view social science should be exclusively instrumental rather than a goal-setting discipline. But in studying what is, we cannot totally rule out what ought to be. In human life, the motives and ends of action are part of the process by which action is achieved and are essential in seeing the relation of the parts to the whole. Without the end most acts would have no meaning and no interest to us. But there is, nevertheless, a difference between taking account of ends and setting ends. Whatever may be the possibility of complete detachment in dealing with physical things, in social life we cannot afford to disregard the values and goals of acts without missing the significance of many of the facts involved. In our choice of areas for research, in our selection of data, in our method of investigation, in our organization of materials, not to speak of the formulation of our hypotheses and conclusions, there is always manifest some more or less clear, explicit or implicit assumption or scheme of evaluation.

There is, accordingly, a well-founded distinction between objective and subjective facts, which results from the difference between outer and inner observation or between "knowledge about" and "acquaintance with," to use William James's terms. If there is a difference between physical and mental processes—and there seems to be little occasion to talk this important distinction out of existence—it suggests a corresponding differentiation in the modes of knowing these two kinds of phenomena.

Physical objects can be known (and natural science deals with them exclusively as if they could be known) purely from the outside, while mental and social processes can be known only from the inside, except in so far as they also exhibit themselves externally through physical indexes, into which in turn we read meanings. Hence insight may be regarded as the core of social knowledge. It is arrived at by being on the inside of the phenomenon to be observed, or, as Charles H. Cooley put it, by sympathetic introspection. It is the participation in an activity that generates interest, purpose, point of view, value, meaning, and intelligibility, as well as bias.

If then the social sciences are concerned with objects that have meaning and value, the observer who attempts to understand them must necessarily do so by means of categories which in turn depend on his own values and meanings. This point has been stated time and again in the dispute which has raged for many years between the behaviorists among the social scientists, who would have dealt with social life exclusively as the natural scientist deals with the physical world, and those who took the position of sympathetic introspectionism and understanding, along the lines indicated by such a writer as Max Weber.

But on the whole, while the evaluative element in social knowledge has received formal recognition, there has been relatively little attention given, especially among English and American sociologists, to the concrete analysis of the role of actual interests and values as they have been expressed in specific historical doctrines and movements. An exception must be made in the case of Marxism which, although it has raised this issue to a central position, has not formulated any satisfactory systematic statement of the problem.

It is at this point that Professor Mannheim's contribution marks a distinctive advance over the work that has hitherto been done in Europe and America. Instead of being content with calling attention to the fact that interest is inevitably reflected in all thought, including that part of it which is called science, Professor Mannheim has sought to trace out the specific connection between actual interest groups in society and the ideas and modes of thought which they espoused. He has succeeded in showing that ideologies, i.e., those complexes of ideas which direct activity toward the maintenance of the existing order, and utopias—or those complexes of ideas which tend to generate activities toward changes of the prevailing order—do not merely deflect thought from the object of observation, but also serve to fix attention upon aspects of the situation which otherwise would be obscured or pass unnoticed. In this manner he has forged out of a general theoretical formulation an effective instrument for fruitful empirical research.

The meaningful character of conduct does not warrant the inference, however, that this conduct is invariably the product of conscious reflection and reasoning. Our quest for understanding arises out of action and may even be consciously preparatory for further action, but we must recognize that conscious reflection or the imaginative rehearsal of the situation that we call "thinking" is not an indispensable part of every act. Indeed, it seems to be generally agreed among social psychologists that ideas are not spontaneously generated and that, despite the assertion of an antiquated psychology, the act comes before the thought. Reason, consciousness, and conscience characteristically occur in situations marked by conflict. Professor Mannheim, therefore, is in accord with that growing number of modern thinkers who, instead of positing a pure intellect, are concerned with the actual social conditions in which intelligence and thought emerge. If, as seems to be true, we are not merely conditioned by the events that go on in our world but are at the same time an instrument for shaping them, it follows that the ends of action are never fully statable and determined until the act is finished or is so completely relegated to automatic routines that it no longer requires consciousness and attention.

The fact that in the realm of the social the observer is part of the observed and hence has a personal stake in the subject of observation is one of the chief factors in the acuteness of the problem of objectivity in the social sciences. In addition we must consider the fact that social life and hence social science is to an overwhelming extent concerned with beliefs about the ends of action. When we advocate something, we do not do so as complete outsiders to what is and what will happen. It would be naïve to suppose that our ideas are entirely shaped by the objects of our contemplation which lie outside of us or that our wishes and our fears have nothing whatever to do with what we perceive or with what will happen. It would be nearer the truth to admit that those basic impulses which have been generally designated as "interests" actually are the forces which at the same time generate the ends of our practical activity and focus our intellectual attention. While in certain spheres of life, especially in economics and to a lesser degree in politics, these "interests" have been made explicit and articulate, in most other spheres they slumber below the surface and disguise themselves in such conventional forms that we do not always recognize them even when they are pointed out to us. The most important thing, therefore, that we can know about a man is what he takes for granted, and the most elemental and important facts about a society are those that are seldom debated and generally regarded as settled.

But we look in vain in the modern world for the serenity and calm that seemed to characterize the atmosphere in which some thinkers of ages past lived. The world no longer has a common faith and our professed "community of interest" is scarcely more than a figure of speech. With the loss of a common purpose and common interests, we have also been deprived of common norms, modes of thought, and conceptions of the world. Even public opinion has turned out to be a set of "phantom" publics. Men of the past may have dwelled in smaller and more parochial worlds, but the worlds in which they lived were apparently more stable and integrated for all the members of the community than our enlarged universe of thought, action, and belief has come to be.

A society is possible in the last analysis because the individuals in it carry around in their heads some sort of picture of that society. Our society, however, in this period of minute division of labor, of extreme heterogeneity and profound conflict of interests, has come to a pass where these pictures are blurred and incongruous. Hence we no longer perceive the same things as real, and coincident with our vanishing sense of a common reality we are losing our common medium for expressing and communicating our experiences. The world has been splintered into countless fragments of atomized individuals and groups. The disruption in the wholeness of individual experience corresponds to the disintegration in culture and group solidarity. When the bases of unified collective action begin to weaken, the social structure tends to break and to produce a condition which Emile Durkheim has termed *anomie,* by which he means a situation which might be described as a sort of social emptiness or void. Under such conditions suicide, crime, and disorder are phenomena to be expected because individual existence no longer is rooted in a stable and integrated social milieu and much of life's activity loses its sense and meaning.

That intellectual activity is not exempt from such influences is effectively documented by this volume, which, if it may be said to have a practical objective, apart from the accumulation and ordering of fresh insights into the preconditions, the processes, and problems of intellectual life, aims at inquiring into the prospects of rationality and common understanding in an era like our own that seems so frequently to put a premium upon irrationality and from which the possibilities of mutual understanding seem to have vanished. Whereas the intellectual world in earlier periods had at least a common frame of reference which offered a measure of certainty to the participants in that world and gave them a sense of mutual respect and trust, the contemporary intellectual world is no longer a cosmos but presents the spectacle of a battlefield of warring parties and conflicting doctrines. Not only does each of the conflicting factions have its own set of interests and purposes, but each has its picture of the world in which the same objects are accorded quite different meanings and values. In such a world the possibilities of intelligible communication and *a fortiori* of agreement are reduced to a minimum. The absence of a common apperception vitiates the possibility of appealing to the same criteria of relevance and truth, and since the world is held together to a large extent by words, when these words have ceased to mean the same thing to those who use them, it follows that men will of necessity misunderstand and talk past one another.

Apart from this inherent inability to understand one another there exists a further obstacle to the achievement of consensus in the downright obstinancy of partisans to refuse to consider or take seriously the theories of their opponents simply because they belong to another intellectual or political camp. This depressing state of affairs is aggravated by the fact that the intellectual world is not free from the struggle for personal distinction and power. This has led to the introduction of the wiles of salesmanship into the realm of ideas, and has brought about a condition where even scientists would rather be in the right than right.

III

If we feel more thoroughly appalled at the threatening loss of our intellectual heritage than was the case in previous cultural crises, it is because we have become the victims of more grandiose expectations. For at no time prior to our own were so many men led to indulge in such sublime dreams about the benefits which science could confer upon the human race. This dissolution of the supposedly firm foundations of knowledge and the disillusionment that has followed it have driven some of the "tender minded" to romantic yearning for the return of an age that is past and for a certainty that is irretrievably lost. Faced by perplexity and bewilderment others have sought to ignore or circumvent the ambiguities, conflicts, and uncertainties of the intellectual world by humor, cynicism, or sheer denial of the facts of life.

At a time in human history like our own, when all over the world people are not merely ill at ease but are questioning the bases of social existence, the validity of their truths, and the tenability of their norms, it should become clear that there is no value apart from interest and no objectivity apart from agreement. Under such circumstances it is difficult to hold tenaciously to what one believes to be the truth in the face of dissent, and one is inclined to question the very possibility of an intellectual life. Despite the fact that the Western world has been nourished by a tradition of hard-won intellectual freedom and integrity for over two thousand years, men are beginning to ask whether the struggle to achieve these was worth the cost if so many today accept complacently the threat to exterminate what rationality and objectivity have been won in human affairs. The widespread depreciation of the value of thought, on the one hand, and its repression, on the other hand, are ominous signs of the deepening twilight of modern culture. Such a catastrophe can be averted only by the most intelligent and resolute measures.

Ideology and Utopia is itself the product of this period of chaos and unsettlement. One of the contributions it makes toward the solution of our predicament is an analysis of the forces that have brought it about. It is doubtful whether such a book as this could have been written in any other period, for the issues with which it deals, fundamental as they are, could only be raised in a society and in an epoch marked by profound social and intellectual upheaval. It proffers no simple solution to the difficulties we face, but it does formulate the leading problems in a fashion that makes them susceptible of attack and carries the analysis of our intellectual crisis farther than has ever been done before. In the face of the loss of a common conception of the problems and in the absence of unanimously accepted criteria of truth, Professor Mannheim has sought to point out the lines along which a new basis for objective investigation of the controversial issues in social life can be constructed.

Until relatively recently, knowledge and thinking, while regarded as the proper subject matter of logic and psychology, were viewed as lying outside the realm of social science because they were not considered social processes. Whereas some of the ideas that Professor Mannheim presents are the result of the gradual development in the critical analysis of thought processes and are an integral part of the scientific heritage of the Western world, the distinctive contribution of the present volume may turn out to be the explicit recognition that thought, besides being a proper subject matter for logic and psychology, becomes fully comprehensible only if it is viewed sociologically. This involves the tracing of the bases of social judgments to their specific interest-bound roots in society, through which the particularity, and hence the limitations, of each view will become apparent. It is not to be assumed that the mere revelation of these divergent angles of vision will automatically cause the antagonists to embrace one another's conceptions or that it will result immediately in universal harmony. But the clarification of the sources of these differences would seem to be a precondition for any sort of awareness on the part of each observer of the limitations of his own view and at least the partial validity of the views of the others. While this does not necessarily involve the holding of one's interests in abeyance, it does make possible at least a working agreement on what the facts in an issue are, and on a limited set of conclusions to be drawn from them. It is in some such tentative fashion as this that social scientists, even though they are in disagreement on ultimate values, can today erect a universe of discourse within which they can view objects from similar perspectives and can communicate their results to one another with a minimum of ambiguity.

IV

To have raised the problems involved in the relations between intellectual activity and social existence squarely and lucidly is in itself a major achievement. But Professor Mannheim has not rested at this point. He has recognized that the factors at work in the human mind impelling and disturbing reason are the same dynamic factors that are the springs of all human activity. Instead of positing a hypothetical pure intellect that produces and dispenses truth without contaminating it by the so-called non-logical factors, he has actually proceeded to an analysis of the concrete social situations in which thought takes place and intellectual life is carried on.

"The sociology of knowledge" historically and logically falls within the scope of general sociology conceived as the basic social science. If the themes that Professor Mannheim has treated are systematically developed, the sociology of knowledge should become a specialized effort to deal in an integrated fashion, from a unifying point of view and by means of appropriate techniques, with a series of subject matters which hitherto have been only cursorily and discretely touched upon. It would be premature to define the exact scope which this new discipline will eventually take. The works of the late Max Scheler and of Professor Mannheim himself have, however, gone sufficiently far to allow of a tentative statement of the leading issues with which it must concern itself.

Of these the first and basic one is the social-psychological elaboration of the theory of knowledge itself, which has hitherto found a place in philosophy in the form of epistemology. Throughout the recorded history of thought this subject has haunted the succession of great thinkers. Despite the age-old effort to resolve the relationship between experience and reflection, fact and idea, belief and truth, the problem of the interconnection between being and knowing still stands as a challenge to the modern thinker. But it no longer is the exclusive concern of the professional philosopher. It has become a central issue not merely in science, but in education and politics as well. To the further understanding of this ancient enigma the sociology of knowledge aspires to make a contribution. Such a task requires more than the application of well-established logical rules to the materials at hand, for the accepted rules of logic themselves are here called into question and are seen, in common with the rest of our intellectual tools, as parts and products of the whole of our social life. This involves the searching out of the motives that lie back of intellectual activity and an analysis of the manner and the extent to which the thought processes themselves are influenced by the participation of the thinker in the life of society.

A closely allied field of interest for the sociology of knowledge lies in the reworking of the data of intellectual history with a view to the discovery of the styles and methods of thought that are dominant in certain types of historical-social situations. In this connection it is essential to inquire into the shifts in intellectual interest and attention that accompany changes in other phases of social structure. It is here that Professor Mannheim's distinction between ideologies and utopias offers promising directives for research.

In analyzing the mentality of a period or of a given stratum in society, the sociology of knowledge concerns itself not merely with the ideas and modes of thinking that happen to flourish but with the whole social setting in which this occurs. The setting contains the factors that are responsible for the acceptance or the rejection of certain ideas by certain groups in society and of the motives and interests that prompt certain groups consciously to promote these ideas and to disseminate them among wider sections.

The sociology of knowledge furthermore seeks to throw light on the question of how the interests and purposes of certain social groups come to find expression in certain theories, doctrines, and intellectual movements. Of fundamental importance for the understanding of any society is the prominence accorded to the various types of knowledge and the corresponding share of the resources of society devoted to the cultivation of each of these. Equally significant is the analysis of the shifts in social relationships brought about by the advances in certain branches of knowledge such as technical knowledge and the increased mastery over nature and society that the application of this knowledge makes possible. Similarly the sociology of knowledge, by virtue of its concern with the role of knowledge and ideas in the maintenance or change of the social order, is bound to devote considerable attention to the agencies or devices through which ideas are diffused and the degree of freedom of inquiry and expression that prevails. Attention will be focused upon the types of educational systems that exist and the manner in which each reflects and molds the society in which it operates. At this point the problem of indoctrination, which has recently received so much discussion in educational literature, finds a salient place. In the same manner the functions of the press, of the popularization of knowledge and of propaganda, receive appropriate treatment. An adequate understanding of such phenomena as these will contribute to a more precise conception of the role of ideas in political and social movements and of the value of knowledge as an instrument in controlling social reality.

Despite the vast number of specialized accounts of social institutions, the primary function of which centers around the intellectual activities in society, no adequate theoretical treatment of the social organization of intellectual life exists. One of the primary obligations of the sociology of knowledge consists, therefore, in a systematic analysis of the institutional organization within the framework of which intellectual activity is carried on. This involves, among other items, the study of schools, universities, academies, learned societies, museums, libraries, research institutes and laboratories, foundations, and publishing facilities. It is important to know how and by whom these institutions are supported, the types of activity they carry on, their policies, their internal organization and interrelations, and their place in the social organization as a whole.

Finally, and in all of its aspects, the sociology of knowledge is concerned with the persons who are the bearers of intellectual activity, namely the intellectuals. In every society there are individuals whose special function it is to accumulate, preserve, reformulate, and disseminate the intellectual heritage of the group. The composition of this group, their social derivation and the method by which they are recruited, their organization, their class affiliation, the rewards and prestige they receive, their participation in other spheres of social life, constitute some of the more crucial questions to which the sociology of knowledge seeks answers. The manner in which these factors express themselves in the products of intellectual activity provides the central theme in all studies which are pursued in the name of the sociology of knowledge.

In *Ideology and Utopia*, Professor Mannheim presents not merely the outlines of a new discipline which promises to give a new and more profound understanding of social life but also offers a much-needed clarification of some of the major moral issues of today. It is in the hope that it will make some contribution to the solution of the problems which intelligent people in the English-speaking world are facing that his book has been translated.

9

IDEAS AND IDEALS AS SOURCES

OF POWER IN THE MODERN

WORLD

Knowledge as Power

WHEN WE speak of power in a civilization such as ours we are sometimes disposed to look for its sources in natural resources, in size and vigor of population, in technology, in military prowess, in economic organization, in political cohesion, and in social integration. Conversely, we are disposed to ascribe the weakness of a civilization to relative deficiencies in one or more of these elements. Seldom do we take account of the power of ideas and ideals to shape the affairs of men.

And yet, our lore and literature are full of persuasive sayings to the effect that "knowledge is power," that "ideas are weapons," and similar notions extolling the powerful role of ideas and ideals in history and in society. Hand in hand with these glorified notions concerning the force of ideas and ideals goes the exaltation

Reprinted from *Conflicts of Power in Modern Culture*, ed. Lyman Bryson *et al.* (New York: Harper & Row, 1947), pp. 499–509, by permission of the publisher. Copyright 1947 by the Conference on Science, Philosophy and Religion.

of the role of the intellectuals who presumably are the bearers, the creators, and the disseminators of these ideas and ideals. Not until we see examples of a Hitler or a Mussolini running amuck in the world is our faith in the power of reason, truth, and virtue shaken. Even then, we tend to ascribe the evil these men do more to the perversion of ideas and ideals than to ideas and ideals themselves.

There is scarcely any doubt among informed persons concerning the power of ideas as represented, for instance, by science to shape and transform the world in which we live. Ideas as power factors in this indirect sense are virtually universally recognized. But there is considerable doubt whether ideas or ideals *as* ideas or ideals also operate *directly* as power factors. It is appropriate, therefore, to raise some questions about the nature and function of ideas and ideals in the context of a consideration of the role of power in contemporary civilization.

Assumptions Underlying the Analysis of Ideas as Sources of Power

There are many terms we use to designate ideas and ideals, among them: truths, theories, thoughts, knowledge, conceptions, values, beliefs, doctrines, creeds, and ideologies. All of them are ways of talking about factual and normative propositions. What is important is that we should distinguish between these ideas and ideals themselves, and the men who are their originators, bearers, disseminators, and manipulators. What is important also is that we should distinguish between the content of these propositions and the symbols and forms in which they are expressed and the ways in which they are used.

Before we assert that ideas and ideals are sources of power, let us be clear about what we have assumed. Thus, when we say "knowledge is power," do we mean there is something intrinsic about knowledge that will inevitably transform man or the world? When we say that "ideas are weapons," do we mean to imply that no one has to wield them, to give them the power to wound? Is it the ideas and the ideals, or the men who hold them who are powerful? Is it the ideas and ideals, or the contrivances, the movements, and organizations in which they become incorporated that are potent? Is knowledge power, or is it the ability, the will to manipulate or act upon knowledge that is the source of power? Are ideals the determiners of men's destinies whether or not specific groups of human beings become organized around these ideals? Is it the ideas and ideals, or the acceptance of them by men that makes them dynamic and endows them with power? Is it ideas and ideals, or the persuasive power of the words that express them or the voice that utters them that makes them a force in society? Is it the ideas and ideals, or is it education, propaganda, preaching, persuasion, coercion, deception, advertising, and control over the instruments of communication that constitute power? Is it ideas and ideals, or the symbols, slogans, and stereotypes in which they are incorporated that we battle about? Is there greater power in correct ideas and in noble ideals than there is in false ideas and base ideals? Are thoughts dangerous and ideals subversive, or is it what is done on the basis of and in the name of the thoughts and the ideals that constitutes the danger? Is it true that "truth shall make men free" and that *"in hoc signo vinces?"* Are intellectuals *qua* intellectuals powerful, or do they merely have the potentiality of becoming effective in the affairs of men through their social, economic, and political position or their strategic place in society and connection wth its power holders? Can ideas and ideals be eradicated? Is democracy, for instance, an irreversible idea or ideal, or is it merely its wide acceptance under the specific conditions of recent times in the Western world that gives us the impression of an irreversible trend?

These questions are not easily answered. But, if ideas and ideals are sources of power, we need to know in what their power consists and what kind of power they constitute. We need to know, moreover, whether there is a difference in the kind and degree of power of different ideas and ideals or whether all ideas, whether true or false, and all ideals, whether noble or ignoble, are equally pregnant with power.

We know a great deal from the study of history about the conditions under which certain ideas and ideals have originated.

We also know something about the extent to which certain ideas and ideals have been disseminated or accepted, and the conditions under which and the means by which this has been brought about. But we know relatively little about the actual potency of ideas and ideals in shaping human destiny apart from the movements in which they have been incorporated and apart from the ways in which, through science and technology, they have remade the world. Nor are we as yet agreed on the most promising methods of discovering the influence of ideas and ideals upon human conduct, either individual or collective.

Consensus and Social Solidarity

It is well to recall that most people do not make their own ideas or ideals. They unconsciously accept or think further what others have thought before them, and what those around them are thinking. They hold those beliefs which have become established in their society and obey those norms which are reinforced by social sanctions. What gives ideas their credibility and what endows deals with the faith of believers is, first of all, the fact that they are part of the culture in which each member of society is born, guided to maturity, and, for most of us, lives out his life. They have the power to direct men's thoughts and regulate their actions in precisely the same way in which other elements of their culture mold personalities and conduct. They have compulsive power over the members of a society because there is nothing to challenge them and because the whole society has conspired—though often unwittingly—to impose them and enforce them. They are part of the atmosphere each individual breathes; they are the medium in which his intellectual and moral life is lived. Indeed, the uncoerced consensus on the basic knowledge of man and the world and on the principles of right conduct is one of the basic criteria of the existence of a society. Together with a common language these common understandings give a society its most essential ingredient: the capacity for collective action.

The existence of consensus in a society does not, of course, imply the absence of variations in attitudes, ideas, and conduct. We know of no society, not even the most primitive or the most totalitarian, where such variations between individuals and sub-groups do not exist and such deviations from the standards do not occur. But there must be agreement on a limited number of fundamental issues before a society can exist.

Ideas, Ideals, and Local Culture

In addition to imbibing of the intellectual heritage and the intellectual and ethical values of the society into which the individual is born and in which he matures and lives, there are, of course, other means through which ideas and ideals come to play a role in the life of the individual and society. Among these are the formal educational system and the religious institutions. Despite the firm and widespread belief in their efficacy to affect knowledge, belief, and conduct, we have but little reliable evidence concerning the actual effect of teaching and preaching upon attitudes and character, though there is substantial agreement on the power of education to transmit skills and formal knowledge.

Aside from formal education and religious training there are many other channels through which ideas and ideals are transmitted and inculcated. There is the informal discussion in the varied interest groups with which we are identified. In modern urban-industrial society these have varied forms and wide range. Whereas each group attempts to monopolize the individuals' interests and loyalties, in our civilization most persons are identified with a multitude of such groups, each representing only a narrow segment of their interests and none capable of integrating them into a coherent system.

It is increasingly characteristic of our age that mankind the world over is subject to the influences of the organized media of mass communication. Most notable among them are the press, magazines, books, motion pictures, and radio. The distinguishing feature of these new means for influencing ideas and ideals is the fact that they transcend the limits of the family and the local community and local, tribal, and even national cultures.

We are only in the initial stages of the quest for understanding of what these new means for conveying ideas and ideals have done to man and to the world. It should be noted, however, that they are merely *means* of communication and therefore merely potential agencies for influencing men's thought, belief, and action. The ideas and ideals they convey, in however attractive and plausible form, are still the ideas and ideals of someone wishing to transmit them to others who are expected to receive them. The instruments themselves are neutral, whereas neither the ideas and ideals they transmit, nor the motives and purposes of the men who select the ideas and ideals to be communicated to others can be so regarded.

World Communication and the Emergence of World Community

Through the perfection of the new means of mass communication we have come to live in a shrunken intellectual and moral universe. The individual members of the human family have broken the provincial boundaries of their culture and must learn to think, feel, believe, and act in accordance with the progressively enlarging sphere of a world culture.

This does not, of course, mean that the emerging world culture is of the same character as the local cultures to which we are accustomed. The emerging world culture is still, for the most part, a babel of tongues. The flow of ideas and ideals still encounters many obstacles, national, regional, racial, economic, and religious. The ideas and ideals to which men are exposed on a world scale do not possess the plausibility, the charisma, the sacred sanctions, and the other non-rational sources of legitimation inherent in the folk culture of the tribal and local community. These ideas and ideals are not truly cultural elements at all, in the strict sense of the word; they are rather products of civilization. In brief, we are far from a world community.

Aside from the superficial level of acceptance of these ideas and ideals—and this applies more to the latter than the former— there is the matter of integration. Alien ideas and ideals encounter not merely the resistance offered to all extraneous cultural influences, but before they can become incorporated into a new culture they must establish linkages with accepted cultural elements and undergo a process of assimilation. This integration into the life of the new societies whom it has touched is perhaps more advanced in the case of science than in ethics, philosophy, or religion.

Nor should we minimize the transitional disruptive influence which strange ideas and ideals exert upon a culture. This phenomenon has been adequately documented in the instances of a variety of situations, notably the disorganizing influence incident to colonization, mass migration, technological innovations, and missionary enterprises. What is not so readily recognized, however, is the secularizing influence of the widening of intellectual and ethical horizons and the struggle between conflicting ideas and ideals and even the mere coexistence of contradictory ideas and ideals in the same society. The progressive spread of democracy has brought in its wake more widespread literacy and mass education, increasing leisure, wider participation in the political process, and greatly enlarged expectations of mass sharing in the benefits of an advancing technology and civilization. Ideas and ideals thus have a wider audience. But the mere accessibility of information and the mere exposure to ideas and ideals do not offer any guarantee that men will be either more rational or more humane. What is offered them may be information or misinformation; the values to which they are exposed and to which their loyalty is beckoned may be either noble or base. What decides which ideas will triumph is not their truth value, but the effectiveness with which they are presented. An exception may perhaps be noted in the relatively restricted realm of science where training and practice combine to inculcate the practitioner with the passion to reflect reality faithfully and where there is nothing to be gained by fooling oneself, even if in view of the public character of scientific activity it were possible to fool others.

In the case of ideals, however, the situation is much more complicated. It is sometimes difficult to determine what the highest values are, not to speak of the fact that value judgments—as distinguished from facts—are intimately bound up with the whole value system of a culture and with the unconsciously acquired preferences and prejudices of the members of the society in question.

Ideas and Ideals in Power Relations and the Building of a World Community

The mass communication agencies can carry with equal ease, speed, and persuasiveness truths as well as half-truths, propaganda designed to lead to peace or to war, appeals to build a free, peaceful, prosperous, and just world community or slogans designed to make the building of such a world community highly improbable. These alternative possibilities remain whether those in control of intellectual and ethical production and distribution are the state or private individuals. There is no assurance, to use Justice Holmes's phrase, that "the best test of truth is the power of the thought to get itself accepted in the competition of the market,"[1] when the market is highly monopolistic and is manipulated by men or groups of men who do not use an identical measure of value.

The prospect of organizing the world's intellectual and moral leaders and its communication technicians into a separate group conscious of their responsibility does not seem to offer much hope, at least in the foreseeable future, of averting the dangers of ideological war on a cosmic scale. The producers, distributors, and manipulators of ideas and ideals are themselves subject to the same influences that move the power-holders as well as the audience to which they direct their efforts. The actual conflicts, rivalries, and tensions that exist in the world cannot just be talked out of existence. In the face of some values, which in themselves may be laudable, such as loyalty to one's group, factual evidence and the appeal to other and what we consider higher values may prove impotent.

Nor should we underestimate the potential influence of fashion, of mass movements, and of mass hysteria upon the extent and degree to which our ideas and ideals are shaped by irrational factors. We know of theories that have died not from disproof

[1] Abrams *vs.* U.S.

but from boredom, because the currents of scholarly and of popular interest turned to other and what seemed at the time more interesting concerns. The manias and crazes and social myths recorded in history do not reflect too much credibility upon the assumption of the essential rationality of man.

The Role of the Intellectuals

This raises the question of the possibility and desirability of scientific and ethical neutrality. To treat that question adequately would require a treatise by itself. Suffice it to say here that, whatever view we hold concerning the moral standards to be applied to men of science, art, philosophy, and religion, and especially to the growing army of experts and technicians in the mass communication industries, it is unlikely that these standards will be much higher than those of the society at large and especially its dominant power groups. The first and indispensable step toward meeting the responsibilities that rest upon the creators, molders, and disseminators of ideas and ideals is to become fully conscious of their unstated assumptions. By making their hidden values explicit they at least put themselves on the road to intellectual and moral integrity. In a world in which such overwhelming power rests with the opinion industries, the relationship of the "intellectuals" to these power groups is in particular need of constant re-examination.

In the interests of building a world community it is essential that those who deal with ideas and ideals as their stock in trade be clear about the meaning of these ideas and ideals. The task will probably be easier in the case of ideas than ideals. To ideas we can apply the methods of science and thus determine their correspondence to reality. To a certain extent this is possible in the case of ideals as well. We can determine the degree to which they are congruent with the cultural configurations of the groups which are exposed to them. We can analyze the implications of these ideals and point out their mutual interrelations, their internal inconsistencies and contradictions.

Knowing clearly what we are promoting, we can more conscientiously, if not more effectively, make our message clear to others. Being ourselves convinced of the rightness of our ideas and ideals will aid us in persuading others. In this attempt to diffuse what we know and believe we can avoid much of the resistance that we might otherwise encounter by tying our ideas onto the ongoing culture and the problems of life of the people whom we seek to influence. Our ideas and ideals will be more welcome to others if they meet men's needs for security, freedom, creativeness, self-realization, and social participation. Our efforts will be more successful in the long run if, in addition, we maintain our respect for man and refuse to use him as a pawn or an object whose credulity and loyalty we seek to exploit. This requires a clearer recognition than some proverbially naïve teachers, preachers, and other intellectuals have had of the motives and machinations of power groups who seek to use ideas and ideals, through us as their paid or unpaid agents, to influence public opinion and mass action in their own interests. If we know what their game is, we may conceivably refuse to play it. After all, there is no inherent reason why intellectuals should be totally unaware of the facts of life.

Finally, their day-to-day preoccupations are likely to lead intellectuals into the occupational psychosis of overrating the power of ideas and ideals and underrating the realities for which they stand. We need not wait until there is universal agreement on the ideas and ideals by which men live to begin the building of one world and a world community upon which it must be based. The world's intellectuals in the past have been as much a divisive as an integrating force among men. If they approach their high calling with integrity and with understanding of the realities of social life and especially of the actual power forces at work in the world they can serve as agents for creating greater understanding among peoples. Worldwide understanding among intellectuals themselves, such as we have already substantially achieved in the realm of science, is a step in that direction.

There is every prospect that with such effective means of worldwide communication at our disposal, with the increasing accessibility of men everywhere to the ideas and ideals of all other men, with the increasing recognition among even the most remote and "backward" peoples of their interdependence with the rest of the world for their security and prosperity, with the universal infectiousness of the ideas of freedom, democracy, and human dignity, however differently these terms are interpreted by different peoples, and with the increasing worldwide fear of the consequences of war, we can achieve a sufficient degree of consensus to build the beginnings of a world community. In this task ideas and ideals are indispensable instruments.

10

ON MAKING VALUES EXPLICIT

REGARDLESS OF the wide differences of opinion that may be found among social scientists concerning other relationships to the value problem, there seems to be agreement that the social scientists can make a contribution by making the values underlying social policy and human behavior explicit. The question is less one of whether this can be done as it is, how important it is to do it and what methods are best suited to the task.

It is a common experience to discover in many arguments and public debates that the passion to win an argument exceeds the desire to be "in the right." The desire to be the victor and to have one's opinion prevail thus becomes itself a value irrespective of whatever values may be involved in the debate.

There are occasions when we define the desire of our action explicitly. There are passages in the Declaration of Independence and in the Preamble of the Constitution which set forth certain values like: "Life, liberty, and the pursuit of happiness." We can all quote passage from Scripture which set forth certain values explicitly like "Love thy neighbor as thyself." We all can recall political slogans like "Liberty, Equality, Fraternity" or "Peace and Bread" which purport to set up certain values which have helped add dynamism to social movements. The Four Freedoms are a recent example from the area of international politics, and

Previously unpublished.

we can find countless examples of explicit statements of ends written into the charters and bylaws of the many organizations outside of government that make up our complex society. Presumably, there are certain values inherent in such terms as democracy, socialism, communism, freedom, order, progress which have the power to fire man's imagination whether or not the content or meaning of these terms is spelled out concretely.

It does not require profound contemplation or extensive investigation to show that different people attach different meanings to these terms, and that sometimes even though they seem to accept the values designated by a given term, by mouthing the term they may put widely varying content into the term so that the assumption that they agree on values rests upon spurious foundations. As a consequence, instead of talking *to* one another about the same thing, people are talking *past* one another and are thinking of different things while they use the same terms. While I think it is utopian for a universal scientific standardization of these terms, much less of our terms embodying values, I do think social scientists could make a contribution bearing upon the more rational means of policy making by calling attention to the fact that disagreements about values, in so far as values are explicitly stated, often turn out to be agreements, and that what appear to be agreements often turn out to be disagreements.

Aside from the cases where values are explicitly stated there is a wide universe of discourse in which values are not explicitly stated but are kept implicit. Thus, much of the debate that goes on between parties and much of the disagreement about policies might be traced to the fact that the disputants or adversaries have not stated their values or ends overtly, but have left them to be inferred. If, for instance, in the tense situation between the United States vis-à-vis the Soviet Union the values that are at issue could be brought out into the open, and clearly stated, it might turn out there would be quite an area of agreement while, of course, there might also remain a great area of disagreement. It would help, nevertheless, to have the values for which each side stands, and against which each side stands, clearly articulated so that they could be discussed and analyzed in the open. Some of the emotional tension which at present is generated in discussions of "The U.S. vs. the Soviet Union" might possibly subside if this were done, although it is not precluded that clarification of the values which each side symbolizes might also generate new conflicts. To know all is not necessarily also to give all. To know all in such a case might be the occasion for greater bitterness and unforgiveness.

Whether values are explicitly stated, or are inferred from what people say and do does not, of course, always give us reliable evidence on what values people actually hold. As Kant put it, "One should not believe everything they say, nor should one believe that they say it without reason." People sometimes give "lip service" to values without embracing them, because it is expected, because it is respectable, because it is noble or because it is safe or merely because it is fashionable. When they do so, they do not necessarily either have a comprehension of what it means to embrace certain values, nor do they necessarily give evidence of the fact that they are willing to sacrifice anything for these values. It might be possible for social scientists to penetrate into this realm of the genuineness with which values are held and to make empirical investigations of the concepts that people have of the meaning for these values in terms of concrete action and their readiness to sacrifice other values for the attainment of these objectives. What sort of picture do people have in their minds when they talk about peace, freedom, order, progress, democracy, Christianity, communism, states' rights, or any number of other terms which are used to designate values, and what are they willing to do in order to realize the content that they put into these value terms? It should not be too difficult for social scientists to set up investigations designed to give reliable answers to such questions.

It is not inconceivable that if the meaning of Christianity, democracy, equality, liberty, fraternity, and other terms were spelled out a lot of people who think they want them would not be so sure about whether they do want them. It has been said that if a man tried to be a Christian for twenty-four hours he would probably land either in jail or in the lunatic asylum.

This suggests that some people are not merely ignorant of the meaning of the values which they supposedly cherish, but oftentimes use them as rationalizations for other objectives which they seek to realize. Whether men are rational beings or not (and if they are, we must probably admit of a wide range of degrees of rationality), they do seem to be under the compulsion to make their actions appear reasonable to themselves and to others. Rationalization in this sense means the search for "good reasons to act for something that has bad reasons or for which we can give no reasons at all." Thus, I feel, for instance, that when in recent discussions of the civil rights issue we so often find spokesmen for the South reiterating the values of "states' rights" they are using this value term for the purpose of concealing an objective which involves the denial of rights as citizens of a state to a portion of their citizens. It would be naïve, therefore, to assume that these southern spokesmen are advocates of the value of "states' rights" because there is every indication that if these "states' rights" were granted, some of the southern states would use them to deny certain rights to their citizens, and there are many indications also they would not assume the responsibility that presumably goes with "states' rights." Assuming we can determine what values people actually hold and what content they put into these values, there remains the further problem of ascertaining who in a given society or in a given controversial situation holds these values, and who holds contrary values. This could be ascertained by techniques analogous to those used by public opinion students. It might show us what different segments of society had different orientations toward values and might even reveal the factors—traditional, situational, educational and otherwise—that account for different segments of society holding different values or holding the same values.

There is the further question of inquiring into the intensity with which certain values are held or pursued. This might be done not merely on the basis of emotional reactions we get from people when we inquire about these values which might conceivably be measured on a scale, but also on the basis of the order of priority which people assign to certain values as over against others.

Finally, it appears that much of social science discourse which purports to be on a purely factual level turns out, upon analysis, to harbor many hidden values. We have become accustomed to making a very sharp distinction between fact statements and preference statements. Actually, this distinction is not nearly so sharp as it seems. Facts do not lie around in the universe waiting to be picked up. Facts are made by people who select certain aspects of the universe for preoccupation, for observation, for examination, and for commission to and discussion with their values. If some consensus is arrived at, then we have what we call facts.

In contradistinction to facts, values are supposed to be based upon preferences which often implies caprice. What is not so clearly seen is that facts, too, involve at least a certain amount of agreement with others on some assumptions, if only on the assumption of what is worth selecting for observation and what its relevance is to some problem of life and what the criteria of truth are. The problem of objectivity becomes complicated in the social sciences because it is hard to find "facts" that do not imply some assumptions, among those who regard them as facts, which makes them into facts. In some aspects of social science where we seem to be dealing with relatively "pure facts," it turns out upon further examination that value elements are involved, even if only in accounting for why these facts and not other facts have been selected as relevant to a given problem which is under discussion. When we come to define such a term as "efficiency," we find ourselves unable to give it any communicable meaning without some reference to values.

I hope that from what I have said, it is at least plausible to expect that the social sciences will be able to make some contribution to policy-making by taking the task of making values explicit seriously. Those who feel that social science discourse should proceed on a "value free" or non-evaluative plane might be reminded of the difficulty of carrying on such discourse and that if we cannot eliminate values, even if we wanted to, we can at least get along a little better by being aware of them and thus possibly being able to discount for their presence.

III. The Community

11

THE SCOPE AND PROBLEMS

OF THE COMMUNITY

THE IMPORTANCE of and the interest in the community as a subject for sociological study is attested to by a series of distinguished volumes ranging from such theoretical works as Tönnies' *Gemeinschaft und Gesellschaft* and MacIver's *Community* to practical volumes like Steiner's *Community Organization* and Perry's *Neighborhood and Community Planning*. The term "community," like other concepts taken over from common-sense usage, has been used with an abandon reminiscent of poetic license. In the case of some writers community has stood for those organic relationships that obtain in the plant and animal world and that may be found in human relations as well as between organisms of the same or of different species living together on a symbiotic basis. Others have referred to the community as a psychical rather than an organic relationship and have consequently emphasized consensus over symbiosis and collective action over the division of labor.

This seems to be the fundamental difference between the point

Reprinted from *Community Life and Social Policy*, ed. Elizabeth Wirth Marvick and Albert J. Reiss, Jr. (Chicago: University of Chicago Press, 1956), pp. 9–20, first published in *Publications of the Sociological Society of America*, XXVII (May, 1933), 61–73.

of view of Herbert Spencer and that of Auguste Comte. While the former emphasized one aspect of the social complex, namely, the division of labor, competition, and interdependence, the latter regarded consensus, i.e., common culture, common experiences, aims, and understanding as the more fundamental fact in social cohesion. The emphasis upon one or the other of these dual aspects of human group life reappears persistently in the history of our discipline. It is implicit in Sir Henry Maine's distinction between "status" and "contract," in Durkheim's discrimination between the two kinds of mutual dependence or *solidarité*, the one organic and the other mechanical, and it has crystallized in the difference of meaning between "community" and "society," expressed in the works of Tönnies, Max Weber, Park and Burgess, and MacIver.

"Community" has come to refer to group life when viewed from the standpoint of symbiosis, "society" when viewed from the standpoint of consensus. A territorial base, distribution in space of men, institutions, and activities, close living together on the basis of kinship and organic interdependence, and a common life based upon the mutual correspondence of interests tend to characterize a community. Society, on the other hand, has come to refer more to the willed and contractual relationships between men, which, it has been assumed, are less directly affected than their organic relationships by their distribution in space.

There are, then, three basic concepts around which much of the theoretical discussion in sociology has turned: "social group," "community," and "society." Whereas the indiscriminate use of these terms leads to confusion, it becomes necessary, if we are to have fairly stable frames of reference, to state explicitly the meanings we assign to the words we use.

The term "social group" may be conceived of as the broadest, most colorless, and inclusive of the three, referring to any aggregation or association of men that can be thought of as in some way belonging together and having a unity of its own. The importance of such a concept that calls to mind the cohesiveness of individuals is suggested by Josiah Royce when he speaks of the "fecundity of aggregations," implying that there are some things that are true of collectivities that are not true of the individuals composing them. The study of the group or collective aspects of human behavior, which constitutes the major interest of social psychology and sociology, is based upon the recognition of this fact.

Of social groups there may be distinguished two general orders: those that are best conceived as communities and those that can best be understood if regarded as societies. These may, indeed, be the same social groups. Every social group may be said to be distributed in space, although in some this territorial distribution may be of minor significance when compared with other aspects of group life. While, as Park and Burgess say, "an individual may belong to many social groups, but he will not ordinarily belong to more than one community, except in so far as a smaller community of which he is a member is included in a larger of which he is also a member"; it may be an oversimplification of the complexities of life to say, as they say, that "every community is a society, but not every society is a community."[1] It would be difficult to conceive of any social group that does not give evidence of some of the characteristics of community life such as being capable of having its membership plotted on a map. As here used, the word "social group" is the generic term, whereas "community" and "society" are subordinate terms bearing correlative and reciprocal relations to one another.

While the terms "community" and "society" may, when viewed from the standpoint of their historical development, appear to have been vying with one another for the exclusive attention of sociologists, as soon as sociological interests turned from logical dichotomizing and philosophical generalization to the analysis of concrete segments of social life, it became clear that they were not mutually conflicting entities but two mutually complementing aspects of every form of group life. Every social group exists in a territorial, physical, and ecological, as well as in a social-psychological, bond, the two representing opposite poles toward one or the other of which every social group tends more or

---

1   Robert E. Park and E. W. Burgess, *Introduction to the Science of Sociology*, p. 163.

less. For purposes of getting an answer to some questions it is best to conceive of a social group as a community, for others, as a society. They are not two different kinds of group life but two aspects of all human group life.

What makes every community a society is apparently the fact that human social life invariably involves some degree of communication. It is this fact which seems to distinguish the plant and animal communities, on the one hand, from human communities, on the other. Plant and animal communities are of interest to sociologists because they represent in the simplest and most abstract form those symbiotic relationships which are extremely complicated in the human community, where they are obscured through the fact of communication and consensus. There is, as Dewey says, "more than a verbal tie between the words common, community, and communication. Men live in a community in virtue of the things which they have in common; and communication is the way in which they come to possess things in common."[2] Every community thus always has the dual aspects of living together, on the one hand, and participating in a common life, on the other. In the plant and animal world it is quite sufficient to analyze community life in terms of symbiosis and competitive co-operation, the mechanisms of which are, so to speak, built into the organisms. In the human community, however, we have never fully exhausted our powers of analysis until, in addition, we have also understood the participation of the individuals in common enterprises, the sharing of common hopes and ideals, and the mechanisms of communication and social interaction which are not built into the organisms but which exist in language, collective symbols, laws and customs, in short, in a social heritage.

What has made the community an increasingly significant concept for sociologists to reckon with is, first of all, ascribable to its inclusiveness. It has denoted a series of phenomena ranging from the division of labor to collective action, from group life conceived in substantive form to the psychical processes involved in the interaction of personalities. It has thus included virtually the whole range of sociological interests from the territorial base

2 John Dewey, *Democracy and Education*, pp. 1–7.

to collective action, from human ecology to social psychology. In a sense it may be said that the concept "community," through its ambiguous and varying definitions, has been instrumental in calling to our attention the fact that all social phenomena range between these two widely separated poles.

Historically the community has been an expression that emphasized the unity of the common life of a people or of mankind. Even a superficial retrospect, however, reveals that this common life itself has undergone profound changes which have been reflected in changing scientific interests in the community. One of the chief tasks in every human group is that of generating a sense of all belonging together. In the face of the increasing mechanization of living, of national and cultural provincialism, of the more thoroughgoing segmentation of life and the more minute division of labor, this task has become, as MacIver says, "not less necessary but more difficult."[3] In the transition from a type of social organization based on kinship, status, and a crude division of labor, to a type of social organization characterized by rapid technological developments, mobility, the rise of special interest groups, and formal social control, the community has acquired new meaning and has revealed new problems.

At one time territorial, kinship, and interest relations were, apparently, more coterminous than they are now. The folk community was apparently more of a primary group, as Cooley used the term, than the prevailing form of group life is today in Western civilization. As folk life gives way to technological civilization, new bases for social integration must appear if men are to retain the capacity to act collectively in the face of divergent interests and increasing interdependence. The change from status to contract, of which the trend from the family to the state as the predominant form of social organization is representative, and the change from a relatively high degree of local self-sufficiency to a delicately and unstably equilibrated international interdependence, best represented by the change from barter and local markets to international trade, finance, and politics, suggest a wider territorial basis for community life and the tenuous charac-

[3]   R. M. MacIver, *Community*, p. 51.

ter of modern community opinion and action. The territorial limits of modern communities cannot be drawn on the basis of a
single criterion. Every important interest in community life may
have a varying range of influence, and may in turn be subject to
repercussions from without of an indirect and remote sort. The
multiplication of corporate groups in modern times, the wide dispersion of the membership, and the increasing number of ties of
identification and affiliation of the individual with diverse societies often obscure the fact that every society is also in some degree
a community.

There is increasing awareness among the students of collective behavior that the modern community as distinguished from
its older prototype rests upon a different principle of cohesion of
its constituent elements, which may be stated in the contrast between kinship and territory, between sentiment and interest, between status and contract, and between custom and law. The
remarkable fact about community life today is that it is as capable
of collective action as it appears to be, considering the fact that it
has so little besides the mechanism of newspapers and technical
devices to hold it together. The competence of our present-day
publics, aside from the specialized professional, sectarian, and interest groups, is limited to the crudest and most elementary issues. While our problems of community life have become increasingly complicated and technical, our social life has become highly
mobile and tenuous, and its sphere of concerted thought and action as ambiguous and as fleeting as the headlines on the front
page of our metropolitan press. Aside from a few fatuous stereotypes and sensational "human interest" news features we lack a
universe of discourse based upon common meanings and have
failed to develop an adequate technique for integrating the diverse and often conflicting motives of special interest groups. It is
this growing disparity between our interdependence and our capacity to act as a unit, between our need for organization and
the defiance of this need by the trend of modern social life, that
has driven the friends of democracy to despair and has brought
the community organization movement to a state of virtual paralysis. The muckraking movement, the social survey movement, and

the community organization movement may be regarded as three closely related developments based upon the recognition of these facts.

When the territorial units upon which our political organization rests no longer coincide with the areas of economic and cultural organization, there not only results inefficiency in administration, but there may arise problems of community disorganization, such as the breakdown of institutions, political corruption, physical deterioration, vice, crime, and the paralysis of collective action. The vital problems of community life have a disconcerting way of defying politically determined or historically evolving administrative boundaries. From the standpoint of research, which is gradually receiving recognition as a necessary preliminary step in the development of techniques for community planning and control, the most regrettable consequence of the lack of conformity between the limits of the community and those of the administrative areas is the instability and incomparability in time of the units by which basic data, governmental and otherwise, are collected.

The adoption of relatively minute census tracts as the permanent units for the collection of these basic materials for community study serves, at least in part, to meet these difficulties. This discrepancy between natural and administrative boundaries has come to light, in part, through attempts to find and delimit local units for collection and compilation of statistical data, such as the census and other basic social materials. The sociological study of the community in the concrete has thus, by calling attention to a need incident to research, pointed the way for the reorganization of administrative areas. Some of the outstanding difficulties encountered by students of community problems, especially in urban communities, are in some measure attributable to the fact that these problems transcend the official city limits and tend to take on a regional scope. Our interdependence, our mobility, and the new mechanisms that affect collective behavior give to virtually all problems of community life in our culture something more than a local, and sometimes even more than a regional, setting and significance.

As research interests have turned from the more abstract consideration of community life to the study of specific areas, villages, towns, cities, and regions, the importance of relatively stable and comparable unit areas and of continuous moving indexes of changes in community life has become apparent. But here, as elsewhere, facts do not lie around at random merely waiting to be picked up by inquiring sociologists. Data have relevance only to specific problems, and each problem may call for a different set of facts to be discovered, organized, and interpreted in order to be concluded. We must be clear, therefore, on the questions to which we seek answers before we can say what data will be relevant.

In so far as we are interested in the community of scientists, rather than as technicians and politicians, we raise a series of questions about it which are more general, more abstract, and probably more universal than those which arise in the practical affairs of everyday life. In so far as this is true, it should be possible also to formulate data that would be considered the minimum requisite for the sociological study of any community. These data, if our theory is correct, should also prove basic in dealing with practical and technical problems of communal existence. Indeed, any acceptable definition of the community would be fruitful only to the extent that it not merely delimited a field of study but also suggested a set of questions or hypotheses which could provide the basis for specific sets of collected data.

One aspect of every community is its territorial base. To discover the center and the boundaries of a community is therefore a preliminary task in any study. In the past, before the interests of the sociologists were as clearly defined as they are now, the area of a community was either staked out arbitrarily or was defined by political or administrative boundaries. The tendency at present, even in such an official procedure as the definition of metropolitan areas by the census, seems to be to stake out the territory on the basis of definite tests of internal cohesiveness of the community and the determination of the margins of influence of different communities with reference to one another. The Census Bureau, in determining the periphery of metropolitan districts, has employed such criteria as the administrative boundaries, the retail trade areas, the commutation area, the local postal or freight-rate zones. The more we interest ourselves in regions as communities, the more we are inclined to take account of other factors, such as newspaper circulation, wholesale trade areas, banking areas, and wider cultural areas over which a given settlement exercises its dominance.

What applies to regions and larger communities applies in equal measure to smaller areas within the community, such as zones and neighborhoods within cities. Here, as in the determination of the centers and peripheries of larger areas, the sociologists apply empirical tests for the determination of the units by which they collect and organize data. Perhaps the simplest way of looking at an area is to view it as a distribution of population. The mere tabulation of such data for different areas will generally reveal perceptible differences in population composition, such as age and sex ratios, nationality, occupation, and income grouping, which can be correlated with other social data such as home ownership, stability or migration, health, delinquency, and crime rates, insanity rates, voting, political and religious affiliation, and other characteristics of population groups.

The study of the mere distribution of population has been traditionally the interest of demographers. When we conceive of the area as a community, however, and regard it as having a unity of some sort, we pass over from demography into human ecology. The ecologist is interested in the study of processes such as invasion, concentration, segregation, succession, and mobility that obtain among a population in areas considered as units, or communities. In human communities, however, unlike plant and animal communities, we are not dealing merely with space and sustenance relationships, but invariably we find these elementary relationships complicated by economic, political, and cultural factors. Space and time are translated into cost; the struggle for life becomes a struggle for a living, and competitive co-operation becomes conflict and conscious collaboration toward a common goal.

Aside from the distribution and competition of the population, the sociologist sees the community also as a physical mechanism consisting of buildings, streets, facilities for communication and transportation, and a complex of technical devices through which an area is transformed into a human habitat. The distribution of population affects, and is affected by, not merely the character of the landscape, but also such factors as land values, types of land use, accessibility, both in time and in cost, and the technical devices available for community life. The web of life in which human communities are enmeshed is incomparably more complex and technical than that of the plant or the animal community.

Another approach to the community is suggested if one thinks of it as a constellation of institutions. These include not merely such formal and established social structures as schools, churches, courts, business houses, and settlements but also such phenomena as families, neighborhood organizations, political parties, rooming houses, gangs, clubs, newspapers, and recreation centers. Institutions have a history and a natural history which is linked to, and a segment of, the communities in which they arise. They might be studied from the standpoint of their location, from the point of view of the spatial distribution of the people in whose life they function, the changing roles they play in community life, and as competing and conflicting with one another in their effort to enlist the interest and loyalty of the population. It is primarily in this aspect of community life that the interest of the community organization movement has centered, but it is only now that we are beginning to collect the data which would have made the community organization movement a more fundamental and efficacious effort than it was.

A more distinctly social-psychological approach to the community is represented by the view of a community as a constellation of types of personalities. The more objective and external data about communities mentioned above need obviously to be supplemented by the more subjective material to be obtained only through personal contact with, and the personal documents of, human beings. The statistical data contained in the census figures can be made meaningful only through the understanding of the culture of which personalities are the active, dynamic constituent parts. Every community may set certain limits to the possibilities for personal development; there is usually a wide range of personality types to be analyzed and classified in every community; and there are, as Adam Smith observed, some types of personality that can only be found in great cities. The distribution of competence, talent, and genius may be very uneven in the various areas of a city, and in country and town. In some communities distinctive types of personality may be found which are unique to the area and are a faithful mirror of its life. The concentration of specific types of personalities in specific areas where they find or create for themselves a hospitable culture is one of the factors which has given distinctive color to the city.

The social problems of a community may be thought of as arising out of the conflicts between attitudes, values, personalities, institutions, and economic, racial, political, and cultural groups. These conflicts may be conceived of as indexes of social change, of growth, and of disorganization, and can be better understood if seen as parts or symptoms of a larger community configuration, which, from the standpoint of the sociologist, may be resolved into ecological, economic, technological, cultural, and political phases.

Three types of tasks suggest themselves in order to make this material transcend the mere collector's interest and make it both scientifically and practically useful: (1) The facts about community problems must be ascertained by the uniform and continuous collection of basic data to make them usable as indexes of social change, of growth, and of disorganization. (2) These facts require correlation with one another so that they may be seen as aspects of a larger whole, namely, the totality of community life. (3) The insights to be derived from viewing these problems as indexes of fundamental interrelated community changes should be valuable in suggesting a co-ordination of techniques for treatment and for planning. The local and regional studies made at Chicago, the regional survey of New York and its environs, and the various specialized activities that have recently been co-ordinated on a national scale in the Public Administration Clearing House in Chicago are symptomatic and possibly prophetic of a new outlook on the community. If we are to plan sensibly for the future

we must know something about the present and about the processes that are at work in the transformation of our life even while
we are studying it. Neither abstract theories nor empirical facts
will give us a sound basis for action unless we recognize the necessity for the careful and extensive empirical work that must lie
between theoretical analysis and practical programs.

A great deal of enthusiastic effort has been, and is still to some
extent being, devoted to what is called community organization.
This may be conceived of narrowly as including merely local efforts on a common-sense basis to readjust institutional facilities
to supposed community needs by the establishment of new institutions, by legislation, or by arousing collective action. But it may
also be conceived broadly (taking account of local, regional, and
wider territorial interrelations) based on the continuous rather
than the sporadic collection of facts, viewed as an inclusive whole,
and analyzed in terms of basic social processes. There is a recognized need for the latter type of community organization which
takes on the character of social planning.

As in every crisis, so in the present emergency there is no
dearth of panaceas for the reconstruction of social life on a more
adequate basis. Some believe that the hope of our social order lies
in the return to the local ties of the neighborhood. The trend of
our civilization, however, has generally been sensed to lead in the
opposite direction. There can be no return to the local self-
contained neighborly community except by giving up the technological and cultural advantages of this shifting, insecure, and
interdependent, though intensely interesting and far-flung, community life, which few would be willing to do. Meanwhile, the
sociological students of the community, whether working on a local, regional, or more inclusive scale, are perhaps wisely devoting
their efforts to the analysis of the more fundamental processes of
community life and social change, upon which alone a sound program of social reorganization can be based. In the present state
of our knowledge every prediction that we may make will undoubtedly be coupled with a great deal of risk, our data being as
fragmentary and as uncertain as they are; but to the extent that
we hope to rely in collective action upon intelligence rather than

luck, the choice is not between prediction and no prediction but between better or poorer prediction. Through rigorous definition of our concepts, through awareness of the interrelation of the various segments of the materials with which we are dealing, through the availability of more accurate and widely comparable data, and through the intensive analysis of more fundamental and perhaps necessarily more abstract problems, the sociological approach to the community gives promise ultimately of a greater measure of social control.

Sciences are distinguished from one another not so much by subject matter as by the different questions that are raised about the subject matter. Not all questions are equally fruitful, but we approach science to the extent that we are able to raise scientific, i.e., abstract, theoretical, and universally significant questions about our subject matter. It happens that the social survey was primarily interested in the kind of fact-finding representative of demography. The muckraking movement was chiefly concerned with exposés leading to collective action. The community organization movement centered its interest principally on the institutional aspects of community life. Important as these movements were in their day, being practical movements and techniques, they were only secondarily concerned with raising questions of scientific interest.

Courses on the community will doubtless be offered in universities in the future as they have been in the past, and it is to be hoped that practical effort in community organization and social planning will rise to the opportunities and needs of our times, but these activities are not most profitably pursued as a sociological monopoly. In the long run, if the sociologist is to justify himself as a scientist he will pursue to the utmost his theoretical investigations in human ecology, social interaction, and social psychology, and through the discoveries which he has every prospect of making, and which on a small scale he has already made, in these more abstract questions he will ultimately contribute most to the understanding of the community.

12

HUMAN ECOLOGY

HUMAN ECOLOGY as an academically recognized intellectual discipline is considerably younger than our century. It borrowed its conceptual framework and much of its method from plant and animal ecology, which are themselves but recent arrivals in the scientific world. When Ernst Haeckel coined the name for the new branch of biological science in 1869, he sought to call attention to the fact that the structure and behavior of organisms are significantly affected by their living together with other organisms of the same and other species and by their habitat.

Whatever else men are, they are also animals, and as such they exhibit the effects of physical aggregation and of their habitat. Much of what subsequently became human ecology had already been studied in a less systematic and scientific manner by geographers, historians, and philosophers under the general theme of "environmentalism." New impetus was given to the study of human ecology by the interest aroused in the relationship between population and the means of subsistence through the writings of Malthus and by the new understanding of the web of life, including the survival and development of species as postulated by Darwin and the theorists of evolution.

Reprinted from *Community Life and Social Policy*, ed. Elizabeth Wirth Marvick and Albert J. Reiss, Jr. (Chicago: University of Chicago Press, 1956), pp. 133–42, first published in the *American Journal of Sociology*, L (May, 1945), 483–88.

Developments in demography during the nineteenth century and the more accurate description of human settlements as furnished by the human geographers, together with the beginnings of social surveys of specific communities, particularly in England, set the stage for the systematic formulation of problems and the perfection of methods out of which have grown the ecological studies of the last generation.

Sociologists, both rural and urban, were at work studying the human community by methods which subsequently have been called ecological long before human ecology was recognized as a distinctive field of scientific activity. A series of significant maps of the spatial distribution of vital and social phenomena in England had appeared in Henry Mayhew's *London Labour and the London Poor*. Booth's *Survey of the Life and Labour of the People in London* had furnished a notable example of the importance of areal study of the great metropolis. Von Thünen's *Der isolierte Staat* had given a theoretical framework for the understanding of successive concentric zones of land use of a region. The device of graphically presenting population composition by means of pyramids had already been used by pioneers in the United States Census. There had been studies of urban land use, of housing, and of the incidence of poverty, disease, and crime; and there had also been systematic interpretations of these phenomena on high theoretical levels, of which Henry George's *Progress and Poverty* is perhaps the outstanding example. Studies of the physical aspects of the human community had even found their way into sociological textbooks, exemplified by Albion W. Small and George Vincent's *An Introduction to the Study of Society*. C. J. Galpin, in his surveys of rural communities, notably in his *The Social Anatomy of an Agricultural Community*, had indicated the methods for depicting objectively the interrelations between the trade center and the hinterland. In addition, there had been numerous monographs of a more or less scientific nature on specific communities, towns, and cities in various parts of the country showing their growth, their social characteristics, their physical structure, and the incidence of problems such as housing and social disorganization.

It was not, however, until 1915, when Robert E. Park pub-

lished his provocative paper on "The City: Suggestions for the
Investigation of Human Behavior in City Environment" in the
American Journal of Sociology, that what subsequently became
recognized as the ecological study of the human community was
systematically formulated. Park's suggestions stimulated a series
of investigations which, in the course of a few years, led not
merely to the accumulation of a rich body of objective data but
also to an appreciation of the significance of the study of the
community as a physical fact for the understanding of it as a social phenomenon and as a state of mind, and eventually to the
recognition of the role that human ecology might play in the study
of social life generally.

Human ecology, as Park conceived it, was not a branch of
sociology but rather a perspective, a method, and a body of
knowledge essential for the scientific study of social life, and
hence, like social psychology, a general discipline basic to all the
social sciences. He recognized its kinship to, and derivation from,
geography and biology. But he emphasized that, unlike the former, human ecology was less concerned with the relationship between man and his habitat than with the relationship between man
and man as affected, among other factors, by his habitat. In distinguishing it from plant and animal ecology, he stressed the
unique characteristics of man and the human community. He
noted that, unlike plants and animals, human beings in large
measure make their own environment; they have relatively great
powers of locomotion and thus are less attached to the immediate
habitat in which by nature they are placed; they are conditioned
by their capacity for symbolic communication, by rational behavior, and by the possession of an elaborate technology and culture.
Moreover, in human aggregations we find the life of the individuals regulated by conscious controls, by rules, norms, and laws,
and by formal organizations and institutions. These factors introduce into the study of human ecology complications unknown in
the plant and animal world.

The focus of attention of ecological studies has been on localized or territorially delimited social structures and social phenomena. This has given to the community a central position in

the conceptual framework of human ecology. Unfortunately this common-sense term, like all other common-sense terms when used in scientific discourse, has had the disadvantage of ambiguity. The early literature of human ecology was much concerned with the distinction between the community and the society. The former stressed the symbiotic relations, spatial and temporal dimensions, physical structure, competition, and the division of labor; the latter stressed communication, consensus, common norms, values, conscious social control, and collective action. Unfortunately these two ideal-typical aspects of human social life have frequently been confused with concrete realities. Thus there has been a failure to see that all communities are also societies and all human societies bear at least some of the characteristics of communities. Competition, for instance, among human beings never takes the form of a blind struggle for life and survival. Rather, it manifests itself as a more or less regulated and controlled struggle for a living and for status. Whereas in the plant and the animal world the mechanisms of collective behavior, such as there are, are built into the structure of the organisms and can truly be described in terms of reflexes and instincts, the behavior of the human world can be understood only in the light of habit, custom, institutions, morals, ethics, and laws.

Aside from the considerable theoretical literature that has developed in the field of human ecology, the contributions of the discipline have become increasingly manifest as aspects of specific studies of communities and regions. As the ecological interest and techniques developed, almost all American community studies have given increasing evidence of the use of ecological methods and knowledge. This is as true of the studies of rural and urban communities as it is of those of wider regions. It is not merely because the ecological aspect of human social life yields a degree of objective knowledge, in the sense of non-controversial description of physical facts and offers possibilities for a high degree of mensuration and precision, but also because the relevance of the physical base of human social life is increasingly appreciated for the understanding of sociocultural phenomena that human ecology has found an increasingly important place in community studies and, for the matter, in all studies which have an areal dimension.

The emergence of human ecology as a scientific discipline and its recent development have already been adequately reviewed by others.[1] It is necessary in this review to sketch merely the newly developing interests, problems, procedures, and findings of the discipline. As might be expected, the most important developments and achievements of human ecology are not to be found in studies which pass under that label but are associated with empirical studies of rural and urban communities and of regions undertaken by sociologists, by other social scientists, and by specialists in other practical fields such as market analysis, administration, and planning.

Considerable progress has been made in the methods of delimiting the territorial bounds of social phenomena and relationships. This has called into being the concept of the natural area as distinguished from the administrative area. It has been found that the settlement of human beings, the patterning of social institutions, the incidence of social problems, and the intricate network of social interrelationships does not, except by accident, conform to arbitrarily delimited areas and that hence administrative areas only rarely coincide with the ecological or natural areas. In the study of urban life, for instance, the types of land use and the types of residential areas to be found in the city do not conform to the neat lines of precincts, wards, and other political and administrative boundaries. Neither do crime, disease, family disorganization, and, for that matter, political alignments fit themselves into the static patterns of formally adopted areal units. They have patterns of their own, and they shift in accordance with the total conditions of life. Ecologists of humanity have developed the techniques of base maps, spot maps, and rate maps for the more accurate exploration and delineation of the actual

---

1   See R. D. McKenzie, "The Field and Problems of Demography, Human Geography, and Human Ecology," chap. iv in *The Fields and Methods of Sociology*, ed. L. L. Bernard (New York: Long & Smith, Inc., 1934), pp. 52–66; and James A. Quinn, "Topical Summary of Current Literature on Human Ecology," *American Journal of Sociology*, XLVI, No. 2 (September, 1940), 191–226.

incidence and distribution of these phenomena. Burgess' ideal
concept of the growth of the city[2] and the many studies of delinquency, family disorganization, racial and economic distribution,
housing, incomes, and standards of living in rural, as well as
urban, areas have shown that students of social life cannot accept
without considerable modification the presentation and analyses
of data offered them by official agencies which must use arbitrary
administrative areal units. The development of census tracts in
cities, for instance, by the United States Bureau of the Census
represents a recognition of the need for reducing large arbitrary
areal units to the smallest possible units for the purpose of scientific investigation.

Particularly in the study of urban areas and metropolitan regions has it become necessary to discover the actual extent of the
influence exerted by the center upon the periphery. This applies
as much to social institutions as it does to technology and to population aggregates. A metropolis, through its intricate network of
interrelationships, extends its range of influence upon a territory
usually far beyond the orbit of the immediately surrounding urbanized fringe. Because the census gives us a picture of human
settlements in accordance with where people sleep rather than
where they work, we are likely to gain a false impression of the
economic and social entity constituting the metropolis and tend to
conceive of it primarily as a political unit.

The recognition of the factors which underlie the distribution
of people and which account for the differentiation of types of
human settlements has important implications for social control,
especially government. For instance, whereas the criminal is free
to move about, irrespective of political boundaries, the police are
hedged in by rigid lines of areal jurisdiction; and whereas disease
germs are no respecters of administrative barriers, health officials
are often limited to a district. The no man's land on the margin
of two or more jurisdictions, so frequently the favorite location
for contraband activities, is the result of the discrepancy between
natural and administrative areas. The lack of coincidence between

2   Robert E. Park, E. W. Burgess, *et al.*, *The City* (Chicago: University of Chicago Press, 1925), chap. ii.

natural areas (which are defined by the range of actual functions and which are constantly in flux) and administrative areas (which are defined by law and are relatively static) is of particular concern to community organization and planning. Unless the area of community organization and planning is approximately coextensive with the area over which the phenomena to be organized or planned extend, there is bound to be confusion and ineffectiveness.

To the research in human ecology belongs much of the credit for the more realistic conception of the community and the region. The Fifteenth Census of the United States (1930), in its special monograph on *Metropolitan District*,[3] took explicit account of the regional scope of at least our larger urban centers. McKenzie's study of the metropolitan community[4] traced "some of the basic changes that have taken place in American cities since the advent of motor transportation" and "the more important structural changes that are taking place in American settlement" as a result of new technological developments. By taking account of newspaper circulation as one of the factors determining the scope of the metropolitan region and the area of influence of urban institutions, this study suggested a series of subsequent investigations into the ecological aspects of social-psychological phenomena which had hitherto been neglected or were not thought to be subject to objective analysis. The numerous studies which followed on radio-listening areas and on the area of influence of urban institutions, such as the stock exchange, the professional organization, and the health, welfare, educational, governmental, and cultural agencies and institutions, gave ample evidence of the theoretical as well as practical usefulness of this approach.

Nowhere has the new conception of the metropolis found greater recognition than in the field of planning. *The Regional Survey of New York and Its Environs*,[5] the National Resources Committee's *Regional Factors in National Planning and Develop-*

3   Washington: Government Printing Office, 1932.

4   *The Metropolitan Community* (New York: McGraw-Hill Book Co., Inc., 1933).

5   New York, 1927–31.

ment,[6] and its *Our Cities: Their Role in the National Economy,*[7] together with supplementary reports, and such technical planning manuals as *Action for Cities: A Guide for Community Planning,*[8] show the extent to which the ecological point of view, concepts, methods, and findings have penetrated into the art and science of planning. What is true of urban studies is equally true of rural and wider regional analyses and planning enterprises.[9]

Even when planning was primarily physical planning, it offered great hospitality to the methods and findings of human ecology; but since planning has developed to include the economic and social designing or redesigning of the community, human ecology has found an even more important place in it. Planning aims at the optimum use of resources and the rational integration of community life. Such knowledge as the human ecologist has been able to obtain about the location of industry, the distribution, segregation, and succession of population, the areas of influence of social institutions, and the interrelationship between the physical, the technological, the economic, the political, and the cultural aspects of community life has proved itself indispensable.

It should be noted, however, that human ecology has not been merely the handmaiden either of the other social sciences, on the one hand, or of such practical arts as planning, on the other. It has, in recent years, developed a substantial body of scientific knowledge in its own right and has also drawn upon other branches of social science for its data and hypotheses. For instance, studies of communication, public opinion, markets, and voting have contributed immensely to the formulation of the prob-

[6] Washington: Government Printing Office, 1935.

[7] *Ibid.,* 1937.

[8] Published under the sponsorship of the American Municipal Association, the American Society of Planning Officials, and the International City Managers' Association (Chicago: Public Administration Service, 1943).

[9] Cf. Rupert B. Vance, "Rural Life Studies" prepared by the U.S. Department of Agriculture, Bureau of Agricultural Economics.

lems of human ecology, the data with which the discipline works, and the explanations and interpretations toward which it strives. It should also be noted that, although the most intensive studies of human ecology have been concerned with urban and rural communities, human ecology has also been applied to larger areas and to world-wide phenomena. Thus the patterns of urbanization, the trends of migration, the interrelations between national states, the functions of frontiers, and the problems of minorities, among others, have been studied at least in a preliminary way by the methods of human ecology; and there is every reason to believe that in the future the knowledge gained from local small-scale research will be applied to the world as a whole.

The accumulation of vast bodies of precise, descriptive material and its graphic presentation by means of maps and diagrams has unfortunately led some investigators to assume that the facts are either self-explanatory or that one set of ecological facts can be adequately interpreted in terms of other ecological data. In the ecological studies of delinquency, insanity, family disorganization, religious life, political behavior, and social institutions it has sometimes been naïvely assumed that, once the spatial distribution of people, institutions, functions, and problems has been traced and their concentration and dispersion noted, there remains nothing for the ecologist to do but to relate these phenomena to other ecological data to arrive at valid explanations. This view overlooks the fact that social life is a complex interdependent whole. Material conditions of existence are, of course, important factors in the determination of social structure and personal characteristics and behavior. Subsistence, competition, the division of labor, spatial and temporal arrangements, and distributions are important aspects of the material conditions of existence and, in turn, of social life. But they are not the whole of social life. On the contrary, as has been adequately demonstrated through numerous investigations, types of attitudes, personalities, cultural forms, and social organizations and institutions may have as significant an effect in shaping ecological patterns and processes as the latter have in conditioning social and social-psychological phenomena. Indeed, in view of our present-day knowledge concerning social causation, we might well be predisposed to follow the general principle that physical factors, while by no means negligible in their influence upon social life and psychological phenomena, are at best conditioning factors offering the possibilities and setting the limits for social and psychological existence and development. In other words, they set the stage for man, the actor. We are not yet far enough advanced to say with confidence what importance shall be ascribed to any one factor operating in the complex sphere of the social and the psychological, much less to evaluate the relative importance of physical as distinguished from social and psychological factors.

This does not, of course, mean that ecological studies are irrelevant to sociology and to the social sciences. They furnish the indispensable framework of knowledge upon which social and psychic existence rests. They often aid us in defining and localizing our problems. They aid us in uncovering interrelationships of which otherwise we might not be fully aware, and they suggest the selection of criteria for controlled study. It is as yet questionable to what extent ecological facts may serve as indexes of social and psychological facts. For instance, the use of income, occupation, area of residence, home-ownership, rental, and duration of settlement may well be justified in the analysis of social status; but if social status is not to be thought of as identical with economic status and if, as we might well suspect, economic status itself is the resultant of factors among which those cited are only a few, then the use of such an index as rental for economic status, not to speak of social status, is likely to be misleading. Used judiciously, however, such an index may prove itself useful for scientific analysis, especially when its correlation with other facts of the same order has been established.

The studies showing significant differences in such phenomena as delinquency and mental disorders between different areas of the city are of the utmost importance for the advance of scientific knowledge. The establishment of gradients for rates of personal and social disorganization passing from the center of the city out toward its periphery is a scientific achievement which carries us far beyond the common-sense knowledge we have had hitherto. But it would be absurd to say that there is something in the inlying areas themselves or in the fact that they are close to the center of the city that produces these high rates of delinquency or other forms of social disorganization. It is rather to the relative concentration and segregation of certain population groups living under certain conditions and in a certain culture that we must look for an explanation of these facts. Human ecology thus provides us with one of the hitherto neglected aspects of the matrix within which social events take place and hence with a conceptual framework and a battery of techniques through which these social phenomena can be more fully and adequately understood.

It would be vain, however, to expect human ecology to give us more than a segmental view of the group life of man which sociology seeks to depict and to understand. Working in co-operation with students of social organization and social psychology, human ecologists can furnish a more comprehensive and a more realistic analysis of society than would otherwise be possible. They can introduce into the study of social phenomena objective referents which will anchor the generalizations concerning society, for which all sociologists strive, more firmly in time, in space, and material reality. Human ecology is not a substitute for, but a supplement to, the other frames of reference and methods of social investigation. By introducing some of the spirit and much of the substance and methods appropriate to the natural sciences into the study of social phenomena, human ecology has called attention to the wide areas where social life can properly be studied as if the observer were not an integral part of the observed. This beneficent influence would be negated, however, if the human ecologists were to proceed as if they, together with the demographers and the statisticians, were the only true scientists among the sociologists, or as if they, unaided by others using different approaches, alone could comprehend and explain the complicated and elusive realities in the realm of the social.

13

LOCALISM, REGIONALISM,

AND CENTRALIZATION

ONE OF the *curiosa* that generally could be relied upon by teachers of history to shock the student into a state of horror over the Dark Ages was the description of the countless petty principalities between which a constant war was going on for the authority over the people of Europe. This barbaric state of affairs, which even now moves us, at the least, to a condescending pity for our benighted medieval ancestors who tolerated the intolerable, is not without parallel in the contemporary world. A recent governmental report says: "The public affairs of the American people are managed by some 175,000 different governments— Federal, State, and local. In addition, many of the governments have separate departments working more or less independently on various kinds of public service. The chance for confusion, cross purposes, and wasted effort is almost limitless.[1]

This state of affairs is of sociological significance, for it in-

---

Reprinted from *Community Life and Social Policy*, ed. Elizabeth Wirth Marvick and Albert J. Reiss, Jr. (Chicago: University of Chicago Press, 1956), pp. 143–58, first published in the *American Journal of Sociology*, XLII (January, 1937), 493–509.

1   National Resources Committee, *Progress Report* (Washington, June 15, 1936), p. 1.

volves the essential structure of society and the capacity of its members to act collectively. In the measure that sociology, among other disciplines concerned with the social, is interested in the nature of group life with a view to its possible and eventual rational direction and improvement, the relation between the actual units of social existence and the units of formal social control presents a challenging problem. It is understandable, therefore, that sociologists who are primarily concerned with persons and with groups should so frequently appear to be concerned with areas.

Our political and administrative boundaries grew up as a result of social strife on the battlefield, in legislatures, and in chancelleries. They are not, for the most part, products of dispassionate, rational reflection. Most of them, even in this country, became imbedded in constitutions, laws, procedures, and traditions before the forces set in motion by the industrial revolution had begun to reshape the pattern of social existence and of social intercourse. Institutions, customs, attitudes, and boundaries, like other products of social life, sometimes continue to exist for reasons other than those that brought them into existence. If many of the local political and administrative areas are no longer conveniences in man's daily life, but have become archaic survivals of an age that was economically, technologically, and socially primitive and parochial, it becomes all the more important to examine their function in contemporary social existence and to view them as flexible instrumentalities for the achievement of a more satisfying social life.

Although the spatial aspect of social existence may at first appear as only remotely related to man's quest to maintain and to enhance his freedom in the face of the encroachments of the society of which he is always a part, a mere glance at the historical development of the idea of freedom will reveal its intimate connection with the area that at any one time defines the extent of the human community. Freedom in the epochs preceding our own was not primarily or solely a matter of persons, but of areas. The house, the manor, the village, the principality, and the city— these were the stable anchorages in terms of which a man's status and the scope of his freedom were defined before the advent of the modern national state. It was this areal context which gave the concept of sovereignty its reality and its meaning. The ambiguity of this concept as employed by political theorists until recently was due, in some measure, to the fact that it was treated as if it had become detached from a local base. It is a refreshing sign of a returning realism that the interest group and the region are displacing the concept of sovereignty as the central theme in political research, while the source of sovereign power as residing in the popular will, at least in democracies, is taken for granted. Similarly it is to be noted that in sociological research the increasing emphasis upon actually existing local groups as subjects for analysis has brought an empirical reality into speculations which formerly were often vaporous and ill-defined.

Ever since Plato's *Republic* and Aristotle's *Politics* the question as to what constitutes the most feasible, if not the ideal, numerical or spatial unit of social organization has been a perennial problem with social theorists. The answers have varied and have, in general, reflected the social conditions, the existing technologies, and the more or less limited mental horizons characteristic of different epochs and different localities. There is involved in the choice between local autonomy and centralized control the persistent effort to find a balance between freedom from outside interference, on the one hand, and the security and enrichment of life that can come only from participating in a larger world, on the other hand. The nineteenth century in Europe, having brought to a climax the developments in exploration, invention, enlightenment, expansion of trade, and of political dominion, made its choice in favor of the larger national state as the dominant and inclusive frame of social organization, subordinating, if not displacing, the multitudinous autonomous local units. The struggle to achieve a larger social and political entity, symbolized by the modern nation, was regarded by some as the inevitable outcome of the forces set in motion by the Renaissance and the commercial and industrial revolution; its potential benefits in enriching the life of man were conceived of as worthy of the sacrifice of many of the values hitherto cherished. But others, like Rousseau, held that democracy was possible only in small societies because only there could the majority of the people retain their control over the conduct of common affairs.

Even in our day there are many who attribute a beneficence to the small unit "as the human unit which makes possible a spirit of neighbourhood and unity which is difficult to attain over larger areas,"[2] and who regard bigness, whether of corporations or of political units, as a curse.[3] In France this movement to regain and preserve the advantages of the small local unit against the encroachments of the larger national state took the form of a political philosophy of regionalism. The persistent idea of states' rights throughout the history of the United States may be taken as evidence of a similar apprehension engendered by a government that is great, powerful, and above all distant. It was largely because such a form of political organization was suspected of developing inevitably into a tyranny and of being incapable of responding to the will of the people that Thomas Jefferson, in his zeal to preserve the liberty of the individual and in his anxiety to forestall the encroachments of a powerful centralized state upon the freedom of its local constituent units, counseled:

But it is not by the consolidation, or concentration of powers, but by their distribution, that good government is effected. Were not this great country already divided into States, that division must be made, that each might do for itself what concerns itself directly, and what it can so much better do than a distant authority. Every State again is divided into counties, each to take care of what lies within its local bounds; each county again into townships or wards, to manage minuter details; and every ward into farms, to be governed each by its individual proprietor. Were we directed from Washington when to sow, and when to reap, we should soon want bread. It is by this partition of cares, descending in gradation from general to particular, that the mass of human affairs may be best managed, for the good and prosperity of all.[4]

2   G. D. H. Cole, *Social Theory* (4th ed.; London, 1930), p. 160.

3   Osmond K. Fraenkel (ed.), *The Curse of Bigness: Miscellaneous Papers of Louis D. Brandeis* (New York, 1935).

4   H. A. Washington (ed.), "Autobiography," *The Writings of Thomas Jefferson* (New York: H. W. Derby, 1861), I, Book I, 82.

It is, of course, highly questionable whether even in Jefferson's day the form and practice of the American government ever even approximated the ideal set forth by him, but it is certain that in our day there is no gradation of powers or functions from the most general to the particular as we proceed from the national unit down to the local unit.

The fear of centralization is understandable in a society in which government is regarded as a necessary evil. Obviously, the more powerful the government in such a society is, the more reason the citizens have to fear it and to delegate to it as little power as possible. This may help to account, too, for the insistence upon a government of "checks and balances" which, by retarding if not paralyzing its capacity to act, was believed to insure a maximum of local and individual liberty.

This attachment to a system of distributive social control continues despite the transformation in contact and communication wrought by modern technology. The isolation, the economic self-sufficiency, and the autonomy of the small, independent local unit have been undermined by the development of rapid, efficient, and cheap methods of transportation and communication. The enlargement of the market has accentuated the division of labor. The freedom with which persons, goods, and enterprises can move or be moved from one locality to another, where the restrictions are least and the opportunities greatest, has been tremendously enhanced. This new freedom has liberated the forces that make for greater efficiency and productivity. By emancipating individuals and communities from absolute dependence upon purely local circumstances, their potential stability and security have been increased, provided the instruments of control could be extended to coincide with the enlarged sphere of interdependence that has emerged in recent decades.

The contrast between what was possible before the introduction of modern methods of communication and transportation and what is possible today may be illustrated by comparing the Roman with the British Empire. Although the Romans had a superb system of roads to link the scattered parts of their Empire with the capital, the disintegration of the Roman world is, at least in part, attributable to the fact that the communication system of the ancient world was incapable of knitting so vast and varied a congeries of peoples and territories into an organic unity.[5] Conversely, the apparent efficiency in the administration of the British Empire reflects, in part at least, the improvement in techniques of communication and transportation to a point where the difficulties of maintaining contact virtually have been eliminated.

It would be difficult to exaggerate the significance of news as a factor in the integration of social groups. No aggregation of individuals, however numerous or densely concentrated, can be regarded as a community or a society unless its members are in effective communication with one another and share in the pursuit of common ends. In a small, intimate, local group, the collective goals of which touch the vital life-interests of every member, the appropriate media of communication are spontaneous gestures, rumor, and gossip which give to the social interaction a personal and emotional tone. In larger, more segmentalized, and inclusive groups the media of communication lose some of this expressive quality and take on the more impersonal character of news. Whereas the gossip of the more closely knit local community is primarily concerned with the doings and feelings of men, the news of the larger and impersonal world deals predominantly with things and affairs. It does not follow therefrom that a more heterogeneous and larger group is invariably objective and incapable of responding to sentiments. It implies rather that propaganda and advertising are employed to simulate the type of appeals that have proved effective in more intimate and homely situations. But, on the whole, in the measure that the public takes the place of the crowd and logic takes the place of tradition as the basis for common understandings and agreement, the scope of consensus and of collective action is narrowed and tends to become restricted to secular activities, i.e., to instrumentalities and means rather than to sacred goals and non-rational ends.

Our society can obtain whatever benefits are derivable from large-scale, centralized organization under democratic controls

5   Cf. W. F. Oakeshott, *Commerce and Society: A Short History of Trade and Its Effects on Civilization* (Oxford, 1936), pp. 29 and 41.

only if it learns to utilize the effective techniques of wide-range communication, available for the first time in history, for generating a sense of popular understanding, appreciation, and participation in the formulation of public policies for a very much larger and more heterogeneous body politic than ever before has functioned as a democracy. With such instrumentalities as the radio and the motion picture at our disposal to supplement universal and almost instantaneous news reporting, and with easy personal access to people remote from us in space through travel and the telephone, there is no longer serious reason to assume, as formerly there undoubtedly was, that common sentiments and purposes, individual initiative and responsibility, are incompatible with larger territorial and numerical units of society than those to which we have been accustomed.

Instances both historical and contemporary could, of course, be cited of the successful functioning of centrally directed human associations of enormous range even in the absence of the efficient technology of communication that we now possess. An example is the Catholic church. It is to be noted, however, that it has maintained itself intact only as a spiritual power, and in extending itself over a wider area has been forced to shed most of its temporal and secular authority. Moreover, it no longer enjoys even a spiritual monopoly, and has been more or less successfully challenged by competing denominations in the realm of the sacred as well. It remains, nevertheless, a striking case of continuous, far-flung, centralized government. In our own day the trend toward ever larger centrally controlled units of social organization is perhaps best exemplified by the forms of integration characteristic of the modern state and industry.

An approximate index to the trend toward centralization in government may be found in the shifting proportion of expenditures by the various levels of government. Whereas up to the year 1933 the local governments in the United States still expended more than either state or national governments, in 1934 for the first time in a year of peace the federal expenditures were estimated to have exceeded those of either of the other two levels of government.[6] Some of the money expended by the federal government was in the form of grants-in-aid and subventions to the state and local authorities, in the spending of which the latter exercised a share of control. However much such statistics may be discounted as indexes of fundamental changes in our political structure, either the inability or the unwillingness of local or state governments to provide the necessary revenues for the adequate discharge of governmental responsibility for essential public services to the people is an indication that even if the sentiment of localism is still vigorous, it is not always accompanied by the ability or the will to pay the price. There are some governmental functions, such as the regulation of currency and the control over interstate commerce, that have from the beginning of our national life been vested in the federal government. As modern government has come to be more and more a service institution and as the factors producing and affecting the problems of social welfare have become more intertwined and far-reaching in scope, the dominant role of the national government has become increasingly accepted.

Coincident with, and in part as a result of, the acceptance of machine technology and large-scale production, the scope of centralized economic control has also been expanded. The modern corporation tends toward ever larger units of centrally managed industrial and commercial enterprises. The chain store and the chain factory are in a position to locate and relocate their individual establishments on a much more rational basis than a locally owned and managed store or industrial enterprise, not only because their managements are less restricted by local sentiment and opinion, but also because they are likely to possess a national or international outlook and hence to have access to more comprehensive knowledge of the factors and trends affecting the enterprise. They can open or close single units in the chain as resources, labor supply, markets, transportation costs, taxation, and local legislation make such a step necessary or desirable. Hence

6   National Industrial Conference Board, "Cost of Government in the United States 1933–1935," quoted in *State Government*, IX (September, 1936), 186–87.

the traditional governmental regulatory measures often fail to have their expected effects. It may be possible, for instance, through state or local taxation to drive chain stores out of a given area or to induce factories to move from one locality to another where they are not subjected to taxation or other controls; but the power of local and state governments in general has proved inadequate to deal with the major economic problems created by modern industry and business. The powers and jurisdictional area of the federal government more nearly conform to the actual extent of modern interdependent economic enterprise.

Without considering in any detail the advantages and disadvantages of centralization as contrasted to localism, it might be appropriate to point to some of the bases of the current reluctance to extend the range of government to conform to the enlarged horizons of economic, social, and intellectual organization. In some degree centralization is suspect because it is not in harmony with the settled traditions that have been carried over from pre-industrial society. The homely, small, and familiar group patterned after the family and the local community is felt to be consistent with solidarity, freedom, and peace. The strange and the distant arouse sentimental antagonisms, and are regarded as alien and arbitrary intruders and disturbers in a society that functions almost automatically to provide for the needs and desires of its members. Even when some degree of economic contact exists between such a simple society and the larger world outside, it is not felt to be a serious threat to social and political stability and independence. Under the plantation economy in the United States, for instance, staples such as cotton, corn, and tobacco were being traded in the world market; but about the only significant relationship of the producing communities with the outside world was this pecuniary one. Not until modern capitalism developed into an industrial-financial imperialism did the flag, the Bible, and the dollar come to be associated symbols.

Centralization has a particularly sinister connotation today because it seems to be linked in the minds of many with tyranny and regimentation. Democrats are inclined to shrink from the acceptance of the idea of centralization because they visualize its

eventual development into the corporative state and the dictatorship of a self-appointed élite. These have come to be the measures
which are held out by aggressive Fascist movements as the only
effective remedies for the alleged ills of democracy. Aside from
this transient reminder of Fascist totalitarianism, however, centralized government is essentially distasteful to democratic palates
because it is alleged to breed a haughty, indifferent, and parasitic
bureaucracy to which a society so dominated must pay involuntary tribute and render obedience. But even the most beneficent
intentions, it is sometimes asserted, cannot prevent a centralized
government from becoming wasteful and unresponsive to the actual needs of the people whom it is intended to serve. It will be
wasteful, it is charged, because being far away from the sources
of revenue it will increase officeholders and their salaries; and it
will be unresponsive to the changing local interests because, on
the one hand, distance from the scene will produce ignorance,
delay, and formalization and, on the other hand, the size and
diversity of the electorate will produce only compromises between
the strongest of the pressure groups so that no one ever gets what
he truly wants, and representative government will be nullified.
Individual and local interests, it is feared, will become submerged, and, since only a very few can aspire to the seats of authority, individual and local initiative and responsibility will be
dulled. Only in extremely critical situations, therefore, will a democratic society voluntarily submit to centralized power.

Conversely the advocates of centralization have not been without impressive facts and rationalizations. Aside from emphasizing
the inevitability of the trend toward larger and more integrally
directed social, political, and economic units in the modern world,
they argue that only in a large unit can we obtain the benefits of
the division of labor, attract outstanding talent to the positions of
leadership, achieve economies through large-scale operations and
the elimination of duplication, and avoid the pettiness and parochialism that derive from localism—assuring the members of society the peace that comes with power, the magnificent undertakings that only a large unit can afford, the due consideration of the
balanced needs of an interdependent world, and the freedom of

movement and opportunity for full self-development that are hampered by provincial barriers and limited goals.

Whatever the apologies for each of these conceptions of social organization, the trend toward centralization seems to be undeniable and consistent with the technological development of recent decades. The promise of greater military security in the larger unit seems, moreover, to be objectively demonstrable. Similarly the enhancement of economic productivity through the greater division of labor unmistakably argues in favor of larger aggregations, as does the greater possibility of orderly, balanced, or planned development.

Above all, however, it must be recognized that there are some functions that only a large unit can undertake if they are to be done at all. This applies pre-eminently to the assumption of risks. It might very well be that certain highly developed states in the American commonwealth with diversified industries could successfully undertake unemployment insurance programs for their citizens, but it is equally probable that certain others could not. Had it not been for federal grants to the states for education, the improvement of rural life, roads, emergency relief, housing, and public works of various types, it may well be supposed that some sections of the country would today be even farther from a tolerable average standard of social well-being than they now are.

The functions that a society, and particularly a modern government, carries on for its members are so diverse that the question might well be raised whether the advantages or disadvantages that are alleged to be associated with centralization are inherent or incidental, and whether they apply to all functions alike. There probably is more than a simple or single answer to these questions. To cite an instance relating to one of the newer and more significant functions of modern government, namely, public welfare activities:

Although it often asserted that services locally controlled are more likely to be flexible, adjusted to need, and well administered than systems dependent upon more remote control, the history of local administration of social service shows, in general, exactly the reverse to be true. As local units of administration become smaller and more like the integral or primary community in character, administration appears to be less efficient. At the other extreme is National administration under which it is extremely difficult to vary rates of compensation or relief in accordance with legitimate differences between geographic areas. Expansion or contraction of relief funds and relief loads by the central government in accordance with National conditions and resources often appears to local communities to be arbitrary and ruthless in character. Such change might be accepted more readily if the localities had a voice in the decision. In accordance with experience in some European countries, grants-in-aid to States and through States to local communities are viewed by many in America as constituting a "middle way" of great promise. . . .[7]

What applies to social work has been found in varying degree to apply to public health, housing, education, public safety, and probably to most other governmental services. In the last analysis, therefore, much will depend in the formulation of one's attitude upon the values he attaches to individual freedom and collective security, to personal initiative and social order. A long line of sociologists, including Charles H. Cooley, have reminded us of the fact that the individual and society are not antagonistic and incompatible elements but that they are two aspects of the same thing. It may not be out of place, however, to quote a recent, singularly lucid utterance on this perpetually misunderstood theme as it relates to freedom in the modern world:

From time immemorial, there have been those who fought for individual liberty just as others have fought for collective action. These two sets of ideals are sometimes represented as alternative and mutually exclusive states; the more there is of the one the less can there be of the other. . . . The observable facts are that human beings do react to one another in such a manner as to direct their actions to common ends, and the means taken to achieve a common end habitually involve a high degree of collaboration. Associated with these activities, the individuals are found to entertain sentiments about each other, about their common ends, their collaboration, and about

[7]   Katharine F. Lenroot, address at Third International Conference on Social Work, July 13, 1936 (*Public Welfare News*, IV [August, 1936], 2).

groups as such. In general, people are found to place a high value upon social activities and upon societies.

People are also found to place a high value on what they refer to as individual liberty. It is also to be noticed that many people obtain the satisfactions of this liberty, whose habitual actions and thoughts are guided by a high regard for the activities and thoughts of others. In fact, people obtaining the satisfactions of individual liberty are very apt to be just those who participate to a high degree in the sentiments and activities of their own society. This suggests that there can be no necessary inconsistency between the claims of individuals and the claims they make for their societies, although conflicts between the two have not been infrequent in practice. We might go further and state that in general, the satisfactions of individual liberty are rarely experienced except within the framework of a fairly coordinated group or society. . . . Naturally, it does not follow that every type of social organization is equally likely to yield this particular satisfaction.[8]

Having found it impossible to make a choice on rational grounds between localism and centralization as the ideal form of social organization, except by taking account of the values and purposes which a society or an individual takes for granted, one may conclude perhaps that they are not really alternatives at all, or at least that they cannot be adequately understood so long as they are viewed as mutually exclusive frames of organization. The question is rather—taking our society as we find it and recognizing that modern economic life and especially technology have profoundly shattered its internal consistency and solidarity and have altered its metes and bounds in many important respects— what are the benefits to be derived for certain purposes from one or the other type of organization and to what extent is each type of integration compatible with other aims to which we or other sections of society are committed? If our chief ends are military, we are likely to prefer a centralized authority, while for other purposes we may prefer a maximum of local autonomy. As a shrewd, democratically minded observer recently put it: "It is

[8]   T. N. Whitehead, *Leadership in a Free Society: A Study in Human Relations Based on an Analysis of Present-Day Industrial Civilization* (Cambridge: Harvard University Press, 1936), pp. 227–28.

probably safe to say that all thoughtful students of American government agree that it is desirable to have every function handled by the most localized unit of government which can do the work adequately."[9]

But it is precisely the question: Who can do what most adequately?—the term "adequately" being used in a broad and inclusive sense to take account of the principal interests of the members of a heterogeneous community—to which at present no unambiguous answer can be given. There are obviously some functions of which no reasonable person would like to see the family deprived. In our society as a whole, as we find it today and as it has evolved historically, there are probably a good many functions which, all things considered, the local community had better continue to perform. Others we would assign to the states or the federal government. From what has been said before, it is clear that while some things may be lost in assigning certain vital social services to as large a unit as the nation, it is imperative to do so if some of these functions are to be carried on effectively or at all.

In the attempt to avoid the dangers of extreme centralization, on the one hand, and to overcome the inefficiency of an archaic localism, on the other hand, a number of programs of governmental reorganization have been put forth, some of them quite feasible within our present constitutional framework and others calling for a more drastic revision of our nominal federalism. These programs are of interest to us only in so far as they seek to evolve a form of organization which would resolve the seeming conflicts between freedom and order, democracy and efficiency, flexibility and security.

Other things being equal, in the distribution or redistribution of functions to the various levels of government, it is preferable to build on those institutions and forms that we already know than to create them *de novo*. It has become fairly clear to competent students of such specific phenomena as population movements, crime, recreation, family disorganization, and economic distress

[9]   Henry W. Toll, "The States: Cooperation or Obliteration?" *State Government,* IX (November, 1936), 229.

that these problems defy analysis and control if they are treated on the basis of arbitrarily set local administrative areas. Hence they have found it necessary to seek areal units which were suited to their purposes. If the concept of the region had not already been in use, they would have been forced to invent it. But it is quite evident that the concrete reality of the region, when viewed from the standpoint of a given phenomenon such as crime, does not always coincide with the region when treated from the standpoint of education, recreation, taxation, or industry. The possibilities as well as the difficulties involved in the adaptation of administrative areas to a variety of functions have been clearly stated in a recent report of the National Resources Committee on *Regional Factors in National Planning.*[10] Similar studies have been made of individual regions, among them the *Pacific Northwest,*[11] the *New England Region,*[12] and the *St. Louis Region.*[13] The latter is of particular interest since it typifies the peculiar problems presented by the growth of great cities into metropolitan districts which often transcend state and even national boundaries. The problems of social control presented by the new technology of electric-power transmission, which are foreshadowed in the above-cited report on the Northwest, are already a challenging reality in the Tennessee Valley where an *ad hoc* governmental authority, based upon flood control and navigation, is now operating over an area including parts of several states.

While the division of the country into regions with their limits fixed by boundaries established on the basis of one problem or set of problems might solve some of our difficulties, it would undoubtedly create new ones, for it would inevitably do violence to the integrity of the areas of other problems.[14] A variety of alternative and supplementary devices has consequently been suggested. Among them are various forms of interstate agreements, such as interstate commissions to consult on a number of prob-

10   Washington: Government Printing Office, 1935.

11   *Ibid.*, 1936.   12   *Ibid.*   13   *Ibid.*

14   See Major Charles J. Calrow, "Reflections on Regionalism," *State Government,* IX (September, 1936), 193–95.

lems and interstate compacts and *ad hoc* authorities perhaps best exemplified by the interstate crime compacts, the Interstate Commission on the Delaware River Basin, and the New York Port Authority. A somewhat unique situation is presented by the unprecedented growth of metropolitan regions, which has brought large aggregations of people into the orbit of a central dominant city where life must be carried on under a peculiar set of circumstances. In order to deal more effectively with their acute and special problems unhampered by the restraints and obligations imposed by the states in which they are located, the large cities have attempted to recapture a modicum of freedom to deal with their own problems in a manner best suited to their circumstances, which generally are quite different from those prevailing in the rural areas that often dominate the state governments. This movement, known as "Home Rule,"[15] has made some progress in some American cities but is being effectively resisted in others. A similar but more radical aim is beng pursued through the proposal to endow cities with independent statehood. For the present this movement appears to be utopian in character for the rurally controlled states are likely, for reasons of revenue and of prestige, to block any attempt to "cut the heart" out of their dominions. Although more than half of our total population was urban (in 1930) only twenty-one of the forty-eight states had more than 50 per cent of their population in urban places. This may aid in accounting for the fact that we still live in a rural society politically.

What might at first glance seem to be a relatively simple problem, namely, the reconciliation of localism and centralization, is, as has been indicated, complicated by the circumstance that the conflict is not merely one between territorial units but between interests and functions that defy areal definition. A return by administrative devices to local autonomy would probably not be an automatic solution to the quest for representative democracy, for a community is not merely a territory but a group of persons and a set of institutions and a body of interests in interaction.

[15]   See Albert Lepawsky, *Home Rule for Metropolitan Chicago* (Chicago, 1935).

Even though a region cannot be so delineated as to satisfy all the requirements of a multifunctional, segmentalized, self-governing community, the regional approach to the problems of collective living has much to offer in the way of prospects for remedying some of the more glaring anomalies in our contemporary social existence. The planning movement, which has gained considerable ground lately partly as a result of the challenging problems of waste, privation, and disorder thrown into focus by the depression, gives some hope to our society of extricating itself from the paralysis brought about by our inability to adjust our technology and our social structure to our needs and aspirations. The planning idea and the emerging techniques that go with it are still in too amorphous a stage to lend themselves to precise analysis and evaluation. Their fundamental core, however, seems to consist in the attempt to achieve some sort of integration of the various elements in communal life through the rational direction of all the available resources to the socially to-be-defined end of a more satisfying existence.

Social planning assumes that free societies and democratic governments with their broad distribution of political powers are not or need not be essentially more helpless and wasteful than dictatorships. But even with the assumption that centralized autocracies can act more efficiently in critical situations than distributive democracies that impose checks on the promptness, the secrecy, and the arbitrariness of their elected representatives, the democratic experiment may still be defended on the ground that it is the most feasible compromise between efficiency and freedom.

It is precisely because democracies cannot proceed to order the lives of citizens without their consent that planning is a more significant and a more complicated function in a democracy than in a dictatorship, In a self-governing society, as distinguished from an autocratic one, it is not a single individual or a small group that sets the goals for the achievement of which planning is an instrument, but the citizens themselves. The planners may be able to help them to choose more wisely by informing them of the implications and the mutual compatibility of the various goals that are being considered, of the alternative means of reaching them, and of the probable costs involved in resources, as well as in personal and cultural values. In a dictatorship, in contrast, the planner's task is simply to implement the preconceived goals revealed by the oracle.

Planning in a democracy, therefore, cannot be regarded as the mere sum of physical planning, economic planning, and social planning. If, in view of the possible reluctance on the part of some, instead of using the term "planning," we may speak of intelligent foresight and rational ordering and direction of appropriate means to given social ends, it must be clear that such an activity must operate with the physical resources—natural and cultural—with the laws and institutions, and with the capacities, the attitudes, and interests of men. Of these only the physical resources are merely means; all the rest are ends as well as means. Some of the major difficulties of contemporary industrial society seem to arise in large measure out of the fact that our economic and technological changes have far outdistanced the relatively slow readaptation of our institutions, ideas, and sentiments. Planning, through its emphasis upon integration and the intelligent and orderly pursuit of achievable social goals, which in a free society are not imposed from without or above but self-selected in the course of democratic interplay of ideas and wills, is at least one promising alternative to violence and chaos.

14

THE LIMITATIONS

OF REGIONALISM

SEMINAL IDEAS are so rare that when we meet them in the scientific world we tend to embrace them with more than justifiable enthusiasm. Almost inevitably, as a consequence, we are disposed to overextend them and to make them the basis of a cult. To a certain extent this has happened in the case of the regionalism concept. Other writers have emphasized the fruitfulness of the idea. It is my task to call attention to its limitations.

I am reluctant to undertake to deflate the idea of regionalism. The idea has a venerable history; it has furnished many fruitful insights into the life of man in society at various periods and it has done much to correct and supplement other one-sided perspectives. It should be noted at the outset, therefore, that in undertaking this critical task there is no intention on the part of the author to minimize the significant clues, for the understanding of the complexities of social life, and the many practical suggestions, for the solution of social problems, which have come from the regional approach.

Reprinted from *Community Life and Social Policy*, ed. Elizabeth Wirth Marvick and Albert J. Reiss, Jr. (Chicago: University of Chicago Press, 1956), pp. 159–71, first published in *Regionalism in America*, ed. Merrill Jensen (Madison: University of Wisconsin Press, 1951), pp. 381–93.

The regional idea owes its scientific vitality to the fact that it offers a naturalistic and empirically verifiable theory for the interpretation of history. It affords a check on other competing theories in that it keeps the investigator's feet planted on the solid ground of the physical conditions of existence, though it must be admitted that it has not prevented him from letting his imagination soar to the heavens. The view of man in society, however, which singles out the interconnections between the human habitat and the complex fabric of social arrangements, ways of life, ideas and ideals, must be recognized for what it is, namely, a one-factor theory, which taken alone will furnish only a one-sided, and hence distorted, picture of social reality. To be scientifically valuable, it must be supplemented by and integrated with other perspectives affording other equally plausible and meaningful interpretations.

From time immemorial the attention of thinkers in many parts of the world has been directed to the spatial or areal aspects of human existence and to the physical substructure upon which communities and societies rest. Some of these notions have been elaborated into cosmic theories purporting to explain the origin and persistence of certain institutions in certain places on the basis of climate, rainfall, topography, natural resources, and similar factors. The development and the diffusion of civilization and the rise and fall of empires have been traced to such "environmental" conditions. The prevalence of democracy or autocracy, of monotheism or polytheism, of urbanism or agrarianism, and of variant forms of family, community, or national life has been depicted as more or less determined by such physical facts of nature. The influence which such a writer as Montesquieu has exerted upon Western thought is directly traceable to the vigor and persuasiveness with which he documented such a theory.

It would be foolish to deny that through such an approach much light has been thrown on many of the mysteries of cultural uniqueness and similarity; but it would also be naïve to fail to see that such simplistic interpretations of the complexities of social life have obscured other equally significant elements and have led to distorted versions of the complex and seemingly capricious course of human affairs.

There are many and varied conceptions of regions encountered in the rich and rapidly growing literature being produced by scholars and scientists representing a wide range of interests. Geographers, historians, anthropologists, linguists, artists, economists, sociologists, political scientists, administrators, architects, engineers, and planners—all have been attracted to the idea and have contributed to its elaboration. The various notions of the region which have emerged from these different sources present many nuances of meaning. To some, the region is an area defined by one or more physical characteristics such as rainfall, length of growing season, character of soil, vegetation, contours, and similar features. To others, it is an area delimited by the prevalence of one or more cultural characteristics—such as language or dialect, costume, form of social organization, type of architecture, use of given tools, acceptance of a given religion, practice of certain social customs—which distinguish the region from adjacent areas or other regions. This is what the anthropologists have called a culture area.

To be distinguished from such natural and cultural areas defined in terms of homogeneity in respect to one or more traits is the conception of the region as an area set off from other areas by barriers of various sorts. Mountains, deserts, rivers, lakes, and oceans are the most obvious of these barriers. No less potent, however, may be the artificial, i.e., man-made, barrier such as state and national boundaries and trade, exchange, and customs regulations, which inhibit contact between different areas and which in turn tend to confine the activities of a given area and isolate it from others.

There is a third conception of the region which, in contrast particularly to the first mentioned (which implies homogeneity of characteristics), rests upon interdependence. In a region so conceived the component parts are not necessarily similar or identical but stand in a relationship of significant interdependence or integration of life in one or more respects. Such a region finds difficulty in delineating its boundaries, but is more likely to have a salient or dominant center; whereas the types of regions described above can be more readily defined in terms of their periphery but may not give evidence of the existence of a focal point which dominates the life and activities of the area. An example of this third type of region is the trade area, which is delineated by the network of economic interconnections that holds it together and which can be described in terms of the radii of influence which extend from the center outward. The importance of such regions in historical and contemporary societies may be indicated by pointing to the role of rural trade centers, metropolitan regions, and cultural and political capitals, which extend their tentacles out in all directions and influence the life of their regions in varying degrees.

Such regions cannot usually be set off from adjacent regions by sharply defined lines because, in the first place, the center of dominance may have varying range in respect to the various functions it performs for the region and, secondly, because the periphery may shade off or fade into a no man's land where it meets the influences exerted by a competing center of dominance. The listening areas of radio stations, the circulation areas of newspapers, the ticker services of stock exchanges, the wholesale or retail trade areas of a metropolis, and the drawing area of a medical center, a university, an orchestra, an opera, or a museum may give us indications of how far in its complex functions a center extends in its influence and where it comes into collision with a competing center. Those of us who have labored in the field of metropolitan regions and who are aware of the many and varied functions that tie such regions together are in a position where we must warn others against the naïve acceptance of regional definitions based upon a one-factor criterion, and even more against the disposition to accept the boundaries, when once defined, as permanent. Regions based upon the principle of interdependence and the dominance of a focal center are not only vaguely defined but are subject to infinite flux.

A fourth type of region is an areal unit defined in terms of an *ad hoc* problem. If we would control contagious disease, crime, slums, traffic, or other community problems, we must find suitable areal units of administration corresponding to the areas over which these problems extend and taking account of the factors which underlie these problems. An area which is suited to one purpose may not be adaptable to another purpose. The TVA, which, it should be noted, has multiple objectives—national defense, navigation, and flood control—is such an area; and one of the issues it faces is precisely attributable to the several, and perhaps even mutually conflicting, functions for which it has been established. The New York Port Authority would not seem to be a suitable pattern on which to build other regional services such as the control of railroad or highway traffic, much less the orderly redevelopment of slums or the control of crime in the New York area.

With the development of local, regional, and national planning it has become increasingly important to seek improved techniques for defining the scope of the strategic functions with which planning agencies must deal. In the course of such efforts, the problems posed by the multifunctional planning area—one that will reconcile the residential pattern of the community with the industrial, the transportation, the public-service, the cultural, and the political pattern—have become readily apparent. Ideally, a planning region should be one that comprises the territory within which all of the problems of the community can be treated adequately. But the area which affects a central community and the area affected by the central community in one vital way or another encompass the world. Hence planning regions must of necessity always be based upon compromise and in practice turn out to be more or less unsatisfactory compromises.

What has been said about such *ad hoc* regions as planning areas is, of course, only a particular instance of other single- or multiple-function regions. It suggests that the administrative region, or *ad hoc* region, is a contrast conception which may be put in juxtaposition to the "natural area" as viewed by human ecologists. Nature does not always carve out neatly the lines that set off one area from another, nor does man in his works always obey the dictates of nature. While the natural and the cultural landscape often coincide, they also often clash. Historical factors which have shaped the outlines of cities, counties, states, and nations may impose rather arbitrary patterns upon the features of the human habitat and may themselves in the course of time become as significant as nature itself. Thus, for instance, when some of our states were laid out, rivers were designated in many instances as the boundaries between them. At the same time, rivers were also significant arteries of transportation and thus conditioned the sites of the towns. As a result, we face the problem today of having over twenty of our principal cities located on state boundaries—a situation which, since many of these cities have grown to metropolitan size, creates complicated interstate problems of administration. The planning region is an attempt to overcome the handicaps imposed upon those who have the responsibility of dealing with the actual and emerging problems of today by the rigid and in many instances unsuitable outlines of administrative areas. The planning region represents a recognition of and an answer to the fact that human social life does not always conform to the metes and bounds set by nature; that ongoing life tends to spill over not merely these natural barriers but also the arbitrary or historically conditioned political and administrative units; and that if man is to be a better master over his fate, he must, by all the intelligence he can command, seek to shape the most appropriate units of organization for his collective needs.

This depiction of types of regions has been undertaken here to call attention to the fact that in the concept of region we are not dealing with a single and unambiguous idea but rather with a variety of notions and approaches. To use the regional concept as if it were one clear and univocal term is to make for misunderstandings and confusion rather than clarity. There now remains the task of drawing from this delineation of the various dimensions of the concept implications which will indicate its proper uses and limitations.

It seems useful to discuss the fruitfulness and at the same time the limitations of the regional concept by considering the region first as a fact and then in turn as a hypothesis, as a practical tool for social engineering and as a state of mind and social movement.

All of these conceptions of the region involve a spatial or areal approach to social phenomena. If we do not mean by the term "region" to call attention to the fact that we are looking at life in terms of the space dimension and the interest in location and position which that implies, then the term "region" has no intelligible meaning whatsoever.

It is well to begin this consideration of the spatial aspect of human social life by noting the fact that men and all that they work with and live with and create are located somewhere in space. It is helpful to us in understanding man's relationship to his fellow-men to take into account his relationship to his habitat. His habitat is furnished to him, however, only in part by nature. It is in part also molded by himself. Nature sets the stage; but it is man that is the actor. Nature furnishes possibilities and sets limits. It is among these possibilities and within these limits that man can choose.

Climate, topography, resources, and other aspects of nature are not distributed evenly or uniformly around the world. The depiction of the characteristics of the natural landscape furnishes the most elementary factual basis for the delineation of regions.

Just as regions are physical facts of nature, so they are also facts of culture. Peoples, languages, forms of social organization, institutions, customs, and practices are also distributed in space. To point out their location and their movement is to call attention to a no less important fact of regionalism than the regional aspects of nature.

To define the areas on the earth's crust where certain kinds of human beings live in a certain degree of density, making their living through particular sets of activities, building particular kinds of structures, following particular kinds of customs, pursuing certain interests, meeting specific types of problems and seeking to solve them in specific ways, is a legitimate and necessary task which properly engages the scholarly labor of many persons throughout the world. Geographies and histories of specific areas, ethnographies, statistical compilations, linguistic atlases, and economic, political, sociological, and psychological studies are available in abundance, testifying to the fruitfulness of the labor that has gone into this far from finished description. While certain local units such as continents, nation-states, cities, and regions have become conventionally established in the course of scientific work for the purposes of collecting, classifying, and presenting this material, there is by no means universal agreement on what the most feasible areal units are for dealing with these data. The basis on which many previous areal units were carved out obviously is no longer suitable for our purposes. We are not collecting population statistics today for the area which once was the Holy Roman Empire; and in our attempt to obtain useful statistics on the population of metropolitan cities we are attempting desperately to break through the difficulties which have hitherto kept us from getting comparable data on the suburban fringe surrounding central cities.

The fact of regionalism must therefore be recognized in determining the manner in which the student of social life collects the data that will enable him to discern the differences between areas which are worth recording. The determination of the regional units which promise to be most useful for the understanding and control of social life depends not merely upon the facts thus discovered but also upon the purposes for which they shall be used.

Moving from the consideration of regions as fact to the region as hypothesis, we note that scholars and scientists and men of imagination are not usually content with description alone. They also seek interpretation and explanation. The concept of region thus becomes a tool of research, a possible way of explaining the incidence and distributions which have been found to exist. Regionalism in this sense offers a theory accounting for the interrelations between things. The doctrine that physical conditions of existence influence the character of peoples and their cultures has been so often set forth by notable figures in our intellectual history that it is often taken for granted as an established fact. The general hypothesis that men who live under different physical conditions become and are different sounds plausible enough, as does the more specific hypothesis that men who live differently think differently. In order to turn these rather general aphorisms into useful scientific hypotheses, however, we must ask: What correlations, if any, exist between specific cultural characteristics in a given area and specific conditions of nature, and what factors or processes account for this correlation? Culture, we can say with a good deal of assurance, does not spring directly or automatically from the soil or the atmosphere. It develops, rather, through an intricate process, and the most dissimilar cultural phenomena have been found to exist in the most similar environments, and vice versa. If any relations between natural habitat and social and cultural characteristics exist—and there is a high probability that they do—they must be shown to exist in actuality. They cannot be assumed, but, unfortunately, the literature of regionalism has too frequently taken them for granted.

Moreover, while we may have sound reason for inferring interconnections between regional habitat and regional culture in the initial stages of man's conquest over and adjustment to nature, civilizations as they mature tend to emancipate themselves from the soil and the natural context out of which and in which they developed. It is well to remember that things may continue to exist for reasons other than those that brought them into being. The momentum of established institutions and habits is so great that often it requires a cataclysm to uproot them.

Not only must we take account of the impact of past history and practice, which may be quite autonomous of the dictates of nature (for nature, as has been pointed out, merely offers possibilities and sets limits), but we must be particularly alert to the profound influences of communication and movement through which a technology, an institutional form, an idea, or an ideal can be diffused widely throughout the world. Even if regional contexts between natural and cultural facts should become established in a given area, we must always, especially in modern times, reckon with the power of communication and transportation—with the mobility of men and ideas—to undo regions.

There is the third view of regionalism, which envisages it as a tool of administration, of control, and of planning. The region in this sense is a tool in social engineering. The delineation of such regions, to be effective, obviously cannot proceed without taking due account of the region as a fact and the region as a set of interrelations between facts. To do otherwise would be to seek to

impose artificial areal patterns of formal control upon human relations, which have a tendency not to be bound by rigid lines.
Moreover, as the studies of the National Resources Committee
have so convincingly shown, various purposes require different
areal scope, and it is difficult to find any criterion that will satisfy
the multiple demands of adequacy. Even if such a criterion or set
of criteria could be found, the dynamics of life would soon make
it archaic. Short of considering the whole world as a single region,
which would be self-defeating, there is no other regional arrangement, of lesser scope, which will fully satisfy the many interests
that clamor for recognition. The best we can do is to make the
most reasonable compromises we can invent, which means weight-
ing some functions more heavily than others, and to keep our lines
of demarcation flexible enough so that they can be adjusted to
changing needs and possibilities. It would be self-deceptive, however, to proceed as if the crude approximations we now make to
an adequate regional arrangement were anything more than improvisations.

This is not to deny that, irrespective of their historical origin,
the regional units that we construct for purposes of administration, planning, and social engineering may themselves result in
the emergence of patterns which have important, and sometimes
unforeseen, consequences. If we view such little countries as Luxembourg, Belgium, and Holland in the light of the tribal, dynastic, and historical factors that help account for their present independent position as nation-states, we may, of course, rationalize
ex post facto the justification or inevitability of their independent
existence. This, however, should not obscure the fact that they
have such uniqueness as they possess and are afflicted as they are
with problems as small independent nations, in large part, because they have had such a long experience of living under the
particular administrative arrangement which separates them from
each other by boundaries which in the light of present-day needs
are utterly indefensible. If we were planning them anew, with a
view to present-day conditions and problems, we probably would
not retain them as separate administrative areas and independent
political units.

There may have been a time when a better defense could be made for the independent existence of our forty-eight states than can be made today, but it is a fact that their independent existence for so long, with the consequent patterning and differentiation of life that has grown up between them, is today one of the strongest reasons for their continued independent existence. Surely, ideally speaking, a more economical and efficient arrangement of the territory comprising the United States of America could be devised today than that under which we are operating, but it is unnecessary to argue the futility of such a proposal, however practical it may be, in the face of the vested interests and the inertia which stand in the way. A system of law and administration, with its network of functional interrelations, once developed, comes to have great potency for its own self-continuance and for shaping many of the other aspects of the regional complex of life which it embraces.

There are, however, many factors at work which soften the sharp demarcation lines between administrative regions and which may be invoked to transform them into more realistically designed units to meet the conditions and problems of contemporary civilization. The arrival upon the scene of national labor organizations, engaged in collective bargaining on a national scale eventuating in nationwide contracts, tends to wipe out wage, income, and cost differentials that formerly marked off one region from others. The national income tax and national grants-in-aid, which redistribute part of the national income in accordance with regional needs, also national minimum-wage legislation, postal rates, mail-order houses, and many other instances which could be cited, tend to minimize differences in the ways of life of regions and weave the separate regions into a broader national living unit. The fact should, of course, not be overlooked that many vestiges of regional differentials continue to exist. Nor should we minimize the threat—if it be a threat—that a pluralistic pattern of civilization, comprising many unique regional forms of expression, is being gradually transformed into a more standardized national pattern.

Regionalism presents a fourth aspect as a state of mind, as a way of life, as a mode of collective consciousness, as a social movement, and as a cult. The three types of factors considered above do eventually combine to produce a settled way of life and a characteristic consciousness. People who live long enough under similar conditions might be expected to develop some similarity of traits. People who continue to live together under conditions of mutual interdependence and are subjected to the same influences from identical sources might similarly be expected to develop a sense of mutual interdependence and to share a sense of common belonging. Thus regions develop a conception of themselves and acquire a more or less stereotyped conception in the minds of others who think about them or who have relations with them. Out of this common mode of life grow a coalescence of interests and an identification with the symbols expressive of these common interests. This heightened regional sentiment and sense of belonging may be accentuated by conflict or rivalry with other regions. The differences between the South and the rest of the nation on the subject of civil rights tend to strengthen rather than to minimize the regional consciousness of the South, at least for the time being. Regional discriminatory freight rates and similar economic schisms make for regional definition of interests and states of mind which express themselves dramatically in regional political alignments. Regional sentiments may have their constructive uses in mobilizing for region-wide action, but they may also be perverted into regional chauvinism.

Regionalism may thus take the form of a social movement. The cultivation of the arts based upon regional themes or reflecting the regional atmosphere has in some parts of this nation resulted in the crystallization of regional "schools." Whether these regional schools in literature or the arts are the faithful expression of the regional way of life or whether they are an attempt motivated by the tourist trade to manufacture an artificial regional culture is a question which the present writer is not competent to answer. In France regionalism is not merely a sociocultural movement but a strong political force based upon the protest of the provinces against the centralized control and dominant influence of the capital. In its extreme form regionalism leads to isolation, parochialism, separatism, and secession. As a counterpoise to gigantism, to uniformity, to standardization, and to overcentralization it can have wholesome effects; but these legitimate aspirations can also degenerate into regional cultism and jingoism and lend themselves to exploitation by political and cultural demagogues.

In summary, then, regionalism is not one thing but many things. The failure to discriminate the many distinct factors that underlie the emergence and persistence of regions is a serious fault of present-day scholarship and research. It has led to the failure to distinguish between genuine and spurious regions. Areas of homogeneity have been mistakenly represented as areas of integration. It has been mistakenly assumed that physical regions also inevitably constitute economic, cultural, and political regions.

If the mark of a community is interdependence and the mark of a society is consensus, it follows that many areas which have been conceived as regions are neither communities nor societies, for they show no convincing evidence of a common basis of existence or of a collective consciousness.

As a tool for the discernment of interrelations between habitat and culture the regional concept has great value, provided we do not assume what needs to be proved, namely, that these correlations actually exist, and proceed to analyze the processes that account for these correlations. Regionalism, which is the way of viewing social life in areal terms, is, after all, only one possible perspective of human beings living together. To regard it as the only one leads to distortion of reality. As a one-factor explanation of the complexities of social life it can become a false and dangerous doctrine; but seen as a supplement to and corrective of other one-factor explanations—such as the economic, the sociocultural, and political factors—it can have great value.

Regionalism as a dogma can easily degenerate into a cult. As the basis for a social movement it offers a potent counteragent against the leveling influences of standardization, uniformization, and overcentralization. But it can also become a desperate and futile protest against the tides of progress which, stimulated by the technology of mass communication and mobility, make possible ever wider areas of integration of social life and thus have the potentiality of raising the level of human well-being by a wider sharing in the fruits of civilization. It is well to be aware of the regional aspect of human existence and to cultivate a sensitivity to regional influences.

It is important also to remember that there is no magic in the regional idea. It can lead to the falsification of the facts. It can become a futile effort to squeeze life into a rigid mold, and it can become a vain gesture to retard the integration of life on a wider and more inclusive scale.

15

RURAL-URBAN DIFFERENCES

THE SEPARATE development of rural and urban sociology
in the United States is a regrettable historical accident. It was
due in some degree to the availability of relatively large funds
to agricultural experiment stations and to the absence in our government of a department concerned with cities and urban life,
corresponding roughly to the functions of the Department of
Agriculture in the case of rural life. The urban studies of the
National Resources Committee marked the first public recognition of this fact.

Because of the administrative separation between rural and
urban sociological research, methodical analysis of rural and urban likenesses and differences is lacking today.

The recent profound changes in the technology of living, especially in the United States and to some extent all over the world,
have made such notions as we have about rural and urban likenesses and differences obsolete. The city has spilled over into the
countryside. City ways of life have in some respects taken on a

Reprinted from *Community Life and Social Policy*, ed. Elizabeth Wirth
Marvick and Albert J. Reiss, Jr. (Chicago: University of Chicago Press,
1956), pp. 172–76, which was taken from an uncompleted manuscript and
an "abstract" in typescript which were the bases for a talk on this topic
at the University of Wisconsin late in 1951. At the time of his death Wirth
was apparently using these materials to prepare an article with this title
for publication in the *American Sociological Review*.

rural cast, particularly in the suburbs. On the other hand, industry, which hitherto was characteristic of cities, has gone into the countryside. Transportation has made the city accessible to rural people. The radio and, more lately, television promise to produce a virtual revolution. The time has come for a re-examination of the meaning of the concepts "urban" and "rural."

The difficulties that stand in the way of a rigorous comparison of rural and urban modes of life and problems are many, nowhere more numerous than in the United States and the countries of the Western world where the fusion of the two is becoming an inescapable fact. Urbanism is no longer synonymous with industrialism, and ruralism is no longer identified with unmechanized labor. Since social contact is no longer intimately dependent upon personal relations, size of community and location are of less significance for the mode of life. The standardization of ways of living tends to make rural life as we have known it look archaic in many respects; we look upon it more and more as a survival from an earlier era.

In "Urbanism as a Way of Life" I attempted to describe the city as a particular form of human association. The assumption obviously was that at the other pole of the city stood the country. I indicated then that "for sociological purposes a city may be defined as a relatively large, dense, and permanent settlement of socially heterogeneous individuals" and attempted to develop a series of interrelated propositions which I thought could be distilled from the existing knowledge of the city based upon the postulates which this minimal definition of the city as a social fact suggests.

Whatever we might discover about the city in this manner would manifestly have to be checked against what we know or could find out about human settlements which are not cities, i.e., against the country. Only after such a comparison was made would we be able to say that we had selected the significant aspects of urban life which made the city a distinctive form of human association. But just as cities differ, so do rural settlements differ from one another. In respect to each of my criteria of urban life—numbers, density, permanence, and heterogeneity —cities represent a vast continuum shading into non-urban settlements. The same is true of rural settlements be they rural non-farm settlements, villages, or scattered open farm areas. To lump the great variety of cities and rural settlements respectively together obscures more than it reveals the distinctive characteristics of each.

To set up ideal-typical polar concepts such as I have done, and many others before me have done, does not prove that city and country are fundamentally and necessarily different. It does not justify mistaking the hypothetical characteristics attributed to the urban and the rural modes of life for established facts, as has so often been done. Rather it suggests certain hypotheses to be tested in the light of empirical evidence which we must assiduously gather. Unfortunately this evidence has not been accumulated in such a fashion as to test critically any major hypothesis that has been proposed.

I do not wish this remark to be misconstrued as an indictment of the rich body of concrete materials that has been accumulated on what are called cities and what are called rural communities. My criticism is directed rather against the mechanical and relatively unsophisticated manner in which we have identified city and country. Here as in so many other fields students of social life have relied heavily upon the data gathered by others; since in our case so large a part of the data has its source in the various governmental censuses which for purposes of classification must necessarily use arbitrary definitions preferably based upon quantitative criteria, we have fallen into the trap of regarding these arbitrary definitions as actual entities, corresponding to something existing in social reality.

What is even more regrettable is the fact that having taken this arbitrary dichotomy as a base—it should be pointed out that technically it is a trichotomy: urban, rural non-farm, and rural farm—we have built our own data upon the same foundation and thus compounded the error. I might add parenthetically that even in respect to this system of classification the reliable knowledge that we have is far from adequate. One looks in vain in the textbooks about urban or rural sociology for a careful, detailed, and reliable comparison of city and country on the basis of: size of family, mortality, marital status, education, ethnic and racial

origin, occupation, wealth, income, housing, religion, politics, recreation, stratification, mobility, contacts, associational membership and participation, consumption, savings, illness, physical defects, mental disorder, delinquency and crime, family organization, marriage practices, sex life, rearing of children, and many
other facts on which continuous time series would seem to be
indispensable. This, however, is a deficiency that with patience
and diligence might, in the course of a few years, be overcome.

The development of such series for the United States and the
rest of the world, while devoutly to be wished, will not cure the
fundamental difficulty I mentioned earlier. What we look forward
to is not the piling up of a vast body of reliable, continuous information if this labor is to be largely wasted on a basic system
of classification such as we have used up to now. The factor-by-
factor analysis of any problem in terms of which rural and urban
settlements have shown significant differences—whether it be
vitality rates, crime rates, family expenditures, political affiliation
and participation, or any one of a great number of aspects of human behavior—leads to sterile results. From a sampling of a
number of studies, including my own, of the ways in which rural
and urban people are supposed to differ, I have found that if we
allow for each of these functional factors, virtually all of the differences between rural and urban behavior are accounted for
without our resorting to the alleged urban and rural natural
dissimilarity.

If this should prove to be the experience of students generally,
a new approach seems to be called for. What we wish to know is
not so much how a settlement of 2,500 differs from one of 2,499
inhabitants, nor even how one kind of human settlement as a
settlement differs from another, but rather how one mode of human association which may be closely related to a type of human
settlement conditions behavior and problems. This general question for purpose of analysis should lead us to ask how numbers,
density, and heterogeneity affect the relations between men. For
such a purpose we might have to ignore the statistically defined
categories of urban and rural and deal rather with degrees on
a continuum.

Population in large numbers suggests individual variability, relative absence of intimate personal acquaintanceship, segmentalization of human relations and their anonymous, superficial, impersonal, transitory, and utilitarian character. Density may be expected to bring about and accentuate diversification and specialization and, given larger numbers of heterogeneous people, to bring about that unique condition of the coincidence of close physical contact with great social distances, glaring contrasts in mode of life and status, complex patterns of segregation, and the predominance of formal controls. Other associated phenomena should also, if our view of human nature in different social settings is correct, be found in accentuated form in the urban settlement: intensified mobility both physical and social, instability of life, flexibility of social structures and institutions, and differential participation of individuals in a great variety of conflicting, competing, and intersecting groups with a high rate of turnover, through which individuals find expression for their interests and meet some of their major life needs.

It is to these and similar *social* characteristics that students of urban and rural life must turn for a realistic understanding of the manner in which type of settlement is associated with mode of life and state of mind. It is important to note that the urban and rural modes of life are not necessarily confined to urban and rural settlements, respectively, for the reasons mentioned earlier. The same man who is the farm laborer from April to September is also the city hobo from October to March. The large-scale agricultural organizations may be no less impersonal than large-scale labor unions or manufacturers' organizations. I have seen forests of television antennae in rural areas of Pennsylvania and noted the absence of such antennae in large blocks of the slums of Chicago. Is the Negro tenant or sharecropper in Mississippi any more closely associated with the farm owner than a similar employee of a steel company in Pittsburgh with the plant manager?

Rather than taking our conjectured rural-urban types for granted, we might turn to what we actually find under specified conditions of life associated with what we call urban and rural communities.

IV. Social Problems and Planning

16

CULTURE CONFLICT

AND MISCONDUCT

THE HISTORY of criminology as a science is a record of the successive fumbling with anthropological, psychological and sociological hypotheses which have not brought us appreciably nearer to an understanding of the problems of misconduct. In the attempt to explain delinquency we have been repeatedly shifting our attention from the personality to the surroundings and have emphasized first one, then another biological, psychological, or cultural fact, usually to the exclusion of all others. In stressing culture conflict as one of the possible factors in delinquency we are merely selecting for special investigation one of the items in the sociological approach and are neglecting for the moment other factors both situational and personal. In the face of the imposing series of exploded theories of criminality, prudence dictates that a new theory avoid the persistent error of claiming universal applicability. It should be frankly stated at the outset, therefore, that not all delinquency is explained by culture conflict and not all of life's experiences and social relations involve culture conflict. But, if the social psychologists are correct, conscious mental life arises out of conflict situations. Still it would

Reprinted from *Social Forces*, **IX** (June, 1931), 484–92.

be an exaggeration to speak of conflict as a universal etiological principle. There are so many significant problems on which it has an immediate bearing that it is not necessary to magnify the importance of this principle to convince others of its usefulness. There have been several widely accepted theories of sociology which have been constructed around the central notion of conflict. For our purposes, however, we need a much more specific and workable conception than these universalistic theories imply. It is the merit of William Healy to have called attention to the relationship between mental conflicts and misconduct. The sociologist might raise the question whether these mental conflicts as they appear on the inner, personal side of life are not sometimes paralleled by culture conflicts when viewed from the standpoint of the social world.

The records of social agencies concerned with the behavior problems of individuals, in their emphasis on the details of biological heredity, on psychometric tests, on psychiatric diagnoses generally reflect the fashion that happens to prevail at the moment with reference to the sciences of human behavior. In our conventional case records we often find, largely due to medical, psychological, and psychiatric bias, a fairly detailed account of the personal characteristics of the individual, but relatively little about the cultural setting, the group customs out of which the individual's behavior at least in part flows. One is tempted to ask: Is it not as important to record the sometimes grossly conflicting family traditions of the paternal and maternal ancestors as to trace their respective childhood diseases?

Whatever may be the physical, the psychological and the temperamental differences between various races and societies, one thing is certain, namely that their cultures are different. Their traditions, their modes of living and making a living, the values that they place upon various types of conduct are often so strikingly different that what is punished as a crime in one group is celebrated as heroic conduct in another. The obvious fact about the relativity of social values is so strikingly expressed in some of our earliest sociological literature, such as Sumner's *Folkways*, that one may indeed wonder why it has not furnished the starting-point for the sociologists' research into delinquency and crime. The ethnological evidence, which we are not considering here, seems to indicate that where culture is homogeneous and class differences are negligible, societies without crime are possible. A small compact, isolated, and homogeneous group seems to have no difficulty in maintaining its group life intact, in passing on its institutions, practices, attitudes, and sentiments to successive generations and in controlling the behavior of its members. Punishment, at least in the formal sense, as we know it in our society, is unknown and unnecessary in such a community. The control of the group over the individuals is complete and informal, and hence spontaneous. The community secures the allegiance, participation, and conformity of the members not through edicts of law, through written ordinances, through police, courts and jails, but through the overwhelming force of community opinion, through the immediate, voluntary, and habitual approval of the social code by all. The individual in his conduct is supported and fortified by the group as a whole. Even in such a community personal rivalry and friction and the impulsive violation of the mores may perhaps never be ruled out entirely, but such a community can at least be relatively free from external and internal cultural schisms which are the source of much of our own social strife and personal and social disorganization. On the other hand, for example, one needs only to spend some time in Germany, especially if one knew that country before the war with its reverence for law and order, its thrift and its honesty, to realize what a disorganizing effect a mutation of cultural values may exert upon human conduct. Such mutations, however, may be produced not merely by social upheaval, but also by migration, by social contact, and less abruptly, by the ordinary process of attempting to transfer a tradition from one generation to the next.

Most human beings, living in a civilization akin to our own, are exposed to experiences that carry back to varied cultural settings. To understand their problems of adjustment, therefore, it is necessary to view the personalities from the perspective of their cultural matrix and to note the contradictions, the inconsistencies, and the incongruities of the cultural influences that impinge upon them. The hypothesis may be set forth that the physical and psychic tensions which express themselves in attitudes and in overt conduct may be correlated with culture conflicts. This hypothesis may, to be sure, not always prove fitting. If a program of adjustment based upon such a theory does not prove fitting and effective, another explanation for the conduct in question must be sought. In singling out culture conflicts we are merely pointing to one variety of many causal explanations of human conduct and conduct disorders, which may at the same time furnish valuable clues for therapeutic measures.

Whatever differences of opinion may exist between our contemporary schools of sociological thought, there is one proposition on which all would agree, viz., that human conduct presents a problem only when it involves a deviation from the dominant code or the generally prevailing definition in a given culture, i.e., when a given society regards it as a problem. Our traditional legal conceptions of crime in terms of guilt, involving the determination by means of rigidly stereotyped process whether the accused has violated the prescribed code or not, is in large measure responsible for the arbitrary way in which we have been accustomed to evaluate social behavior, moral conduct, delinquency, and crime. The fact that we distinguish between crime and delinquency and are beginning to make legal process broader and more elastic, as the development of the juvenile court indicates, is a striking recognition of the inadequacy of our conventional method of viewing and treating misconduct, and of our determination to break away from iron-clad legalistic restrictions. Our refusal to see misconduct in the relative perspective of the cultural setting in which it occurs and which makes it into the peculiar problem that it is, has been fostered in no small measure by the official conception of crime in which the determination of the guilt of the offender and the appropriate punishment were the chief points around which the proceedings turned. Not until we appreciate that the law itself—even if in extremely arbitrary form —is an expression of the wishes of a social group, and that it is not infallibly and permanently in accord with the cultural needs and definitions of all the social groups whom it seeks to restrain, can we begin to understand why there should be crime at all. As Dr. L. K. Frank has put it:

The law, both statutory and common law, sets forth the socially sanctioned ways of carrying on life which the social scientists are busily engaged in studying. In doing so, the law, theoretically, provides patterns of behavior for all life situations which, if observed in the individual's conduct, would enable him to avoid any conflict, or at least would protect him if any conflict did arise. . . . Moreover it is clear that in so far as there are shifts and changes in the material and non-material culture of a group the very existence of rather fixed and established patterns, legally sanctioned and legally enforced, tends to increase the difficulties of the individual and to foster personality deviations, because the individual is being forced by the cultural movements into the use of new patterns of behavior which lack legal sanction and by so much create in his mind conflicts which may be resolved in frank disregard of the law, both criminally and civilly or a more or less serious mental disorder.

Dr. Frank points out how significant it is for those concerned with the offender and the mentally deranged

to begin to understand and consider more carefully the role of cultural tradition and institutional life in the patterning of human behavior and its modification. This is especially important at the present time since it is evident that no small part of the behavior deviations represent efforts to encompass adjustments where the cultural traditions and the institutional patterns are in process of change. This suggests that every major category of behavior deviation may be considered as an index of a social disturbance of which the social scientists as a group may not be sufficiently aware.[1]

The prevalence of culture conflict as a factor in delinquency strikes one most forcefully when one is dealing, as one so frequently is in American cities, with immigrant families. And it is quite natural that this should be so, for the most obvious distinguishing characteristic of the immigrant is not his physical organism but his foreign culture. Much of what is strange and baffling

[1]   *First Colloquium on Personality*, The American Psychiatric Association, p. 25.

in the behavior of the immigrant and especially his children dis-
appears if he is thought of as an individual living in a dual
cultural milieu. The mysteries of behavior found in the life of the
immigrant rarely are intelligible to us if we fail to reckon with
the fact that in the immigrant family and community we find not
a homogeneous body of sentiments, traditions, and practices, but
conflicting currents of culture and divergent social codes bidding
for the participation and allegiance of its members.

If we examine the statistics of crime which take account of
the existence of immigrants and their children we have an important clue to a neglected factor in delinquency which has wide
bearings and many implications. Sutherland points out that:

> The "second generation" of immigrants generally come into contact
> with the courts as delinquents more frequently than the first gener-
> ation. The Census report of 1910 which shows the opposite can be dis-
> regarded because of the lack of homogeneity in the groups compared.
> Laughlin's study of prisoners in 1921–22 resulted in criminality rates
> as follows:
>
> Native white, both parents native-born 81.84
> Native-born, both parents foreign-born 91.14
> Native-born, one parent native-born and one foreign-born 115.58

In 1920 in Massachusetts per 100,000 population fifteen years of age
and over the following numbers were committed to penal and reform-
atory institutions for adults: 120 native-born of native parents, 226
native-born of foreign or mixed parents, and 143 foreign-born. This
is in general the rating of the three groups: native-born whites of
native parents have the smallest number of commitments, foreign-born
whites rank second, and native-born of foreign parents or mixed
parents (the second generation) rank highest.[2]

The fact that second-generation crime should be even more
prevalent than first-generation crime does not seem difficult to
understand when we note that the immigrant himself, living, as
he generally does, in an isolated immigrant colony, even though
he has not assimilated New-World standards, is at least supported
and controlled by Old-World traditions, which are, to a large ex-

2   E. H. Sutherland, *Criminology*, pp. 100–101.

tent, reproduced in the immigrant colony, be it Chinatown, Little Sicily, or the Ghetto. Under these circumstances, whatever the differences between native and immigrant culture may be, personal morale and community control are maintained. But the second generation is differently situated. The immigrant child, especially if born in America, does not have the life-long and exclusive attachments to the folkways and mores of the Old-World group that the parents have, who have been reared in the customs and traditions of their people and in whom the memories of the Old World call forth a strong emotional response. The child, because of the relative weakness of his attachment to the Old-World culture, and because of his greater mobility, has greater opportunity of making intimate contacts with the American social world than the parent whose contacts are generally confined to the society of his own countrymen, often within the confines of the immigrant colony itself. What is of greatest significance, however, is the circumstance that the child soon becomes incorporated into a neighborhood—a play—and a school group, frequently into a gang, where he establishes primary relations with other foreign and native children. It is under conditions such as these—in the course of intimate and spontaneous contacts—that assimilation takes place. The Americanization of the immigrant parents takes place, if at all, through the medium of the children. In the immigrant family the child thus comes to play a role not unlike that of the missionary between cultures. The term "Americanization," as Park and Miller point out, is not used popularly among immigrants as we use it. They call a badly demoralized boy "completely Americanized."[3] This explains, in part, the fact that the character of the second generation's crime should be different from that of the first generation, as is pointed out by the investigation of the United States Immigration Commission of 1910, in which it was found that the crime of the second generation resembled that of the natives much more nearly than that of the immigrants.[4]

My own studies, particularly in the Jewish group, have shown

3   *Old World Traits Transplanted,* p. 288.
4   *Report of the U.S. Immigration Commission, 1910,* pp. 14–16.

that those social agencies which deal primarily with immigrant families have a unique opportunity, through the attention which they might devote to the collection and interpretation of these cultural facts, to make a contribution not only to the understanding of delinquency in their own cultural group but to delinquency in general. For culture conflicts are by no means confined to immigrant families, but they occur in other families and communities as well, especially where, as is the case in city life, contacts are extended, heterogeneous groups mingle, neighborhoods disappear, and people, deprived of local and family ties, are forced to live under the loose, transient, and impersonal relations that are characteristic of cities. It would be false to suggest that through the extension of social contact under modern conditions of life we are invariably and indefinitely extending the range and depth of culture conflicts. On the contrary, we often find evidence of harmonious blending and fusion of diverse cultural heritages, in the course of which new cultural constructs emerge which are accepted as natural by successive generations, and which organize and give meaning to the conduct of the individual. But it is nevertheless always important to be alert to situations in which culture appears in a state of flux and to understand the processes of change and transition.

Our conduct, whatever it may consist of, or however it might be judged by the world at large, appears genuinely moral to us when we can get the people whom we regard as significant in our social world to accept and approve it. One of the most convincing bits of evidence for the importance of the role played by culture conflict in the cases that have come to my attention, is the frequence with which delinquents, far from exhibiting a sense of guilt, made the charge of hypocrisy toward official representatives of the social order such as teachers, judges, newspapers, and social workers with whom they came in contact. Whether this charge is correct is not as important as the fact that the delinquent believes that these guardians of the social order must be aware of the conflict which he feels. Miss Van Waters remarks pertinently:

> When young people violate sacred family traditions and smile complacently, with no loss of self-esteem, it is *not* because they have become

anti-social; it indicates probably that they dwell in some other island of social culture which smiles upon their activities, and which is endorsed by some powerful group of adults. Almost all delinquencies of youth are expressed social standards of a part of the adult community which is under no indictment, and which flourishes without condemnation.[5]

We may be able to determine statistically that certain regions in the city have more delinquency than others, but we will not be able to interpret the localization of crime adequately until we see that in each area we may be dealing with a different community and that in each community we may find a different set of conflicting strains of cultural influences and mutually antagonistic groups. For these reasons the high delinquency rates in each part of a given conglomerate cultural zone may be widely different. There may even be communities in which delinquency is part of the cultural tradition. Not only does each community have a culture differing from that of every other community, but each gang and each family has a culture of its own which is in competition with other cultures for the allegiance of the individuals. It is important, therefore, to determine whether in our studies of delinquency in the aggregate we are dealing with natural areas or with cultural areas. And within each cultural area it is important to know to which cultural groups within the area or outside of it, the delinquent expresses his primary loyalty.

When a community, a family or a gang acquires traditions of delinquency they serve as codes for the individual just as religious or political traditions exert a controlling influence. A person's loyalty to his gang may account for his misbehavior in his family and his delinquency in the community. The backing of a gang makes it easier for the individual to meet culture conflict situations with a delinquent form of behavior, for the gang is essentially a conflict group and tends to sanction a delinquent mode of conduct as contrasted with the standards of the society represented by the law and the police. If we fail to see that a gang has a moral code of its own—however immoral it may appear to the rest of us—we will not be able to understand the solidarity, the

[5]   Miriam Van Waters: *Youth in Conflict*, p. 128.

courage and the self-sacrifice of which gangsters are capable. We will not understand then why the criminal with the longest criminal record is often in a position of leadership, why certain crimes are regarded with greater resentment by criminals than by noncriminals, nor why gang justice inflicts the heaviest penalties upon those who commit the greatest of all underworld crimes, namely betraying a member to the police.

This point of view may help also to understand more adequately the phenomenon of recidivism. Recidivism is not merely a matter of acquiring proficiency in a given type of offense, but may be regarded as a series of successively similar situations and as a symptom of a deepening culture conflict which takes on more definite form as the offense is repeated. The commission of the same offense on the part of the individual is not merely made possible by the continued presence of similar opportunities, it is not merely a matter of facility and convenience on his part, but it may also be symptomatic of the emergence of a characteristic set of attitudes toward the social norms and of persistent pressure from a social group such as a gang. As Burgess, in his study of parole violations, has shown, the number of violations has tended to increase with the number involved in the crime; regularly the lowest rate was found where a man had no associates in crime, to the highest rate where he had five or more associates.

The first prerequisite for the cultural approach to delinquency is, obviously, at least as thorough a knowledge of contemporary cultures, as we have of the cultures of primitive peoples. We should be able to have a more thorough understanding of Polish delinquents because of Thomas' *Polish Peasant,* just as we seem to have a more thorough understanding of all immigrants because of the Carnegie Americanization Studies. But we are far from even an elementary knowledge of the differences in emphasis of social values of the many cultural groups that make up our social life. The sociologist has developed a technique of community analysis as shown in recent studies which ought to furnish the background for the research into delinquency. The beginnings of similar analyses of family groups, of play-, school- and gang-groups have been made. We can no more dispense with such studies in a scientific study of crime than the farmer can carry on scientific agriculture without a thorough knowledge of the soils and the other media in which plants grow.

The sociological study of delinquency, however, does not end with a general description nor even a careful analysis of the cultural milieu of the individual. On the contrary, the study of the culture on the objective side must be complemented through a study of the personal meanings, which the cultural values have for the individual. The concept of culture and the concept of personality do not stand in opposition to one another. A culture has no psychological significance until it is referred to a personality, and vice versa, a personality is unthinkable without a cultural milieu. The sociologist, moreover, is not primarily interested in personality, but in culture. But culture is not some sort of substance that passes from one generation to the next, or from one individual to another, by means of a biological mechanism, or a simple process of transference. The culture of the group, that is to say the customs, are based on the habits of the individuals, grow out of changes in the habits of individuals and are broken down by the coming together of individuals with different habits. Ordinarily customs are passed from adults to children and in the process emotional elements appear, especially when contradictory impulses are involved. If the human personality is conceived of, as the sociologists propose, in terms of status or position in society, then it is evident that all of us being members of a number of social groups, each with a culture of its own, we are called upon to play a number of sometimes grossly conflicting roles. Upon the mutual compatibility of these cultures and consequently of these rôles will depend in large measure the efficiency of our adjustments and the integration or disorganization of our personality. The study of the constitutional factors which may condition a person's capacity or tendency to react to these situations in one way or another cannot, of course, be left out of account; but it must be admitted that what the sociologist is particularly fitted to discover in a given case is not to which biological or psychological type the individual belongs, but the social type he represents.

If the conduct of the individual, as has just been suggested, is

seen as a constellation of a number of rôles either integrated or
mutually conflicting, each of which is oriented with reference to a
social group in which he has some sort of place, we can appreciate
the significance of understanding these cultures for the control of
the conduct of the individual. But the important features of each
cultural situation are not immediately evident to the observer and
do not constitute objectively determinable data. They must be
seen in terms of the subjective experiences and attitudes of the
individual, which, as our experience shows, can best be determined by means of autobiographical expressions and by naïve
utterances, especially those which reveal what he assumes to be
obvious and generally taken for granted.

A culture conflict cannot be objectively demonstrated by a
comparison between two cultural codes. It can be said to be a factor in delinquency only, if the individual feels it, or acts as if it
were present. This cannot usually, as I have found, be determined
on the basis of interviews with him alone, nor on the basis, merely, of his subjective reactions as contained in autobiographical
materials. Not until we collect and analyze the opinions and attitudes of different members of the same family or gang to which
the individual belongs, do we see the culture conflict clearly revealed. Our attitudes represent for the most part the reflected
judgments and conceptions of others, who do not necessarily live
in the same culture in which we live, and who do not, therefore,
have the same perspective and values that we have. These differences in attitudes and values are often the measure of the distance
that separates us from others. In the immigrant family nothing is
more startling than the gulf that separates the older generation
from the younger. One of the most characteristic expressions of
the awareness of this conflict, as I have found it in children, is the
conviction that they belong to an outcast group. This gnawing
feeling of inferiority deprives the individual of the group sanction
which is necessary to preserve personal morale. Such a culture
conflict frequently eventuates in what Menninger has called the
"isolation type of personality." He says:

Seclusiveness, self-consciousness and other symptoms ordinarily regarded as typical of the "schizoid" personality may characterize a per-

sonality rendered incapable, rather than undesirous of social contacts, by childhood influences. That is to say that there may indeed be an inherited "constitutional" type of unsocial personality, but in addition an acquired type. This latter type is produced by artificial denial of the proper opportunities for social contacts, by such barriers as geographic isolation, religious and economic differences in the neighborhood, pathological parents, real physical defects and blemishes, and imagined physical or psychic inferiority.[6]

On the other hand, the same feeling of inferiority may express itself in compensatory behavior in the form of a flagrant violation of the social code.

We have already cautioned against the notion that all delinquency is caused by, or involves culture conflict. It is equally important to point out that not every case of culture conflict inevitably leads to delinquency. It is not the culture conflict that makes the individual delinquent, but his inability to deal with it in a socially approved way. There are many avenues open to a person in such a situation.

"It appears," as Professor Thomas has said, "that in a given critical situation one person may readjust on a higher level of efficiency, another may commit a crime and another go to a hospital for the insane"[7]

Delinquency represents merely one way in which the conflict may be expressed if not resolved. Other avenues, given a certain type and situation, may lie in the direction of rumination, phantasy, brooding, and suicide. A third form which this heightened self-consciousness might take is the effort on the part of the individual to secure the acceptance of his cultural values—no matter how delusional they may be—by others. Such a person, far from becoming a criminal, may develop into a prophet, a reformer or a political leader.

In general, culture conflict, as I have encountered it in my cases, may eventuate in delinquency under the following types of situations:

6   Karl A. Menninger, "The Isolation Type of Personality," *Abstract of Proceedings of 7th Meeting of the Orthopsychiatric Association.*

7   W. I. Thomas, *Colloquium on Personality,* p. 8.

1. Where the culture of a group, to which the individual belongs, sanctions conduct, which violates the mores or the laws of another group, to whose code he is also subject.

2. Where the individual belongs to a group in which certain forms of conduct have a different meaning and where there is a difference of emphasis in values from that in the dominant society.

3. Where the individual belongs to a group, whose very basis of organization is conflict with the larger society, from which the individual feels himself to be an outcast. This is obviously true in criminal gangs.

4. Where we have societies in which formal law is at variance with tradition, such as, for instance, where the use of alcohol is sanctioned by tradition but forbidden by law.

5. Where social life is very mobile and where culture is in a state of flux, such as in those areas of cities where there is no organized family or community life and where the social framework, which ordinarily supports the individual in his conduct, disintegrates or fails to function.

6. Where the individual belongs to a group which is itself the product of the incomplete blending of different cultural strains, such as a family in which father and mother belong to different racial or religious groups.

7. Where an individual belongs to a group in which he finds himself dissatisfied and stigmatized, but from which he cannot readily escape into the group that he considers superior.

From the standpoint of social therapy a number of tentative suggestions may be set forth:

Obviously, as in mental conflict, one of the first therapeutic tasks is to bring the person into a frame of mind where he can reflect upon the conflict and see it in the perspective of his total experience. In this connection it is important to observe that culture conflicts are real, even if they are only imagined, or exist merely in the phantasy of the child. The significance, from our standpoint, of childhood and adolescent experiences in the family and in other intimate groups is the disposition to acquire a sense of loyalty to the values and the code which this social world imposes upon the developing personality, and which we are naïvely inclined to accept as natural. Subsequent social contacts will perhaps never be completely assimilated to this original heritage.

But in the social treatment of individuals who have encountered difficulties in this process the reconciliation of these different contradictory elements is an important educational problem which requires a thorough appreciation of their personal meaning. Rationalization and sublimation may sometimes prove effective in overcoming conflicts. One method of therapy, which certain European psychotherapists are employing with delinquents in proletarian groups, is to "bring them out of their individualistic private circle and make them class conscious, and thus furnish their everyday life with new social significance." (Karl Lenzberg, Düsseldorf, in a paper at the International Congress of Individualpsychologie, Berlin, 1930.) We have learned that even mentally defective children can be placed into a social milieu which does not demand more in the way of adjustment than they are capable of. And we know also that children who are dishonest in one schoolroom may be honest in the next, that those who cheat in one game often do not cheat in another. In most instances it is not the fear of punishment that makes them honest, but the identification with a cultural ideal or the emulation of a person, such as a teacher, who symbolizes that ideal. Even honesty is not a virtue in all situations.

Besides the therapeutic effort with the individual, the most significant effort toward readjustment of culture conflict difficulties is to reconstruct the cultural milieu in such a fashion that the individual will not be called upon to play fundamentally contradictory roles in his daily conduct. This may be achieved, among other methods, by migration, by family, school, and vocational adjustment, and by supervised recreation.

But whatever therapeutic measures we may undertake, a necessary prerequisite for their success is a more intensive effort on the part of social workers to observe, to record, and to understand the symptoms of cultural maladjustments, and for sociologists to carry further their analyses of culture so that they will not merely have a more thorough understanding of the various cultural configurations that occur in our present-day society with their varying emphasis on social values, but also a greater mastery of the techniques by which the personal meanings of these values for the individual may be discovered.

17

THE PROBLEM

OF MINORITY GROUPS

As THE nature of the peace becomes a matter of public
discussion, the minorities question again moves into the center of
world attention. It is becoming clear that unless the problems involved, especially on the continent of Europe, are more adequately solved than they were after the first World War, the prospects
of an enduring peace are slim. The influence which the United
States will exert in the solution of these problems abroad is con-
tingent upon the national conscience and policy toward minorities
at home, for it is unlikely that our leaders in their peace-making
will be able to advocate a more enlightened course for others than
we are able to pursue ourselves.

The minorities question in all parts of the world is coming to
be more and more indivisible as internal disturbances in any one
country become a threat to the peace of all and as the ideals and
ideologies originating in one group are soon shared by others in
remote corners of the earth. In this shrunken and interdependent

Reprinted from *Community Life and Social Policy*, ed. Elizabeth Wirth
Marvick and Albert J. Reiss, Jr. (Chicago: University of Chicago Press,
1956), pp. 237–60, first published in *The Science of Man in the World
Crisis*, ed. Ralph Linton (New York: Columbia University Press, 1945),
pp. 347–72.

world, social movements of all sorts assume a progressively universal character and recruit their supporters and adversaries among peoples near and far, irrespective of national boundaries. The implications of this trend are of special significance to the United States since, aside from its traditional championship of movements of liberation of oppressed peoples, virtually every minority group in the world has its representatives among our population. Our domestic and our foreign policies are thus closely bound up one with the other.

We may define a minority as a group of people who, because of their physical or cultural characteristics, are singled out from the others in the society in which they live for differential and unequal treatment and who therefore regard themselves as objects of collective discrimination. The existence of a minority in a society implies the existence of a corresponding dominant group enjoying higher social status and greater privileges. Minority status carries with it the exclusion from full participation in the life of the society. Though not necessarily an alien group the minority is treated and regards itself as a people apart.

To understand the nature and significance of minorities it is necessary to take account of their objective as well as their subjective position. A minority must be distinguishable from the dominant group by physical or cultural marks. In the absence of such identifying characteristics it blends into the rest of the population in the course of time. Minorities objectively occupy a disadvantageous position in society. As contrasted with the dominant group they are debarred from certain opportunities—economic, social, and political. These deprivations circumscribe the individual's freedom of choice and self-development. The members of minority groups are held in lower esteem and may even be objects of contempt, hatred, ridicule, and violence. They are generally socially isolated and frequently spatially segregated. Their subordinate position becomes manifest in their unequal access to educational opportunities and in their restricted scope of occupational and professional advancement. They are not as free as other members of society to join the voluntary associations that express their interests. They suffer from more than the ordinary amount of social and economic insecurity. Even as concerns public policy they are frequently singled out for special treatment; their property rights may be restricted; they may not enjoy the equal protection of the laws; they may be deprived of the right of suffrage and may be excluded from public office.

Aside from these objective characteristics by which they are distinguished from the dominant group and in large measure as a result of them, minorities tend to develop a set of attitudes, forms of behavior, and other subjective characteristics which tend further to set them apart. One cannot long discriminate against people without generating in them a sense of isolation and of persecution and without giving them a conception of themselves as more different from others than in fact they are. Whether, as a result of this differential treatment, the minority comes to suffer from a sense of its own inferiority or develops a feeling that it is unjustly treated—which may lead to a rebellious attitude—depends in part upon the length of time that its status has existed and in part upon the total social setting in which the differential treatment operates. Where a caste system has existed over many generations and is sanctioned by religious and other sentiments, the attitude of resignation is likely to be dominant over the spirit of rebellion. But in a secular society where class rather than caste pervades the stratification of people, and where the tradition of minority status is of recent origin, minorities, driven by a sense of frustration and unjustified subordination, are likely to refuse to accept their status and their deprivation without some effort to improve their lot.

When the sentiments and attitude of such a disadvantaged group become articulate, when the members become conscious of their deprivations and conceive of themselves as persons having rights, and when they clamor for emancipation and equality, a minority becomes a political force to be reckoned with. To the individual members of such a group the most onerous circumstance under which they have to labor is that they are treated as members of a category, irrespective of their individual merits. Hence it is important to recognize that membership in a minority is involuntary; our own behavior is irrelevant. Many of us are identified with political, social, and intellectual groups which do not enjoy the favor of the dominant group in society, but as long as we are free to join and to leave such groups at will we do not by virtue of our membership in them belong to a minority. Since the racial stock from which we are descended is something over which we have perhaps least control and since racial marks are the most visible and permanent marks with which we are afflicted, racial minorities tend to be the most enduring minorities of all.

It should be noted further that a minority is not necessarily an alien group. Indeed, in many parts of the world it is the native peoples who constitute the minority, whereas the invaders, the conquerors, or the newcomers occupy the status of dominating groups. In the United States the indigenous Indians occupy the position of a minority. In Canada the earlier French settlers are a minority in relation to the more recent English migrants. In almost all colonial countries it is the "foreigners" who are dominant and the indigenous populations who are subordinate.

Nor should it be assumed that the concept is a statistical one. Although the size of the group may have some effect upon its status and upon its relationship to the dominant group, minorities are not to be judged in terms of numbers. The people whom we regard as a minority may actually from a numerical standpoint be a majority. Thus there are many parts of the South where the Negroes are the overwhelming majority of the inhabitants but, nevertheless, are an unmistakable minority in the sense that they are socially, politically, and economically subordinate.

It may even be true that a people may attain the status of a minority though it does not become the object of disesteem, discrimination, and persecution. If it considers itself the object of such inferior treatment, an oppression psychosis may develop. If a group sets itself apart from others by a distinctive culture and perpetuates itself in this isolated condition long enough, the social distances between itself and others may grow so great as to lead to the accumulation of suspicion and non-intercourse which will make it virtually impossible for members of these groups to carry on a truly collective life. Lack of intimate knowledge and of contact with others may in the course of time generate an incapacity for mutual understanding and appreciation which allows mental stereotypes to arise which the individual cannot escape. What matters, then, about minorities is not merely their objective position but the corresponding patterns of behavior they develop and the pictures they carry around in their heads of themselves and of others. While minorities more often than not stand in a relationship of conflict with the dominant group, it is their nonparticipation in the life of the larger society, or in certain aspects thereof, that more particularly marks them as a minority people and perpetuates their status as such.

It is easy enough to catalogue the minority peoples in various parts of the world in accordance with a set of criteria such as race, national origin, language, religion, or other distinctive cultural traits. Thus it is possible to define the areas of the world where one or another racial, ethnic, linguistic, or religious group occupies a subordinate status with reference to some other group. In different parts of the world different groups are consigned to minority status. A given racial, ethnic, linguistic, or religious group may be dominant in one area and be the minority in another. Similar variations are found throughout history. Groups which in one epoch were dominant may in another be reduced to subordinate status. Because of the colonizing enterprises of some of the nation-states of western Europe a large part of the rest of the world has been subordinated to their political rule, their economic control, and the technology and culture which the European settlers managed to superimpose upon the peoples and areas which they brought under their domain. On a world scale, therefore, there is an extraordinarily close association between the white western Europeans as colonizers and conquerors and their status as dominant groups. Correspondingly, there is a close association between the non-white peoples of the world as the conquered and enslaved peoples and their status as minority groups. There are notable exceptions, however, both in time and in space. In an earlier period of European history the yellow peoples of the East overran vast stretches of the European continent and for a time at least reduced the natives to inferior status. There had been similar, though temporary, invasions of Europe from Africa in the course of which Negroid groups became dominant over the white Europeans. Similarly, the enterprise and military prowess of the Japanese has led to the subjugation of vast stretches of the Orient beyond their island empire which contain many areas and great populations of non-Japanese stock, including European whites. On the whole, however, the expansion of European civilization to the ends of the earth has been so irresistible that from a racial viewpoint, virtually the world over, the whites constitute the dominant group and the colored peoples the minorities.

We are less concerned, however, in this analysis, with racial minorities than with ethnic minorities, and hence it will be well to examine in some detail the linguistic, religious, and national minorities within the white group in Europe and in America. The existence of such groups in virtually every European and American country calls attention to the fact that the modern nation-states into which we are accustomed to divide the world and to which we are wont to ascribe a high degree of ethnic homogeneity are far from being as closely knit by intermarriage, inbreeding, social intercourse, and freedom of opportunity for everyone as the stereotypes of national cultures appear to indicate.

In Europe and in America there are today vast differences between the status of different ethnic groups from country to country and from region to region. In prewar Poland under the Czarist regime the Poles were a distinct ethnic minority. When they gained their independence at the end of the first World War, they lost their minority status but reduced their Jewish fellow Poles to the status of a minority. As immigrants to the United States the Poles again became themselves a minority. During the brief period of Nazi domination the Sudeten Germans of Czechoslovakia reveled in their position of dominance over the Czechs among whom they had only recently been a minority. The European immigrants to the United States from such dominantly Catholic countries as Italy and Poland, for instance, find themselves reduced from a dominant to a minority group in the course of their immigration. It is not the specific characteristics, therefore, whether racial or ethnic, that mark a people as a minority but the relationship of their group to some other group in the society in which they live. The same characteristics may at one time and under one set of circumstances serve as marks of dominant status and at another time and under another set of circumstances symbolize identification with a minority.

It is much more important, therefore, to understand the nature and the genesis of the relationship between dominant group and minority group than it is to know the marks by the possession of which people are identified as members of either. Once we know that almost any distinctive characteristics, whether it be the physical marks of race, or language, religion, and culture, can serve as criteria of membership in a minority, we will not be inclined to construct a typology of minorities upon the marks by which they are identified. A fruitful typology must rather be useful in delineating the kinds of relationships between minorities and dominant groups and on the kinds of behavior characteristically associated with these types of relationships.

An adequate typology of minorities must, therefore, take account of the general types of situations in which minorities find themselves and must seek to comprehend the *modus vivendi* that has grown up between the segments of those societies in which minority problems exist. There are a number of axes alongside of which the problems of minorities range themselves. Among these are: (1) the number and size of distinct minorities in the society in question; (2) the degree to which minority status involves friction with the dominant group or exclusion from participation in the common life of the society; (3) the nature of the social arrangement governing the relationship between minority and dominant groups; and (4) the goals toward which the minority and dominant groups are striving in quest of a new and more satisfactory equilibrium. A survey of historical and contemporary minority problems along these lines will probably not cover the whole range of minority problems and to that extent the typology will be partial. At the same time it should be understood that as long as the relations between minority and dominant groups are fluid—and wherever they do not rest upon long-accepted and settled premises—any rigid typology will prove unsatisfactory. Conversely where the minority's relationship to the dominant group is definitely structuralized and embedded in the mores, laws, and institutions, a typological approach may be highly rewarding.

The number of minorities in a country appears to have a significant effect upon minority-dominant group relations. Where there is just one minority, the attitudes of the dominant group are molded by the unique characteristics of that particular minority. This tends to bisect the country into two contending groups. This happens to be the case in Belgium where the Flemings and Walloons stand in relationship of dominant and minority groups, respectively, to each other. The situation is quite different in the United States, where aside from the Negro, the Indian, and the Oriental, who constitute our leading racial minorities, we have many ethnic minorities, consisting of our European immigrant groups and their descendants and such religious minorities as Catholics, Jews, and Mormons, in a predominantly Protestant country. A singular and unique minority must absorb all of the anxieties, frustrations, fears, and antipathies of the dominant group. But if dominant group attitudes are directed toward a number of minorities, some of these may escape relatively easily and often at the expense of the others. There is little doubt but that the Negro in the United States has become the principal shock absorber of the antiminority sentiment of the dominant whites. The Negro in this country has been so clearly our leading minority that in comparison with his status the ethnic minorities have occupied a relatively dominant position. Indeed the attitude of the ethnic minorities toward the Negro differs little from the attitude of the long-established white Protestant settlers. Where there are several distinct minorities in a country the dominant group can allow itself the luxury of treating some of them generously and can at the same time entrench itself and secure its own dominance by playing one minority against another.

Similarly, the extent to which a minority differs from the dominant group conditions the relations between the two. Where the groups differ widely in race and culture and are thus easily distinguishable in appearance and behavior, the lines separating them tend to persist without much overt effort. Where the dominant group is the bearer of an advanced civilization and the subordinate group is without modern technology and is characterized by a folk culture, as is the case in colonial situations, the dominant group can maintain its superior position simply by manipulating the military and administrative machinery. Where, however, the respective groups are of the same racial stock but differ only as regards language, religion, or culture, the tension between them becomes more marked, and the attempts at domination of the minority become more evident. The segregation of minority groups may be relatively complete or only partial, and their debarment from rights and privileges may be negligible or severe. Much depends upon their relative numerical strength and the extent to which they are believed to constitute a threat to the existing order.

The nature of the social relationships existing between the dominants and the minorities comes closer than either of these factors to illuminating the problems that arise. When the relationship between the two groups is that of master and slave, of rulers and ruled, of exploiters and exploited, the conflicts that arise are those characteristic of situations of super- and subordination. They become essentially power relationships involving on the part of the dominant group resort to the sanctions of custom, law, and force, whenever persuasion, prestige, and the manipulation of economic controls do not suffice. Where the minority occupies the position of a caste, the sanctions of religion and custom may be quite adequate, but in secular societies the perpetuation of a group in minority status requires the manipulation of public opinion and of economic and political power, and, if these fail, the resort to violence.

Thoroughgoing differences and incompatibilities between dominant and minority groups on *all* fronts—economic, political, social, and religious—or consistent and complete separation and exclusion of the minority from participation in the life of the larger society have tended toward more stable relationships between dominant and minority groups than similarity and compatibility on merely *some* points and the mere segmental sharing of life on a few frontiers of contact. The granting of some political and civil rights to hitherto submerged groups has inevitably led to the claim for the full rights of citizenship and of equality of opportunity in other respects. Slavery as an institution in the Western world was moribund as soon as the religions of the white man invested the Negro with a soul.

While the above criteria might give us a basis for the classification of minorities, they do not come as close to the actual minority problems that plague the modern world as we can come by analyzing the major goals toward which the ideas, the sentiments, and the actions of minority groups are directed. Viewed in this way minorities may conveniently be typed into: (1) pluralistic; (2) assimilationist; (3) secessionist; and (4) militant.

A pluralistic minority is one which seeks toleration for its differences on the part of the dominant group. Implicit in the quest for toleraton of one's group differences is the conception that variant cultures can flourish peacefully side by side in the same society. Indeed, cultural pluralism has been held out as one of the necessary preconditions of a rich and dynamic civilization under conditions of freedom. It has been said in jest that "tolerance is the suspicion that the other fellow might be right."

Toleration requires that the dominant group shall feel sufficiently secure in its position to allow dissenters a certain leeway. Those in control must be convinced either that the issues at stake are not too vital, or else they must be so thoroughly imbued with the ideal of freedom that they do not wish to deny to others some of the liberties which they themselves enjoy. If there is a great gulf between their own status and that of the minority group, if there is a wide difference between the two groups in race or origin, the toleration of minorities may go as far as virtually to perpetuate several subsocieties within the larger society.

Even in the "sacred" society of medieval Europe dominated by the Church, there were long periods when heretics were tolerated, although at other times they faced the alternatives of conformity or extermination. The history of the Jews in medieval Europe offers ample evidence of the ability of a minority to survive even under minimum conditions of toleration. It should be noted, however, that at times the margin of safety was very narrow and that their ultimate survival was facilitated by the fact that they formed an alien cultural island within the larger Christian world and performed useful functions such as trade and commerce in which the creed of the dominant group would not allow its own members to engage. The coexistence of the Jews and Christians in the same countries often did not transcend the degree of mutuality characteristic of the symbiotic relations existing between different species of plants and animals occupying the same habitat but which are forced by their differential structure to live off one another. It involved a minimum of consensus.

The range of toleration which a pluralistic minority seeks may at first be quite narrow. As in the case of the Jews in medieval Europe or the Protestants in dominantly Catholic countries, it may be confined to freedom to practice a dissenting religion. Or, as in the case of the ethnic minorities of Czarist Russia and the Austro-Hungarian empire of the Hapsburgs, it may take the form of the demand for the recognition of a language as the official medium of expression for the minority and the right to have it taught in their schools. While, on the one hand, the pluralistic minority craves the toleration of one or more of its cultural idiosyncrasies, on the other hand, it resents and seeks protection against coerced absorption by the dominant group. Above all it wishes to maintain its cultural identity.

The nationalities of Europe, which in the nineteenth and early twentieth centuries embarked upon a course of achieving national independence, began their careers as pluralistic minorities bent merely upon attaining cultural autonomy. Some of these minorities wished to recover and preserve their cultural heritage. This was the case in Poland, for instance, which sought to recover from Czarist Russia a measure of religious and linguistic autonomy. Czech and Irish nationalism was initiated under similar historic circumstances.

It would be an error, however, to infer that the claims for cultural autonomy are generally pursued independently of other interests. Coupled with the demand, and often precedent to it, there proceeds the struggle for economic and political equality or at last equalization of opportunity. Although the pluralistic minority does not wish to merge its total life with the larger society, it does demand for its members a greater measure of economic and political freedom if not outright civic equality. Ever since the revolutionary epoch of the late eighteenth century the economic and political enfranchisement of minorities has been regarded not merely as inherent in the "rights of man" but as the necessary instrument in the struggle for cultural emancipation. Freedom of choice in occupations, rights of land-ownership, entry into the civil service, access to the universities and the professions, freedom of speech, assembly, and publication, access to the ballot with a view to representation of minority voices in parliament and government—these and other full privileges of citizenship are the foundation upon which cultural freedom rests and the instruments through which it must be achieved and secured.

Throughout the period of awakening of dominant ethnic minorities in Europe in the nineteenth century and subsequently in all parts of the world the first stages of minority movements have been characterized by cultural renaissances. The primary emphasis in this stage of development has been upon accentuating the religious, linguistic, and cultural heritage of the group and driving to obtain recognition and toleration for these differences. This movement goes hand in hand with the clamor for economic and political equality. In the course of such movements what at first are marks of inferiority—a homely folk tongue, an alien religion, an obscure lore, and eccentric costume—are transformed into objects of pride and positive group values in which the intellectuals among the minority take an especially avid interest and the promotion of which becomes the road to their leadership and power. The aim of the pluralistic minority is achieved when it has succeeded in wresting from the dominant group the fullest measure of equality in all things economic and political and the right to be left alone in all things cultural. The atmosphere of liberalism in which pluralistic minorities developed has emerged since the Renaissance and has found expression in the movements for religious toleration at the end of the sixteenth century; it was further elaborated by the constitutional bills of rights wrested from absolute rulers in the course of the English, American, and French revolutions, and found formal acceptance on a world scale in the minorities clauses of the treaties at the conclusion of the First World War. If the legal provisions of the minorities clauses have not been fully observed in practice, they have at least furnished a standard by which the relations between minorities and dominant groups may be more universally appraised by enlightened world opinion. If formal resolutions on such matters are valid as signs of the trend of opinion, the Catholic, Jewish and Protestant Declaration on World Peace, of October 7, 1943, may be adduced. On the Rights of Minorities this declaration says: "National governments and international organizations must respect and guarantee the rights of ethnic, religious and cultural minorities to economic livelihood, to equal opportunity for educational and cultural development, and to political equality." More important than such utterances, however, is the most advanced practice to be found among the nations of the world. Of these the practice of the Soviet Union with its minority peoples appears to be the outstanding example. There the recognition of pluralistic minorities has become the accepted national policy.

It should be recognized, however, that pluralistic minorities, like all structures expressive of dynamic social movements, are merely way stations on the road to further developments. They move on inexorably to other stages where correspondingly new types of social structures emerge. Unlike the pluralistic minority, which is content with toleration and the upper limit of whose aspiration is cultural autonomy, the assimilationist minority craves the fullest opportunity for participation in the life of the larger society with a view to uncoerced incorporation in that society. It seeks to lose itself in the larger whole by opening up to its members the greatest possibilities for their individual self-development. Rather than toleration and autonomy, which is the goal of the pluralistic minority, the assimilationist minority works toward complete acceptance by the dominant group and a merger with the larger society.

Whereas a pluralistic minority, in order to maintain its group integrity, will generally discourage intermarriage and intimate social intercourse with the dominant group, the assimilationist minority puts no such obstacles in the path of its members but looks upon the crossing of stocks as well as the blending of cultures as wholesome end products. Since assimilation is a two-way process, however, in which there is give and take, the mergence of an assimilationist minority rests upon a willingness of the dominant group to absorb and of the minority group to be absorbed. The ethnic differences that exist between the minority and the dominant groups are not necessarily an obstacle to assimilation as long as the cultural traits of each group are not regarded as incompatible with those of the other and as long as their blending is desired by both. The "melting pot" philosophy in the United States which applied to the ethnic minorities but excluded the racial minorities, notably the Negro, in so far as it was actually followed tended to develop both among immigrants and natives an atmosphere conducive to the emergence of a crescive American culture to which both the dominant and minority groups contributed their share. This new culture, which is still in the process of formation, comprises cultural elements derived from all the ethnic groups constituting the American people but integrates them into a new blend.

The success with which such an experiment proceeds depends in part upon the relative numbers involved and the period of time over which the process extends. Although since the beginning of the nineteenth century the United States absorbed some 38 million immigrants from abroad, the influx was relatively gradual and the vast spaces and resources of the continent facilitated the settlement and absorption of the newcomers. America was a relatively young country, dominated by the spirit of the frontier and by a set of laws and social ideals strongly influenced by the humanistic, liberalistic doctrines of religious toleration and the rights of man. This, together with the great need for labor to exploit the vast resources of the continent, contributed to keeping American culture fluid and its people hospitable to the newcomers and the heritages they brought with them. No one group in the United States had so much power and pride of ancestry as to be able to assert itself as superior to all others.

Nevertheless, as the immigrants came in great waves and as the wide margin of economic opportunity shrank periodically, outbursts of intolerant and sometimes violent nativism and anti-alien feeling became manifest here too. As newer immigrant groups followed older waves, the latest comers increasingly became the objects of prejudice and discrimination on the part of natives and older immigrants alike. Moreover, as the various ethnic groups concentrated in specific areas and in large urban colonies and thus conspicuously unfolded their Old World cultural heritages, their life became virtually autonomous and hence, by isolation, their contact with the broad stream of American culture was retarded. In addition, their very success in competing with native and older settlers in occupations, professions, and business provoked antipathies which found expression in intolerance movements and in the imposition of official and unofficial restrictions and handicaps.

Although the ethnic minorities in the United States suffer mainly from private prejudices rather than restrictive public policies, their path of assimilation is not without its serious obstacles. The distinctive cultures of the various ethnic groups are not merely assemblages of separable traits but historically welded wholes. Each immigrant group not only has its own language or dialect which serves as a barrier to intergroup communication and to the sharing of common ideas and ideals, but also its own religious, social, and even political institutions which tend to perpetuate group solidarity and to inhibit social intercourse with members of the "out" group. Moreover, each ethnic group in the United States, especially in the early period after its arrival, tends to occupy a characteristic niche in the economy which generates certain definite similarities among its members in occupation, standard of living, place of residence, and mode of life. On the basis of such likenesses within the group and differences without, stereotypes are built up and fixed attitudes arise which inhibit contact and develop social distances and prejudices. Overanxiety about being accepted sometimes results in a pattern of conduct among minorities that provokes a defense reaction on the part of the dominant group; these defense reactions may take the form of rebuffs which are likely to accentuate minority consciousness and thus retard assimilation.

No ethnic group is ever unanimous in all of its attitudes and actions, and minority groups are no exception. They, too, have their internal differentiations, their factions and ideological currents and movements. It should be understood, therefore, that the difference between a pluralistic and an assimilationist minority must be sought in the characteristic orientation and directing social movement of these groups. The Jews furnish an excellent illustration of a minority which especially in modern times has vacillated between these two types. When the "out" group was favorably disposed toward the Jews, assimilation proceeded apace, even in the face of occasional rebuffs and persistent discrimination. When the dominant group made entry of the Jews difficult, when intolerance movements became powerful and widespread, and when persecution came to be the order of the day, the Jews as a minority group generally withdrew into themselves and by virtue of being excluded became clannish. The most conspicuous example of this transformation is to be found in the shift in the attitude of the German Jews who—before the anti-Semitic wave climaxed by the Hitler epic—could have been correctly characterized as an assimilationist minority and whose optimum longing upon the advent of Hitler was for even a modicum of toleration. Among Jews in this country a similar differentiation is contemporaneously found. The older settlers and those who have climbed the economic and social scale seek on the whole full incorporation into the larger society and may truly be regarded as an assimilationist minority; but the later comers and those whose hopes have been frustrated by prejudice, those who through generations of persecution in the Old World retain a more orthodox ritual and a more isolated and self-sufficient community life, generally do not seek full cultural identification with American society at large. To be sure they aspire to full social and economic equality with the rest of the population, but they seek to retain a degree of cultural autonomy.

There is little doubt that the world-wide crisis of the Jewish people, precipitated by fascism and its accompanying wave of racism and anti-Semitism, has forged a new bond of solidarity among hitherto disparate sections of Jewry and has given impetus to a deep pessimism concerning the prospects of ultimate assimilation. But the eventual resumption of the assimilationist trend among the Jewish minorities in the Western world appears to have favorable prospects once the cult of racism declines.

The secessionist minority represents a third distinct type. It repudiates assimilation, on the one hand, and is not content with mere toleration or cultural autonomy, on the other. The principal and ultimate objective of such a minority is to achieve political as well as cultural independence from the dominant group. If such a group has had statehood at an earlier period in its career, the demand for recognition of its national sovereignty may be based upon the cultivation among its members of the romantic sentiments associated—even if only in the imagination—with its former freedom, power, and glory. In such a case the minority's cultural monuments and survivals, its language, lore, literature, and ceremonial institutions, no matter how archaic or reminiscent of the epoch of the group's independence, are revivified and built up into moving symbols of national grandeur.

In this task the intellectuals among the minority group play a crucial role. They can find expression for their talents by recovering, disseminating, and inspiring pride in the group's history and civilization and by pleading its case before world public opinion. Having been rejected by the dominant group for higher positions of leadership, and often having been denied equal opportunity and full participation in the intellectual, social, economic, and political life of the larger society, the intellectuals of such minorities tend to be particularly susceptible to a psychic malady bordering on an oppression psychosis. They find their compensation by plunging into the life of the smaller but more hospitable world of their minority.

The Irish, Czech, Polish, Lithuanian, Estonian, Latvian, and Finnish nationalistic movements culminating in the achievement of independent statehood at the end of the First World War were examples of secessionist minority groups. The case of the Jews may also be used to illustrate this type of minority. Zionism in its political, as distinguished from its cultural, variety has acquired considerable support as a result of the resurgence of organized anti-Semitic movements. The forced wholesale migration out of the countries practicing violent persecution and extermination has changed the conception of Palestine from a haven of refuge in which Jews are tolerated to a homeland to which Jews lay official claim.

The protest against the dominant group, however, does not always take the form of separatism and secessionism. It may, under certain circumstances express itself in movements to get out from under the yoke of a dominant group in order to join a group with whom there exists a closer historical and cultural affinity. This is particularly true of minorities located near national frontiers. Wars and the accompanying repeated redefinitions of international boundaries rarely fail to do violence to the traditions and wishes of some of the populations of border territories. It is generally true that these marginal ethnic groups exhibit more fervid nationalistic feelings than those who have not been buffeted about by treaty-makers.

Secessionist minorities occupying border positions, moreover, generally can count upon the country with which they seek reunion for stimulation of minority consciousness. When France lost Alsace and Lorraine at the end of the Franco-Prussian war in 1871, the French culture of these "lost provinces" became the object of special interest on the part of Frenchmen in and out of these territories. And when these same provinces were lost to Germany at the end of the First World War, a similar propaganda wave on the German side was set in motion. When the Nazis came to power and embarked upon their imperialistic adventures, they made the "reunion with the Fatherland" of such territories as the Saar, Alsace, Lorraine, Eupenet-Malmédy, Sudetenland, and the Danzig Corridor an object of frenzied agitation. By every means at their command they revived the flagging or dormant secessionist spirit among these ethnic groups. They created incidents wherever the slightest pretext existed to provoke violent outbreaks so as to elicit from the neighboring governments countermeasures that could be exploited for the purpose of creating a world opinion that the German minorities in these territories were suffering from extreme persecution and were anxiously waiting to be rescued by the armed might of the Fatherland.

The solidarity of modern states is always subject to the danger of the undermining influence of secessionist minorities, but it becomes particularly vulnerable if the minorites are allied with neighboring states which claim them as their own. Out of such situations have arisen many of the tensions which have provoked numerous wars in recent times.

There is a fourth type of minority which may be designated as militant. Its goal reaches far beyond toleration, assimilation, and even cultural and political autonomy. The militant minority has set domination over others as its goal. Far from suffering from feelings of inferiority, it is convinced of its own superiority and inspired by the lust for conquest. While the initial claims of minority movements are generally modest, like all accessions of power, they feed upon their own success and often culminate in delusions of grandeur.

Thus, for instance, the Sudeten Germans, aided and abetted by the Nazi propaganda, diplomatic, and military machine, made claims on the Czechoslovak republic which, if granted, would have reduced the Czechs to a minority in their own country. The story, let us hope it is legendary, of the slave who upon his emancipation immediately proceeded to buy himself a slave, suggests a perverse human tendency which applies to minorities as well. No imperialism is as ruthless as that of a relatively small upstart nation. Scarcely had Italy escaped the humiliation of utter defeat in the First World War when she embarked upon the acquisition of *Italia Irredenta* far beyond her own borders across the Adriatic. In recent times the rise of the relatively obscure Prussian state to a position of dominance in central Europe is illustrative of the dynamics of a militant minority in quest not merely of a secure basis of national existence but of empire. The none too generous treatment accorded by the newly emancipated Poles between the two world wars to the Ukrainian, White Russian, Lithuanian, Jewish, and other minorities allotted to the Polish state offers another case of the lack of moderation characteristic of militant minorities once they arrive at a position of power.

The problem of finding a suitable formula for self-government in India would probably have been solved long ago if the Hindu "majority," which considers itself a minority in relation to British imperial rule, could have been satisfied wth an arrangement which stopped short of Hindu domination over Moslems. Similarly the problem of Palestine could be brought much nearer a sensible solution if certain elements among Jewish and Arab groups were less militant and did not threaten, in case either were given the opportunity, to reduce the other to the status of a minority.

The justification for singling out the four types of minorities described above for special delineation lies in the fact that each of them exhibits a characteristic set of collective goals among historical and contemporary minority groups and a corresponding set of motives activating the conduct of its members. These four types point to significant differences between actual minority movements. They may also be regarded as marking crucial successive stages in the life-cycle of minorities generally.

The initial goal of an emerging minority group as it becomes aware of its ethnic identity is to seek toleration for its cultural differences. By virtue of this striving it constitutes a pluralistic minority. If sufficient toleration and autonomy are attained, the pluralistic minority advances to the assimilationist stage, characterized by the desire for acceptance by and incorporation into the dominant group. Frustration of this desire for full participation is likely to produce (1) secessionist tendencies which may take the form either of the complete separation from the dominant group and the establishment of sovereign nationhood or (2) the drive to become incorporated into another state with which there exists close cultural or historical identification. Progress in either of these directions may in turn lead to the goal of domination over others and the resort to militant methods of achieving that objective. If this goal is actually reached, the group sheds the distinctive characteristics of a minority.

It should be emphasized, of course, that this typology of minorities is a theoretical construct rather than a description of actually existing groups. We should not expect to find any one of these types to occur in pure form either in history or in the present. All minorities contain within themselves tendencies and movements in which we can discern the characteristic features of one or more of these types. Using such a typology as a tool we are in a better position to analyze the empirical problems of minority situations and to evaluate the proposed programs for their solution.

The basic fact accounting for the emergence of minorities is the lack of congruence between political and ethnic groups. Political boundaries are definite and almost always arbitrary. Cultural and ethnic areas are more difficult to delineate. Political areas can be gerrymandered, whereas cultural areas are the product of growth. Virtually every contest of power between nations, whether around the diplomatic conference table or on the battlefield, is followed by some redrawing of boundaries, leaving cultural pockets enveloped islandlike by an alien sea. Even in the absence of territorial revisions the indeterminant fringes along the frontiers, where marginal groups are interspersed, tend to be chronic danger spots of ethnic friction.

A second factor causing minority groups to arise lies in the fact that culture and people are seldom coterminous. Every living culture must be carried by some people. But culture consists of many elements which may be carried in varying combinations by diverse groups of people. Thus, for instance, a group of people who speak the same language, have the same religion and have an ancient common cultural heritage, are capable of more effective collective action than a similar group with the same religion but different language or the same language but an otherwise different cultural heritage. It is sufficient for the formation of minorities if merely a few of the ethnic characteristics that give them distinctiveness coincide, especially if these include such elements as language or religion. But if a group should by accident of history and geography find itself united on a great range of cultural characteristics and fairly densely concentrated in a compact area so that the contrast between its status and that of its neighbors stands out sharply, the emergence of that group as a minority is almost inevitable.

The genesis of minorities must therefore be sought in the fact that territory, political authority, people, and culture only rarely coincide. Since the disintegration of tribal society the human stocks occupying virtually every area of the world have become progressively diversified. Through the rise of the modern state the parochial principalities of earlier ages have disintegrated and heterogeneous groupings of people and diverse areas have been consolidated into vast political domains. Through conquest and migration formerly compact groups have become dispersed and split up among different political entities. Through modern transportation, communication, commerce, and technology the surviving folk cultures are being increasingly drawn into the vortex of world civilization. There still remain, in various parts of the world, some relatively limited islands of homogeneity and stability in a sea of conglomerate and swiftly moving heterogeneity, but on the whole the civilizing process is leveling them. Minority problems are symptomatic of this profound world-wide transition.

In the long perspective of centuries, therefore, one might expect minority problems to solve themselves. But for the time being they are in need of the best solution we can invent if we would live in peace and promote human progress. Anyone who dispassionately surveys the background of the First and the Second World Wars cannot fail to see that minority questions have played a considerable part in their genesis. Unless these questions are more adequately solved in the next peace than they were in the last, we shall by that failure contribute to an eventual new world conflagration; for in the future even more than in the past these problems will take on cosmic scope, no matter how local their origin. This is not to assert that minority problems are the major causes of international conflict, but merely that in the absence of effective world organization to regulate the play of interdependent economic, social, political, and military forces these problems will continue to produce frictions and to furnish pretexts that may again lead to war.

In modern times, besides the technological and social changes that have profoundly affected the nature and significance of minority problems, there have been set afoot certain ideological forces which bear even more directly upon them. Of these, nationalism, the democratic ideology as applied to persons and groups, and secularism and science seem the most relevant.

The nineteenth century, which has often been called "the age of nationalism," saw the birth of a series of movements of national awakening, liberation, and consolidation resulting in the formation of modern Italy and Germany. It also saw the rapid development of modern empires and the crystallization of such movements as Pan-Slavism and Pan-Germanism, which became formidable threats to a state system based upon the balance of power. The lesser ethnic groups which were involuntarily enveloped by the nascent nations were frustrated and retarded in realizing their national aspirations. There were thus kindled seething movements of unrest which threatened the stability of the newly established states and the peace of the world. Minorities, especially those of the secessionist and militant variety, are in large part by-products of the ideology of nationalism, whose fundamental tenet it was that every people ought to have its own state but which failed to take full cognizance of the fact that political and ethnic lines do not always neatly coincide.

The forces of democracy and of nationalism were closely allied throughout most of the nineteenth century. The coalescence of these two ideologies became the principal weapon of the nationalities which were aspiring to independence at the peace discussions following the First World War. At Versailles the principle of national self-determination was invoked. It was construed to mean the right of every nation to form an independent state. But the conception of "nation" was far from clear and failed to take account of the many lesser ethnic and cultural groups which were not far enough advanced in the life-cycle of minorities to be considered eligible for nationhood and hence statehood. Versailles heard the articulate voices of the secessionist and militant minorities of the time, but failed to hear the softer whispering and petulant pleading of the pluralistic and assimilationist minorities who were put at he mercy of the former without more protection than the pious enunciation of high principles of toleration and non-discrimination.

Woodrow Wilson, in insisting upon the right of self-determination before America's entrance into the war, said: "Every people has the right to choose the sovereignty under which they shall live."[1] When he came to interpret this principle under the Fourteen Points, however, he associated the concept of self-determination not with the freely expressed will of the people but with the criteria of nationality. In the drafting of the peace settlement, as E. H. Carr puts it, "it was assumed without more ado that nationality and self-determination meant the same thing and that, if a man had the objective distinguishing marks of a Pole or a Southern Slav, he wanted to be a citizen of a Polish or Southern Slav state."[2] The peace settlements had as one of their principal objectives the solution of the minorities questions and no doubt did assuage the legitimate claims of a number of oppressed peoples; at the same time they raised a number of new minority problems which hitherto had been either nonexistent or dormant.

The problems and the very existence of minorities rest upon the recognition of the rights of peoples, notably the right of self-determination. Ever since the revolutionary era of the late eighteenth century the liberation of oppressed people has been a cause which has enlisted the support of liberal thinkers. Though some of its advocates thought of this principle—which was implicit in the democratic ideology—as a step toward cosmopolitanism, its immediate effect was to intensify nationalism. The general principle of the Versailles Treaty in effect proclaimed that any group belonging to a minority, whether ethnic, cultural, or religious, was entitled to equal protection and opportunity with others. This principle was easier to proclaim than to put into practice, especially among some of the newly created states comprising former minorities. Having gained their freedom, these militant minorities not infrequently reduced their fellow-nationals with different ethnic characteristics to a state of barely tolerated minorities, and sometimes even made them objects of violent persecution.

In retrospect one of the great shortcomings in the application of the democratic principle under the treaty of Versailles was the emphasis upon groups rather than individuals. Unless the right of self-determination is applied not merely to nations or ethnic

1   *Public Papers of Woodrow Wilson* (New York, 1927), II, 187.

2   Edward Hallett Carr, *Conditions of Peace* (New York, 1943), p. 44.

groups but also to the individual men and women comprising the nation or ethnic group, it can easily degenerate into license to suppress others. If in the coming peace the arrangement for setting up new states and redefining the territories of old ones does not provide a personal bill of rights for all inhabitants and for the protection of the rights of citizenship by an international authority, one of the most tragic lessons of the last peace will have been lost.

Even such an international guarantee of a universal bill of rights will probably prove insufficient to prevent the development of new minorities and the persistence of existing ones. Ethnic, linguistic, and religious differences will continue to divide people, and the prejudices that go with them cannot suddenly be wiped out by fiat. But whereas personal prejudices and antipathies can probably be expected to yield only to the tedious process of education and assimilation, collective programs and policies can be altered considerably in advance of the time when they have unanimous group consent. Law and public policy can go far toward minimizing the adverse effect even of personal prejudices. Moreover, it is for their public policies that we can and must hold states responsible.

The strategy for equalizing the opportunities of minorities has in the past been based upon the doctrine of the rights of man, which presumably applied to majority and minority alike. Only recently, however, has it been recognized that the subordination of minority ethnic groups and racial groups results in great cost to the whole society. From a military point of view it is undesirable because it weakens national loyalties and solidarity. The stunting of minority development reacts unfavorably upon the entire economy. As long as minorities suffer from discrimination and the denial of civil liberties, the dominant group also is not free.

Another ideological factor that has appeared upon the modern scene and has left its impact upon the minorities problem is secularism. The secular trend in the modern world, which manifests itself in the spread of rationalism, science, and the general skepticism toward ideas and beliefs inherited from the past, has already made substantial inroads on parochial cults, on the divine right of some to rule, and on superstitions concerning the innate inferiority of racial and ethnic groups. It promises even greater progress in the future. Rigid caste systems, supported by sacred sanctions, are fast disintegrating. The separation of church and state has advanced to a point where a state religion is already regarded in most countries as intolerable. Even a "holy war" is almost inconceivable in modern times. With the spread of the ideal of equality of opportunity for all men there has come in most countries of the West a greater access for the masses of men, irrespective of race, ethnic affiliation, religion, or even economic status, to educational and cultural possibilities. The findings and methods of science may consequently find greater acceptance. The symbol of "the common man," despite the ridicule to which it has been subjected in some quarters seems to be on the way to making its influence felt the world over.

From anthropological studies of the last half-century we should have gained a recognition of the inapplicability of the concept "race" as applied to the hybrid stocks comprising the European and American peoples. It is not race but culture—linguistic, religious, economic, and social habits and attitudes, institutions, and values—that marks these peoples off from one another. And if science has demonstrated anything, it has shown conclusively that these traits are subject to human intervention, that they can be changed. The possibility of the ultimate assimilability of ethnic groups is thus beyond doubt.

It is coming to be recognized, moreover, that varying religious beliefs and cultural traits need not be a threat to national solidarity and are not necessarily disruptive of national loyalty. The private life of the individual is considered to an ever greater degree inviolable. What is required of the individual and of minority groups is that there be an adjustment to the social order and not necessarily that there be complete assimilation. Isolation of the minority from the body politic and social, on whatever ground it may be based and by whatever means enforced, is increasingly regarded as the road to the perpetuation and accentuation of previously existing differences and as contrary to civilized public policy.

18

RACE AND PUBLIC POLICY

ACADEMIC MEN are inclined to ascribe an importance to knowledge all out of proportion to its actual role in human conduct. This is particularly true when they talk of race relations. Men do not wait until the latest findings of science are in before they begin to feel, think, or act on matters that concern race; and even when new scientific findings come to hand, it does not follow by any means that people will promptly change their beliefs and actions to conform to them.

Race and Reason

This is not to argue the futility of the search for tenable knowledge about race and race relations, but merely to indicate the limits of its effect upon practice. In the beginning was the act, not the thought. Frequently men cling tenaciously to a belief even in the face of overwhelming evidence of its falsity. They often persist in a type of conduct which is flagrantly contradicted by both the factual premises upon which it supposedly rests and its practical outcome. And yet, if we are pursuing knowledge for any other reasons than its own sake, we must assume that ultimately,

Reprinted from *Community Life and Social Policy*, ed. Elizabeth Wirth Marvick and Albert J. Reiss, Jr. (Chicago: University of Chicago Press, 1956), pp. 334–53, first published in *Scientific Monthly*, LVIII (April, 1944), 302–12.

if not always, knowledge does make a difference. Many illustrious examples from history support this assumption. Although the displacement of superstition and dogma by science even in the fields of technology and medicine, to take but two instances, has by no means been as rapid and as automatic as might be wished, in social affairs, in matters that affect religion, the family, nationalism, and race, scientific findings have made their way into belief and action even more slowly. This appears to be due not merely to the supposed fact that scientific findings in these latter fields are less certain and more personal, but rather to the circumstance that established beliefs and practices in these matters have an almost sacred character and are not subject to secular, objective scrutiny. In matters of race even a Hitler or a Goebbels may pose as an expert and be accepted as such by millions, whereas probably no one would accept them as experts in medicine or engineering. We must assume, nevertheless, that the search for truth by the methods of science is at least as important in the realm of the social as it is in the realm of the physical and biological and that ultimately here, too, the truth shall make men free.

The Nature of Race Prejudice

What we know and what we do not know about race would be merely a prosaic academic matter if it were not in the minds and actions of men associated with some of the most acute practical problems of human relations in our day. These problems range from personal idiosyncrasies and antipathies to violent mass conflict and the clash of national and international policies. It is the latter type of problem that constitutes the subject of this paper. But before treating the subject of race and public policy, a word needs to be said about race relations as personal relations.

All of us have our likes and dislikes, our preferences and antipathies. We prefer certain foods over others; we have our personal tastes in clothing and furniture; we ride hobbies and have our blind spots in art and in recreation; we have our passionate affections and our equally deep-seated revulsions toward other persons. All of these, however, are matters of little if any public concern. We regard them as private affairs.

Our tastes, our preferences, and our antipathies, however, are not altogether of our own making and the result of our own personal experiences. For the most part our personal pattern of race relations is made for us by the culture in which we live, just as our behavior patterns in other respects bear the imprint of the group to which we belong. We have preconceived attitudes toward objects and persons that we have never met. These attitudes tend to be more verbal than actual. It is difficult for us to work up very much enthusiasm for, or antagonism against, people whom we have never seen, although we may have stereotyped notions about how we are to react to the symbols representing these unfamiliar persons. In a race-relations survey made some years ago on the Pacific Coast, a considerable proportion of native-white Americans who were questioned exhibited a markedly distant and unfriendly attitude toward Turks, although probably few, if any, of those who held this attitude would recognize a Turk if they met one. Strange as it may seem, the genesis of this attitude may be in part the inadvertent by-product of the Sunday-school experience which many American youths underwent when they dropped their pennies in the collection box to save the persecuted Armenians from the "Terrible Turk."

Prejudices are judgments that we pass on objects or persons before we have had any experience which would give us reasonable grounds for feeling or acting as we do. These "pre-judgments" are the result of our predisposition to lump objects or persons together into classes or categories irrespective of their individual differences or merits. When we treat one person cordially and as an equal, and another in a hostile fashion or as an inferior because the former belongs to our race and the latter to a different race, we are exhibiting a racial prejudice. Whenever we hear people say, "I don't like Americans, Englishmen, Russians, Negroes, Jews, Catholics because they do so and so," we may be sure that what follows the "because" is an attempt to justify on rational grounds an attitude which rests upon emotional bias. No people as large as any of the groups mentioned above are so much alike that the same judgment could conceivably apply to all of them. Our pre-judgments of other people, especially of racial and ethnic groups, are not rationally examined in the light of our own experiences with a substantial number of members of such groups. They are for the most part imbibed by us from the popular beliefs held in our own group, sometimes transmitted unconsciously by our elders and our neighbors through example, sometimes the product of education and not infrequently of deliberate propaganda. The fact that there is no rational or experiential justification for these beliefs, however, does not make them any the less potent.

To most white people all Negroes look alike. Most Americans, even now, find it difficult to tell the difference between Japanese and Chinese, between Koreans, Filipinos, and Puerto Ricans. Only when we get to know certain members of these groups intimately do we begin to distinguish between individuals and to note that there is as much difference between different persons in each of these groups as there is between persons in our own group. Just as we ascribe identical physical traits to them, so we are inclined to ascribe identical mental, social, and moral traits to people whom we know only by their racial labels. Thus, for instance, we attribute a racial odor to Negroes because we have met one or a few individuals whose smell offended us. We forget that perhaps white individuals working in the same occupations or living under comparable conditions might have an equally offensive odor. We meet a member of another racial or ethnic group who cheats us in a business transaction and we immediately ascribe his dishonesty in business to his race, forgetting that if someone of our own group cheated us, we would blame only the individual and have no thought of race. We see someone who is aggressive and, if he belongs to another racial or ethnic group, we blame his race for it. It is a curious fact that we are less inclined when we see something we like in a person of another race to give his race credit for the asset, which, of course, is only an individual merit. Thus once a prejudice toward a racial or ethnic group gets started, it tends to be cumulatively confirmed by subsequent experience and to blind us against all experiences that might prove the opposite.

The Genesis of Race Prejudice

Racial prejudice is associated with the disposition on the part of virtually every human group to think of itself as superior to outsiders. The notion of chosen people is quite widespread. We know of primitive communities the members of which call themselves "men" or "human beings" to distinguish themselves from all outsiders, who are regarded as not quite human. We generally glorify the people whom we speak of as "we," whereas the "others" or outsiders are depreciated and suspected. Although strangers do sometimes have a romantic fascination for us, more often than not we fear them and remain at a respectful distance from them, ready to believe almost anything about them to which we would not for a moment give credence if it concerned a member of our own group. Particularly where these strangers are distinguishable from our own group by such visible marks as color, the tendency to retain them in a category apart is persistent.

Racial prejudices may have their foundation in our own insecurity, be it economic or social. We are reluctant to enter into competition or rivalry with members of groups distinguishable from us by marked physical or cultural characteristics. And when we do compete with them, we are likely to attribute our own failures and shortcomings to some unfair advantage which the others are taking of us, or to our reluctance to put forth our best efforts against unequals. It has been repeatedly found by students of Negro-white relations in the South that the so-called white aristocracy shows less racial prejudice than do the "poor whites," whose own position is relatively insecure and who must compete with Negroes for jobs, for property, for social position, and for power. Only those who themselves are insecure feel impelled to press their claims for superiority over others. This is confirmed by the fact that racial prejudices and conflicts flare up most violently in periods of economic distress when there are not enough jobs to go around. Similarly, when an ample supply of housing is available, people will generally settle in areas where life for them is most congenial and where they can afford to live. But when housing facilities are limited, the Negro may find it difficult to obtain living space, especially when it involves displacing whites.

It takes an exceptionally objective person to accept responsibility for his own failures and frustrations. It is much more convenient to put the blame on another and to invent a scapegoat, especially if that scapegoat has already been groomed for the role by history and circumstance. In the southern part of the United States it might be the Negro; in the Southwest it might be the Mexican or the Indian; on the Pacific Coast, the Oriental; in the great cities, the immigrant or the Jew. We choose as whipping boys those who are easily accessible, easily identifiable, relatively defenseless, and who give us a plausible provocation by actual or imagined competition.

Once a prejudice has become established it tends to perpetuate itself. It becomes part of the atmosphere to which we are exposed from infancy on, not only by what we are officially taught, by what we read, and by what we hear in conversation, but also by subtle gestures and jokes. The desire to conform to what the "best people" do, believe, and say is strong in all of us, and if they happen to hold these prejudices, we tend, though quite unconsciously, to emulate them. Furthermore, these prejudices hold us at a distance from the victims of the prejudices. We never give ourselves a chance to meet on intimate terms those against whom we are prejudiced. If by circumstances we are thrown in contact with them and find no confirmation of our prejudices, we tend to regard these individuals as exceptional cases and still go on believing that others of that race fully deserve the treatment they get. On the other hand, when we meet a member of a race against whom we do not hold prejudices and find him obnoxious, we either never identify him with the group to which he belongs or treat him merely as an obnoxious and unfortunate individual. The groups against whom we hold prejudices, therefore, start out with an initial handicap in their relations with us which they are rarely given the opportunity to overcome. The burden of proof that they are not obnoxious and inferior is upon them.

Being thus regarded as inferior and being excluded from free association and from equal opportunities, the members of a racial group who suffer from prejudice may come not only to feel inferior but also through unequal opportunities and rewards, actually to be inferior. Correspondingly, the holders of the prejudice may become confirmed in their smug feeling of superiority by being able to point to the evidences of their own superior achievement.

There is no evidence to show that race prejudice is any more inherent in human beings than tastes, preferences, and aversions in other matters. Race prejudice is not an instinct nor an innate tendency, but an attitude which has to be acquired, a mode of behavior which has to be learned. Newborn infants do not have it. Young children are generally free from it, and such experimental evidence as we have leads us to believe that it can be both taught and untaught. The mere fact that in different parts of the world, among different peoples, in different epochs of history, and under differing circumstances these prejudices differ widely should lead us to see how modifiable they are.

Factors Affecting the Decline of Race Prejudice

It is relevant to ask, therefore, what can be done about these prejudices. The problem is not solved by the obvious and oft-given advice that we should get to know members of the other race more intimately. Unfortunately, to know all is not always to forgive all. The more intimate we become with one another, the more, to be sure, we shall understand one another, but it does not follow that the more intimate we become, the more affectionate we become. Intimate knowledge of others may lead us to like them more, but also to dislike them more than we did before.

Students of race relations have noticed that prejudice tends to decline when the group that is the victim of the prejudice is no longer in direct competition with the group that holds the prejudice. The greater the security of a group, the less provocation it has to generate and maintain prejudices against other groups. Some improvement in race relations, therefore, might be expected by minimizing or eliminating the causes of economic and social insecurity among all men.

It has also been found that it becomes more difficult to maintain race prejudice when the members of the group against whom the prejudice is directed are no longer easily identifiable, when the marks—whether physical or social—by means of which we classify and label them fade out. Since the Negro is so distinctly marked by physical traits, the prospect that prejudice toward him will disappear is less than the prospect of the decline of prejudice toward racial and ethnic groups less visibly different from ourselves. But even among Negroes it should be noted that many thousands of mixed bloods are annually incorporated into the white group or at least pass among the white group unrecognized as Negroes. The more anonymous our society becomes, the more likely it is that individuals can pass from one side of the color line to the other unnoticed.

Similarly, race prejudice tends to decline when enough exceptions are made. If we have the opportunity to meet a sufficient number of exceptional members of the group against whom a prejudice exists, then the rule to which they are the exception is undermined. Self-respecting individuals of a minority group will, of course, be reluctant to accept special treatment. They will not be flattered when someone says, "All Negroes are so and so, but you are an exception," or "I meant no harm, because some of my best friends are Jews." But if the person who holds the initial prejudice meets only persons of the minority groups who are exceptional and none who conform to his stereotype, the stereotype may finally give way. Just as we have attitudes toward Negroes, however, long before we have met a Negro, so we must not expect these attitudes suddenly to vanish once we have the evidence which contradicts them. As our experience which contradicts our stereotypes grows, there is at least the likelihood that our attitudes will eventually be modified. Education, therefore, as it enriches our experience can become a factor destructive to prejudice.

We have had it reaffirmed recently, if we had not known it already, that race prejudice is likely to decline when the larger group, say the nation, is threatened by an external enemy. When there is an enemy without, the differences within are minimized. Thus in a period of war we realize more clearly than ever before that racial, religious, and other prejudices constitute a danger to our national unity, and it begins to dawn upon us that, however deep-seated our own internal conflicts may have been, they are as nothing compared with the conflicts between us and our enemies.

Consequences of Race Prejudice

Racial, ethnic, and religious prejudices can become seriously divisive forces in society. They are particularly demoralizing in a democracy, where men profess to believe in equality of opportunity. They make our ideals seem impracticable and impossible of realization. They destroy our belief in our own integrity and our ideals. They tend to make us esteem our fellow-men, not on the basis of their individual merit or contributions to society, but on the basis of some fact or alleged fact over which they have no control whatsoever.

Particularly when we are engaged in a struggle against anti-democratic forces do these prejudices become inimical to the national interest. If the dignity and autonomy of the human personality which we profess to respect means anything, it means that we confer status upon an individual, not by virtue of the group into which he was born, but on the basis of his performance. We regard this as one of the principal differences between a caste order—which we began to outlive when we abolished slavery—and a free society. Whereas in a caste order individuals and families occupy a fixed status from which they cannot escape and which they cannot and do not wish to alter, in a society like ours there is, theoretically at least, a possibility of relatively free movement up and down the social scale and there is the ever present incentive to take advantage of this possibility.

By maintaining racial prejudices we make it possible for our enemies to say "You, too, regardless of your professions to the contrary, practice racial discrimination." What is more, the existence of these prejudices is a factor in undermining the loyalty of the group that is the victim of them. They prevent the nation from gaining the benefit of the maximum contribution and full participation of all of its members in the common cause. Just as they cripple the victim, so these prejudices also warp the holders. They make them blind to what they do not wish to see; they breed arrogance and bigotry; and not infrequently they lead to wanton aggression and unprovoked violence.

Despite the fact that there is no scientific justification for linking the physical characteristics that distinguish the major groups of mankind with intellectual or moral virtues or defects, this linkage constitutes the very heart of race prejudice. Similarly, although there is no justification in science for linking a given language, religion, class, party, or nationality with a given racial group, conflicts that are essentially economic, political, religious, or intellectual come to be regarded as racial. What we do not like about others in our economic, political, religious, and social intercourse, we can under certain circumstances attribute to their race. Race prejudice thus comes to be transferred to groups which may not be racial at all. The prejudices derived from one source can be used to reinforce and substain the prejudices arising from a very different cause.

In the past, racial myths have been invented to account for the rise and fall of empires, to justify and to resist revolutionary movements, to rationalize slavery, war, and imperialistic adventures. Racial prejudices have been used to make discrimination in economic opportunities, in education, in immigration, and in social relations seem just and reasonable. They can be used to weld together peoples who have otherwise little in common, just as they can be used to tear asunder groups which history and a common social heritage have welded into a unity. They have been for a long time and are currently being used by our enemies as a powerful weapon against us.

Private and Public Prejudices

While the race prejudices of individuals appear to be largely matters of private concern, they are by no means purely private, either in origin or in their consequences. To the extent that they are the product of the prevailing social stereotypes, they can be modified as other collective images are subject to alteration by education and propaganda. They can be affected for good or ill by laws, official practices, and public policy. They can perhaps be dealt with more effectively by indirect than by direct attack, for they are deeply imbedded in the structure of our society and hence can be basically altered only as society itself is altered. Such prejudices do not flourish in a wholesome society where all the members enjoy a substantial measure of security, where no group feels itself exploited and dominated by another group, where group conflicts are at a minimum, or, if acute, are equitably resolved in accordance with freely accepted rules of the game. In an orderly, stable, prosperous, and enlightened society these prejudices cannot easily become diffused among substantial sections of the people. What is most important, however, is that in such a society it is virtually impossible to build organized movements upon them.

Race prejudices, like all attitudes, are not only contagious but are cumulatively reinforced by the day-to-day social interaction that goes on in a society. Eventually they crystallize into customs and not infrequently they are written into laws. When race attitudes become organized into social movements and thus acquire the vehicles of organizations, ideologies, symbols, and techniques for their dissemination and sanction, they become significant factors in the shaping of public policy. In this manner private prejudices become matters of utmost public concern.

Evolution of American Racial Policy

The United States has not been free from race movements; at different times and in different parts of the country different groups have been the object of organized race prejudice. From its first settlement to the present this nation has followed a succession of public policies involving race discrimination. Our earliest and most dramatic instance of public policy with reference to race emerged with the first contact of the white settlers on this continent with the native Indian population. The indigenous Indians, representing as they did an obstacle to white settlement, found themselves chronically in open war with the whites and were ultimately subjugated by the technically superior invaders. Until very recently the Indians were not allowed to share the rights of citizens, and those who were not exterminated were reduced to the subordinate status of wards of the government and confined to reservations.

Far more important than the Indian, at least from the standpoint of numbers, is the Negro in the United States. Ever since the day when he was first imported as an indentured servant or slave from Africa, he has constituted the principal stock among our people subjected to both official and unofficial differential treatment based upon difference in race. Since the Negro constitutes nearly one-tenth of our total population and is the principal victim of racial discrimination, his treatment may serve to illustrate the relation between race and public policy.

Neither in the American Colonies nor in the newly formed nation was the Negro included among those who enjoyed the rights of citizenship and equal protection of the law. He was assigned to an inferior place and in general remained in the place assigned to him, although sporadic rebellions testify to the fact that he did not always meekly accept his position as permanent. During the period of slavery the Negro was effectively subordinated to the whites by custom, public policy, and law. To be sure, not all Negroes nor all slaves were treated alike. Some slaves either purchased or were granted their formal freedom. The house servants were on the whole in a more intimate personal relationship with their masters than were the field hands, and the treatment of the former was considerably more humane. But slaves were property, and, despite their unique human qualities, as property they were considered in a category apart from the rest of society. A body of law and judicial decisions grew up defining the relationship between whites and Negroes. These legal sanctions heaped upon custom constitute the principal body of race legislation in America. Among the earliest racial legislation are prohibitions of intermarriage between Negroes and whites.

In the course of the Civil War and the collapse of the legal and political support of slavery, the power, privileges, and authority of the masters were weakened. But formal emancipation did not bring either actual freedom or real equality. New laws were considered necessary to define the new relationships between the races when the old caste order collapsed. The nation's attempt to superimpose a new pattern of race relations upon the South and to force equality by law, as evidenced by the Reconstruction measures, proved unsuccessful and produced bitter reaction. Before the Fourteenth Amendment placed limits upon the states, eight of them passed "black codes" to make the new status of the Negro coincide as nearly as possible with the old. The "black codes" imposed restrictions upon Negroes, limiting their choice of occupations, and attempted to tie the former slaves to the plantation economy. They regulated labor and circumscribed the black worker's freedom of movement.

Among the legislation restricting the freedom of the Negro are the segregation laws, or "Jim Crow" laws, enacted by most of the southern states. Under these laws the states which made any provision at all for the education of Negroes did so under the condition of the separation of the races in the schools. Similar separation was enforced in public assemblies, including churches, on common carriers, in hospitals, and in penal institutions. The Negro was further subjected to dfferential treatment in the courts; he was dealt with more severely for committing certain offenses against whites, especially sexual offenses. In some jurisdictions he was excluded from juries and limited in his capacity to testify against whites. Negro suffrage, where it existed at all, rested upon unequal terms with white persons.

The Fourteenth Amendment, which granted the Negro "equal protection of the law," was met by a negative response from the South that induced Congress to pass a series of Reconstruction acts beginning in 1867. Military governments were established in several of the southern states and the existing governments declared illegal. The Fifteenth Amendment, in 1869, was followed by a second series of Reconstruction acts, sometimes referred to as the "Force Bills," designed to lay a constitutional basis for the enforcement of the amendment. With the influx of carpet baggers from the North and the ascendancy of a strong Negro political organization in the South, some of the more flagrant anti-Negro measures enacted between 1865 and 1867 were repealed. Under the impact of this order imposed from without and flagrantly in conflict with custom and attitude in the Solid South, southern whites rallied to consolidate their strength and even turned to extralegal means to regain supremacy. The Ku Klux Klan was merely the most prominent of a number of organizations that sprang up throughout the South to intimidate the Negro and to restore the dominance of southern whites. The Democratic party became the white man's party and managed in most of the southern states to rewrite into the laws the repressive and discriminatory legislation which the amendments were designed to outlaw.

Among the legislation calculated to disfranchise the Negro was the so-called "grandfather clause," which limited the suffrage to those who were lineal descendants of persons who were entitled to vote at some point in time when Negroes were excluded. Since the Supreme Court declared these laws to be unconstitutional in 1915, other devices to restrict Negroes from exercising their right to vote have been resorted to, among them property requirements, the poll tax, and literacy tests which whites were allowed to circumvent but which were invoked in the case of Negroes. In addition, when other means failed, the Negroes were effectively debarred by intimidation from registration and voting.

Contemporary American Racial Policy

Both by custom and by law a Negro in the United States is today subjected to differential treatment in almost all aspects of life. Without attempting to treat all the forms and aspects of racial discrimination, it may be well to cite the principal fields in which the Negro today suffers from grossly unequal treatment.

On the political scene the Negro in large areas of the South is still effectively debarred from the franchise. This is done not only through the poll tax but also through his virtual exclusion from the primary by the Democratic party, which in effect had come to regard itself, with the sanction of the courts, as a private social club. What applies to voting applies equally to the holding of public office. Even in the case of appointments under federal civil service regulations, the Negro finds himself accepted only in inferior positions, grossly under-represented, and to a large extent segregated. This is even more true in the state governments except in those northern urban areas where the Negro enjoys considerable political power and hence can exact certain limited concessions from the patronage dispensers.

In the armed forces racial lines are clearly recognized. The Negro soldier is on the whole strictly segregated into colored units. There are few Negro officers and they never command white units. Although in our earlier history Negroes had distinguished records in the United States Navy, only recently has the Negro again been eligible for our naval forces in any other capacity than as messboy, and he has not yet achieved officer rank.

Some governmental agencies on the federal level have recognized the importance of race relations as they affect their specific activities and have appointed special personnel, such as race relations consultants, to deal with these problems. Valuable as their function has been, these race relations consultants, who are generally Negroes, are frequently put into the impossible position of having to serve as shock absorbers to protect the policy-making officials against Negro protest, while at the same time they are powerless to deal with the grievances of the Negroes arising out of unequal treatment and race discrimination.

In the awarding of war production contracts by the federal government, in accordance with congressional action, clauses have been written into the contracts prohibiting racial discrimination in employment. By executive order of the President a Fair Employment Practices Committee has been established to minimize discrimination against Negroes in defense industries, but unfortunately this committee has little power aside from the weapon of publicity to deal with violations.

Segregation legislation in the southern states provides for "separate but equal accommodations" for the two races. In fact, however, separate accommodations have rarely meant equal accommodations. This "Jim Crow" legislation applies not merely to segregation in public institutions but to private facilities as well, including places of amusement, restaurants, and even cemeteries.

Although there is ample evidence of discrimination against Negroes by legislative action, the unequal treatment of the Negro goes beyond the scope of law. Though in theory he receives the equal protection of the law, in fact he must suffer virtual exclu-

sion from juries inadequate facilities for his defense, the prejudice of the police, prosecuting agencies, and judges who are
generally white. He faces the disadvantages that come from un-
favorable organs of public opinion, hostile public sentiment, and
the ever present danger that if legal methods for denying him justice are not effective, mob violence will take its place.

That the Negro has suffered from unequal public services is
such a commonplace fact that it hardly needs mentioning. A notable exception is the equitable treatment of the Negro under the
federal relief program during the depression and under the provisions of the Social Security Act, save as in practice state and
local administrators of these measures have been able to nullify
the intent of the federal government to avoid discrimination in
relief and welfare measures. There is overwhelming evidence to
show, however, that not merely in the South but in the North as
well the Negro has received inferior police protection, sanitary
facilities, medical care, housing, recreation, and education.

It is particularly in the field of education that racial discrimination has been most widespread and has reacted most unfavorably upon the long-term prospects of attaining equality of opportunity for the Negro. It happens that the southern states which
segregate the Negro in the schools are also the poorest states and
would be able to furnish only mediocre educational opportunities
even if they had to maintain only a single school system. A dual
school system, however, imposes increased financial burdens upon
these economically disadvantaged areas and generally results in
grossly inferior school facilities and educational opportunities for
Negroes. This tends to perpetuate the already existing inequalities
by depriving the Negro of opportunities to rise in the economic
and social scale.

There is a long history in the United States of attempts to impose residential segregation upon the Negro by law and local ordinances. Recent Supreme Court decisions having undermined
the constitutionality of these acts, property owners have resorted
to private arrangements between themselves known as "restrictive
covenants," which debar Negroes almost as effectively from free
choice of residence as if the segregation were enforced by law. As

SOCIAL PROBLEMS AND PLANNING

yet there is no definitive decision by the Supreme Court invalidating such private contracts on the ground that they are contrary to public policy.

Even where the Negro is not subject to discriminatory treatment by law, he is nevertheless severely handicapped by custom and public policy. This is manifested in the singularly consistent imposition of unequal standards of merit and recognition accorded to the Negro in the professions. Even northern institutions relatively free from public pressure, such as higher institutions of learning and professional associations, only rarely admit Negroes and offer them opportunities to make their contributions on equal terms with whites. With the possible exception of the arts, the Negro is thus made dependent upon the more limited rewards and recognition that he can derive from his own circumscribed racial group. If it is recognized that success in almost all fields of human endeavor depends not merely upon native capacity but also upon opportunity, hope of reward, and traditions of success, it can be inferred how severe a handicap is imposed upon even those Negroes who have superior talents. Under these circumstances it is no wonder that the economic, political, and cultural advancement of the Negro has been slow. Indeed, the Negro has remarkable achievements to his credit in the face of these severe, chronic, and cumulative handicaps.

Discouraging as the prospect of attaining more nearly equal opportunities for persons irrespective of race might seem to be in this country, there are some signs of a greater awareness of the problems involved and of a willingness on the part of the dominant white group, even in the South, to make concessions to the rising tide of democratic sentiment and enlightenment. Aside from federal legislation and administrative policies already referred to, the Negro's quest for equality of opportunity has been immensely strengthened in recent years by a number of Supreme Court decisions. Among these has been the reaffirmation on April 28, 1941, by unanimous decision of the Supreme Court, that Negroes traveling from one state to another are entitled to railroad accommodations equal to those furnished white persons, which while it does not specifically do away with segregation will com-

pel interstate carriers to provide the same accommodations for
Negroes and whites who buy first-class tickets. Another decision,
of May 26, 1941, held that Congress has the power to regulate
primary elections in the same manner in which it regulates general elections, a decision which, while subject to greatly varying
interpretation, may undermine the Democratic primary system of
the South, which has debarred the Negro from the franchise. Of
special interest are recent court decisions making it mandatory
for states which exclude Negroes from higher educational institutions and professional schools to provide such education of approximately equal quality. A series of decisions in peonage cases
and reversals of lower courts' decisions in criminal cases involving Negroes, on the ground that Negroes were excluded from juries and that the defendants did not receive fair trials because of
their race, have served as a warning to local jurisdictions that the
federal constitutional provisions establishing equal protection of
the law irrespective of race can no longer be so easily evaded. The
public discussion that has resulted from the introduction of anti-
poll tax and anti-lynching bills may be regarded as a further sign
that the nation as a whole is concerned about the nullification of
the fundamental laws by certain states and localities where these
laws run counter to the racial mores.

The bold and outspoken statements of leading personalities
and of organizations—including many in the South—in denunciation of racial discriminaton are a further sign of impending
changes. The development of the CIO as a new labor organization
more nearly free from the established prejudices of the older existing labor groups also augurs well for the enhanced employment
opportunities of the Negro. This trend is strengthened by recent
opinions rendered by the Attorney General holding that contracts
between employers and unions discriminating against Negroes
are invalid. The passage of more stringent civil rights legislation
in such states as New York and Illinois, which recently have received large influxes of Negro migrants, is another wholesome
step. These laws provide severe penalties for deprivation of equal
civil rights including equal accommodations in private commercial
establishments. They provide further for punishment of partici-

pants in mob violence. They reaffirm the right of equal access to employment opportunities. The New York law forbids discrimination by life insurance companies on account of race. These steps are further indications of growing public awareness of the danger inherent in the spread of racial discrimination from the South to other parts of the country. They suggest a slowly emerging public policy designed to attack discriminatory racial practices generally.

War Experiences and Postwar Prospects

There seems little doubt that this recently accentuated awareness of the discrepancy between our national ideals and our actual practices and policies in relation to race is connected with the character of, and our involvement in, World War II. In a very real sense our enemies have thrust the race issue upon us. They have attempted to make this into a racial war, and the important question for America, therefore, is whether the Nazi doctrine of race and the practices that go with it shall make progress in this country and shall be allowed to divide us, to undermine our national solidarity, and to frustrate the exertion of our maximum potential war effort.

At first glance it would seem that in a country as diverse in its racial and cultural composition as ours the propaganda of racism would have little prospect of succeeding and the practices of our enemy in respect to what they call inferior races would arouse universal horror and disgust. But we cannot talk out of existence the racial, religious, and cultural conflicts and prejudices which have flourished among us and which have given rise to organized movements of nativism, know-nothingism, Ku-Kluxism, and other movements of intolerance and bigotry. Our enemies have demonstrated the power of propaganda which can thrive upon latent attitudes of race antagonism and race mythologies, especially in times of crisis and under conditions of personal insecurity. We must expect our enemies to exploit the resentment that racial minorities feel against the restrictions of their constitutional rights to vote, to enjoy the privileges of citizenship, and to receive equal treatment under the law; against discrimination in employment and in public conveyances; against deliberate segregation;

against unequal educational opportunities; against the blocking of their paths of personal advancement; and against not infrequent mass violence. Unfortunately, the stark necessities of war, while they have made us more conscious of the promises of democracy, have also frustrated our ability to fulfil them. Indeed, we have resorted, perhaps unnecessarily, to measures which have widened old and generated new forms of racial discrimination. We have, for instance, indiscriminately herded Japanese residents, irrespective of their citizenship, into relocation centers and thus nullified the dignity of American citizenship and subordinated it to the criterion of race. We have deprived a substantial part of our citizenry, solely on account of race, of the privilege of contributing its full measure of strength to the winning of the war.

Among the bulwarks upon which we rely to protect us from being engulfed by racial prejudices are those found in the Preamble to the Declaration of Independence, in our Constitution, and in the Bill of Rights. There are few peoples in the world who have affirmed as high a set of principles as these to guide their public policy. Far as we have been from actually realizing the ideals expressed in these noble state documents, they do nevertheless constantly remind us that as a nation we cherish the principle of the equality of men before the law and equality of opportunity for all. We know that not all men are born equal and certainly not all are treated as equals, but we have set equality down as a goal toward which to strive and as the criterion for determining the soundness of public policy. We are at least sure of the direction in which we want to move as a nation.

Race relations policies for any nation are no longer a matter of purely domestic concern. They are issues that concern the world as a whole and they will inevitably be an important phase of the task of postwar world reconstruction. All the caste-like arrangements subordinating the colored races to the white group are rapidly crumbling in the spread of urban industrial civilization. The ideals of freedom and human equality embedded in the religious and political heritage of occidental society, which were given new impetus by the American, French, and Russian revolutions, have continued to fire suppressed peoples everywhere with the ambition to improve their status. The protest against exploitation and subordination of one racial group by another has become world-wide. It has awakened the conscience of the dominant groups in all parts of the world to the indefensibility of their exclusive prerogatives based upon race. In the course of the struggle against fascism and its accompanying dogma of racism, the democratic ideology has acquired new vitality. The value of racial equality has acquired such political force in the world that even such nations as Japan in the course of the war have found it advantageous to grant at least nominal freedom to some of their conquered territories in order to make our own promises of freedom to these peoples seem hollow and hypocritical.

Fortunately, our record in the period immediately preceding the World War offers ample demonstration of the fact that we did not need the impelling motive of military expediency to adopt a more enlightened racial policy. Our action toward the Philippines, for instance, lends strength to the belief that we can resist the temptation to impose ourselves as imperial masters over other peoples and that we can win their loyalty and friendship through improving their lot to the best of our ability. Our recent efforts to improve the conditions of life of the people of Puerto Rico, coupled with the suggestion by a responsible official that they be given the right to elect their own governor, offer similar testimony of our decent intentions. Our relinquishment of extraterritorial rights in China and congressional action eliminating Chinese exclusion though beclouded by the fact that these actions were taken under the pressure of war, constitute other proof.

In our own country we have been making strenuous efforts through a more enlightened policy toward the Indian to make good the injustices which were done him. In the case of the Negro, the virtual disappearance of lynchings, the improvement in education, health, housing, and welfare, the resolute steps toward actual enfranchisement the improvement in the administration of justice, and the provision through official and unofficial action of greater employment opportunities are other encouraging signs that have received widespread public support. What is most important of all is that for all minorities we have shown increasing concern to keep the door of opportunity open.

While we are far from having eliminated distinctions in law, custom, conventions, social usages, ritual, and etiquette based solely upon differences in race, we are in our public policy definitely moving in that direction at a faster pace than we have ever done before. It must be recognized, however, that public policy is shaped by the citizenry and that official action cannot in the long run be either too far ahead or too far behind public sentiment and opinion. The public sentiment and opinion that will ultimately shape both public policy and private conduct is becoming more world-wide in scope. America for centuries has been the experimental proving ground for the principle that men irrespective of their race, creed, or origin can live and work together harmoniously for the common good. If we as a nation can keep alive the struggle for the fuller realization of the ideals which we have as yet only imperfectly achieved, we shall gain an immense source of strength against the enemy and we shall have a more certain prospect for building a better world for all mankind.

19

HOUSING AS A FIELD

OF SOCIOLOGICAL RESEARCH

THAT HOUSING is an important practical problem needs no argument. If practical problems are to be dealt with intelligently they obviously require the foundation of sound knowledge. The knowledge required to deal intelligently with housing includes not merely what all of the social sciences have to give but also the technical knowledge which architecture, engineering, art, law, administration, business, and other professions can offer.

Housing is a social activity. As such, sociology has something to learn from it and it constitutes a subject matter for sociological study. Sociology also presumably has some knowledge to bring to housing problems. It is the purpose of this paper to indicate what this two-fold interest of sociology in housing is as a giver and a receiver of knowledge.

Sociology is clearly not the only discipline bearing upon housing, and, conversely, what housers can legitimately ask of sociologists will only give them a partial answer to their problems. What, then, are the principal aspects of housing to which sociological research might address itself, keeping in mind that there are many other disciplines and practical arts and professions which

Reprinted from the *American Sociological Review*, XII (April, 1947), 137–43, read before the annual meeting of the American Sociological Society, Chicago, Illinois, December 27–30, 1946.

have other problems and which seek other answers in the field of housing?

The answer to this question must, it seems to me, be sought in the light of one's conception of the nature and province of sociology. This discipline is concerned with what is true of man by virtue of the fact that he leads a group life. What sociologists must discover about housing, therefore, is all those aspects which are factors in and products of man's involvement in social life. At first glance this may seem to be virtually everything, for the politics and economics of housing, as well as art, architecture and law, business, financing and administration, designing and planning, are also factors in and products of social relations. Upon further reflection, however, the sociological study of housing would turn out to have a fairly delimitable scope or, at least, distinctive emphasis. There are three clearly significant sociological aspects of housing I propose to discuss briefly: (1) housing as a social value, (2) housing in relation to the community, (3) housing and social policy.

Housing as a Value

In housing, as in the study of other social phenomena, it may be well to start with the central question of the social values involved. Hence, I would propose that the sociological study of housing begin with housing as a social value. Everyone in our society is concerned with the realization of this value, and the quest for the achievement of this value by each affects the similar quest by all the others.

Considering the fundamental importance of the question of values, it is rather shocking to find how little we know about the various ways in which housing as a social value has been defined by different civilizations and by different groups in society. The content of this value ranges all the way from the quest for basic shelter to the striving to achieve residential accommodations with varying degrees of luxury, various amenities of life, status-giving qualities and other characteristics, such as the location of the home, the materials out of which it is to be built, the style of architecture, the nature of the furnishings and equipment, the

nature of the community in which it is located and the characteristics of one's neighbors.

Surely we cannot proceed far in the analysis of housing as a
social problem until we know more than we now do about the nature and the extent to which people's desires and expectations in
respect to housing are realized or frustrated. After all, social problems arise only where there is some deviation from a norm or
some conflict of values, or maladjustment in the effort to achieve
these values, which affects a greater or lesser number in society
adversely. We experience no feeling of frustration if there is no
ambition of which we become aware and in the satisfaction of
which we find ourselves blocked. The mere deviation from accepted norms or the frustrations of our desires, however, do not
constitute a social problem unless at the same time there is a recognition that the ends sought are achievable and the means for
achieving them exist or can be brought into being.

One of the ways in which we can approach the subject of housing, therefore, is to attempt to discover the specific content of the
value it constitutes for different individuals and groups in our society. This can obviously not be judged merely by the kind of
housing that people have, for the kind of housing they have is
clearly restricted by other factors than merely their ambitions and
desires or the pictures they carry around in their heads of the
housing they would like to have, or the kind of housing that is
possible in our present state of technological advancement. Fruitful housing research, therefore, might be devoted to the discovery
of the housing ambitions of people and the manner in which and
the degree to which these ambitions are frustrated among different economic and social groups in our society.

It will be immediately apparent, however, to the sociological
student of housing that housing as a value does not stand by itself. It has a place in the hierarchy of values, and this place differs in different cultures and in different strata of society. One
way in which we may estimate the place of housing as a value in
the scheme of values is to ask what other values people are willing to sacrifice in order to achieve housing of a certain quality.
European observers of American life have often been struck by
the fact that many families in the low income groups in the

United States are apparently willing to make a good many sacrifices in order to have an automobile, but relatively few to have a decent house. On the other hand, we have seen from the studies of immigrant groups that some, such as the Poles, will be willing to forego many other items in their standard of living to acquire real property. The popularity of building and loan associations among immigrant groups is perhaps merely another indication of the extent to which a house constitutes a value fairly high up in the scheme of values, and saving for such a house becomes an important family objective.

In this connection it is important not to mistake the actual state of affairs for the underlying attitudes of people. Just because people live in the slums does not mean that they wish to live in them or that they hold housing in low esteem as a value. It may simply be that they are not able to help themselves, and if better housing were offered at a price they could meet, or if other items in their family budget were less demanding, housing would rise to a more important place.

As part of the estimation of housing as a value in American civilization, special attention should be devoted to home ownership. On this subject fairly reliable quantitative data are available. The difference in the degree of home ownership in rural and urban communities, in cities of different sizes and types, and among various income groups, racial and economic groups, has been fairly completely ascertained. It should be noted, however, to what an extent the actual facts deviate from the highly advertised ideal that every American family should own its home and what the factors are that account for this deviation.

It is clear enough that home ownership has much to do with the place of property and housing in the value scheme of different groups. But it should also be recognized that the desire for home ownership and the quest for security in life may be mutually incompatible. Historically, we have been a highly mobile people, as contrasted with most of the peoples of Europe. It is well, therefore, to ask, in the case of home ownership, to what extent it is a value which conflicts with economic security in general and particularly with the ability to take advantage of job opportunities as they may arise in other parts of the city or in other cities. The experience of industries in providing housing for their employees on a paternalistic basis is instructive in this connection. With instability in industry and employment, home ownership may actually become a handicap. The degree to which this is recognized by the population in general may become an important factor in understanding the trends as well as the differentiations in home ownership between different groups.

The mere nominal ownership of a home does not, of course, imply actual ownership. Often it may be, especially in the low income groups and in periods when the housing demand is very great, as it is at present, that families may make a down payment on a home without actually being able to acquire full ownership. In that case their home ownership consists merely in the privilege of occupying the home as long as they can meet the mortgage and interest payments and the taxes.

With the trend toward multiple family structures, especially in metropolitan communities, it becomes physically impossible for most families to own their homes, even if they wanted to, unless, of course, they were willing to associate themselves in some sort of co-operative housing enterprise. An analysis of the factors conducive to co-operative housing would constitute a special problem under the general head of research on housing as a value. There are, of course, a good many other aspects of sociological interest connected with housing co-operatives, such as the degree of homogeneity or heterogeneity of the co-operators, the influences that bring them together, and the elements contributing to the continuity of the arrangement and the success or failure of the enterprise.

Another feature of the analysis of housing as a value centers around the question of housing standards. It has been remarked that a civilization can be judged, at least to some extent, by the minimum housing conditions which a society will tolerate for its members. In the perspective of history, it should be observed that men have lived in shelters of various kinds. They have lived in caves and in mansions. The medieval castles were probably not as habitable as a modern slum home. Modern technology has made possible the continuous improvement in housing standards. We have become acquainted with the interconnections between standards of housing and standards of health and well-being. More and more these standards have acquired social sanction, and because of the recognition of their relationship to health and safety have been incorporated in laws and ordinances. The extent to which these laws and ordinances keep pace with increased knowledge of the relations between housing and other aspects of social life and with progress in technology is in itself a subject of considerable sociological interest. It has been found that standards once accepted tend to develop around themselves vested interests, such as the organized building trades and material manufacturers, and that as a result instead of furthering housing progress they have become obstacles to such progress. This lag would be a particularly appropriate subject for sociologists to investigate.

In recent years a good deal of attention has been devoted by sociologists to the study of the internal arrangement and the equipment of houses. Social status scales have even been developed on the basis of physical facilities in the house. This, however, is merely one small aspect of the very much larger problem of the analysis of housing as a value. This justifies the search for the kind of housing design which would be compatible with the changing expectations and needs of members of the family. Thus, for instance, it would be important to inquire to what extent privacy for the individual members of the family is a value that people seek to realize. Similarly, it would be interesting to discover what adjustments people make in their housing in various stages of the family cycle, such as the kind of housing requirements that they have when the family is young, as over against when the children grow up and seek housing of their own. The relationship between size of family and size of housing units has become a problem of great practical importance in view of the declining size of the family and in view of the now accepted cultural pattern that only the immediate family should occupy the dwelling as over against the previously accepted cultural pattern in which the extended family is the unit to which housing must be adapted. It has been said, for instance, that the absence of a spare bedroom is the best defense against a host of invading relatives. The popularity of the kitchenette apartment, and of two- and three-room units as over against the larger dwellings attests to the changing structure of the urban family.

Housing and the Community

The involvement of housing with community life is clearly a subject of long standing sociological interest. This connection between housing and community life arises out of the fact that at least in the urban community the house does not stand by itself but is part of a neighborhood, a local community and the metropolis. No individual house can be completely insulated against influences of neighbors or the trends prevailing in the community. Moreover, as more and more of the functions of family living become centered in community institutions, the nature of the functioning of and the accessibility to these institutions and facilities becomes important. The degree to which people—individuals and families—find opportunities for participation in formal and informal organizations operating in the community is perhaps as good a test as any of the adequacy of housing. Thus, for instance, a house, even from the standpoint of the property values involved, is judged by the community in which it is located and the people who inhabit that community, by the schools, playgrounds, parks, community centers and public utilities to which the inhabitants have access, and by the incidence of social problems, such as delinquency and crime and community disorganization.

In modern civilization, place of work and place of residence have become progressively divorced. Nevertheless, convenience of access to place of work and shopping center, as well as to other facilities serving the routines of modern living, continue to be matters affecting the desirability or undesirability of a house.

The social status and the standard of living, the racial and ethnic composition of their neighborhoods are issues to which people in our society are sensitive. Only in the slum, where the inhabitants consist of those who cannot afford to live or are not tolerated anywhere else, are the resistances to invasion by lower income and status groups reduced to a minimum.

In view of these facts, sociological research in housing might well be concerned to a much greater degree than it has been with the structure of communities and their relationship to the general pattern of the city; the analysis of different types of communities; the tracing of the process blight; the phenomena of invasion and succession of different population groups in specific areas of the city; the factors underlying the flight from the city and the emergence of suburban communities and, in turn, the fate of these suburban communities as the corrosive influences extend outward from the central city; the attitudes underlying the resistance to the invasion of strange racial and ethnic groups, the methods used to block this invasion and the alternative methods that might be used for building sound communities in which people of various economic strata and racial and ethnic characteristics can live together amicably; the relation of community institutions to housing and the relationship of place of work to place of residence and the role of transportation in the general pattern of living.

These are problems with which in the past the human ecologist, the demographer, the student of community organization and the city planner have been primarily concerned. A more definite focussing of sociological interest upon these issues would be of immense scientific as well as practical significance.

As in the case of the analysis of housing as a complex of values, so in the study of the relationship of housing to the community the question of values cannot be left out of consideration. To know what is good housing involves also knowing what is a good community. This implies that in the analysis of communities, too, a basic prerequisite is an understanding of the wishes and expectations of people and of the possibilities of realizing them under the available or expected state of knowledge, social and economic organization, and technological resources. In the light of such knowledge it is possible to formulate minimum standards for communities and for the individual house. Indeed, at least in the urban community, it is futile to attempt to set up minimum standards for housing without at the same time considering standards for communities.

Housing and Social Policy

A third major aspect of the housing problem to which sociologists might well address their research is that of the formation of public policy. There may have been a time when individuals or families could solve their housing problems mainly on the basis of their own resources and their own decisions. This is becoming less and less true. Even in the case of rural housing, where individualism still has an important place, the meeting of the housing needs and expectations of people is increasingly conditioned by factors over which the individual or the household has little control. The general trend of agriculture, soil conservation programs, credit policy, the relationship to roads, to schools, to markets and to service centers, are becoming increasingly important. In the urban community, the social matrix in which individuals or families solve their housing problems—even in unplanned communities—is increasingly complicated and inescapable.

To begin with, sociologists perhaps more immediately than others might recognize the fact that we do not have a housing industry as we have an automobile industry, and that an individual cannot enter the housing market quite in the same manner as he enters the market for other commodities as a producer or consumer, as a buyer or a seller. A variety of specialized interests and specialized skills is involved in housing activities, over which the individual has little or no control. The housing industry, if we can speak of it as an industry at all, is loosely organized, and the sociologist might profitably address himself to the nature and functioning of this organization.

Moreover, housing is beset at many angles with a public interest which expresses itself in a complex set of public regulations, such as building codes, zoning ordinances, safety and sanitary regulations, to mention only some formal ones, besides the informal regulations set by fashions and neighborhood and community pressures. Besides, the provision of housing involves a variety of more or less organized and articulate interest groups: the real estate fraternity, the mortgage bankers, the architects, the city planner, the materials manufacturers, the building trades laborers, the public officials, the more or less organized property owners, taxpayers, tenants, and a great many more. These interest groups develop into pressure groups whenever public decisions are to be made. What happens in the case of each issue depends in large measure upon the power relationships between the pressure groups and their influence upon such bodies as Congress, State Legislatures and City Councils.

This is particularly apparent in the case of the struggle that goes on in connection with public housing and the determination of the scope of public responsibility for housing, especially of the low income groups, for whom private housing enterprise has not been able to make adequate provisions. Whether or not and to what extent public responsibility exists for achieving a minimum housing standard for all of our people depends again upon the acceptance of certain social values, and hence, here too the problem of values is central. It is around the recognition of certain of these values that housing movements organize themselves, and if the housing movement in various countries in the Western world, including the United States, has gained its peculiar character through the emphasis upon public responsibility, it is due to the fact that, like other social movements of a reform or revolutionary nature, it has set itself the goal of achieving certain social objectives toward which there either exists a public apathy or against which there operates the organized resistance of special interest groups. We shall not achieve an adequate solution of the housing problem, nor shall we make satisfactory progress toward that goal, without a better understanding of the collective behavior of these various groups within the housing movement. Sociologists have both much to learn and to contribute in this connection.

Housing as a Social Problem

The problem of housing illustrates the nature of social problems in general, and from its analysis students of social life can learn a great deal concerning the role of norms, the complexity of the factors and the method of analysis of social problems in general. They can learn, too, something about the division of labor between the various social sciences and the arts and technical and professional specialties that enter into a concrete social issue.

In emphasizing three aspects of the housing problem, as I have done above, I do not mean to imply that there are not many other aspects of housing from which sociologists might learn and to which they might contribute understanding. I have selected these three merely because in the miscellanous approaches to the housing problem that have been in evidence, these are three factors that seem to me to have been particularly neglected. It would, of course, be possible to formulate the sociological interests in housing in a more or less systematic manner, corresponding to the basic branches of sociological knowledge, starting with human ecology and demography, running through social organization, and ending with the social psychological aspects of the subject matter. All of these aspects are, of course, represented in the problem complexes that I have emphasized. It would, for instance, be perfectly appropriate for a sociologist to delve deeply into specific problems connected with housing, such as the relation of housing to family life or the relation of housing to delinquency, family disorganization, community disorganization, and other deviant forms of behavior, or to single out the grossly neglected problem of the housing of the unattached persons in our society, or of the problems represented by the attitudes involved in the acceptance of second-, third-, and even tenth-hand housing as a respectable form of behavior in a society which frowns upon the wearing of secondhand clothes or the acceptance of other handed down personal commodities.

As sociologists we have the skills and the insights, the systematic framework and the background by virtue of our scientific training to view the problem in the perspective of a systematic science. What I wish to emphasize, however, is that in the case of housing we confront, as sociologists, a genuine problem of social concern which should challange us to mobilize our knowledge and to perfect our methods of analysis. We will not make a contribution of value to society if we merely mechanically apply the conventional concepts of our discipline to the problem. I suggest we look at the problem and then see what we have in existing knowledge and methods of approach that appear relevant to gaining a better understanding of it, noting to what extent our knowledge and methods are inadequate, and perfect the knowledge and methods so as to make them more adequate. In the long run this might make us more useful in the world and at the same time give us a more realistic science.

20

THE METROPOLITAN REGION

AS A PLANNING UNIT

IT SHOULD not be necessary in our time to make a case for metropolitan regional planning. The fact of the existence of the metropolis speaks eloquently enough. The problems of metropolitan government, economy, and society plead so insistently for rational treatment that no one who claims membership in the fraternity of planners can ignore them. Despite the abundance of facts to support the contention that the metropolitan region is not merely a figure of speech but a reality, and in the face of the urgent baffling problems which regional involvements pose for every city of metropolitan proportions, planning still proceeds largely as if the city rather than the metropolitan region were the appropriate planning area.

Forward-looking planners have of course for some years past recognized the imperious necessity of finding a planning unit approximating in scope an area congruent with the community to be planned. Some, however, have had no scruples about under-

Reprinted from *Community Life and Social Policy*, ed. Elizabeth Wirth Marvick and Albert J. Reiss, Jr. (Chicago: University of Chicago Press, 1956), pp. 301–13, first published in *Proceedings, National Conference on Planning, 1942* (Chicago: American Society of Planning Officials, 1942), pp. 141–51.

taking urban planning programs as if the region of which the city was a part were nonexistent. Still others have been content, especially since their fees come from a municipal planning agency, to accept planning programs for the city and incidentally, as an afterthought or as part of the ritual, also to take account of the city's regional involvements. As a recent publication puts it:

Almost every city has, outside its political boundaries, residential or commercial or manufacturing areas, large or small, which are economically a part of the central community, sharing its fortunes and needing to cooperate in its policies. The larger area, containing both the city proper and these outlying activities, must, therefore, for its best effectiveness, be planned as a unit. The municipal planning agency will recognize the fact that its study of the city area can be adequate only if it includes the larger metropolitan district of which it is a part. If there is an official regional or county planning agency, willing and able to undertake a cooperative study with the city planning agency, then the larger area could be more adequately studied.

A city agency alone, partly because of legal limitations, partly because of difficulties in securing and spending city funds to study conditions beyond the city limits, may be severely handicapped at the present time. If it is impossible soon to eliminate such handicaps, the city planning agency must do the best it can to consider, in a broad way, the general aspects of the outer region and particularly those planning factors which have their effects both inside and outside the city boundaries.[1]

It is the thesis of this paper that just as no reputable physician would treat a case of scarlet fever by applying local plasters to the erupted parts of the patient's anatomy, so a city planner is indulging in professional quackery by purporting to make a plan for a city which stops abruptly at the corporate limits. Most of the problems that call for the knowledge and skill of the planner in the first place are systemic or region-wide and are not at all or only in slight degree amenable to treatment on the scope of the legally defined municipality.

What, then, are the facts about metropolitan communities

1   Federal Housing Administration, *A Handbook on Urban Redevelopment for Cities in the United States* (Washington: Government Printing Office, 1941), pp. 15–16.

which dictate the appropriate planning area and what are the metropolitan problems the range of which must determine the scope of the city plan?

For some decades past we have been witnessing the emergence and rapid growth of a new type of urban community—the super-city, or the metropolitan region.[2] The concentration of business and industry in the larger urban centers has been accompanied by the outward movement of residents seeking more favorable places in which to live. The desire to escape from the disadvantages, the costs, and the civic responsibilities of urban living has also been shared by industries, which, while not wishing to deprive themselves of access to urban consumer and labor markets, have sought to benefit from the lower costs, especially land and labor costs, by establishing themselves outside the limits of the central cities and beyond the reach of their regulatory powers.

Except in cases where the cities themselves comprise vast areas and thus contain within their boundaries ample undeveloped territory for residential and industrial expansion, there has taken place during the last decade a significant shift in the distribution of urban residents. In general, the cities have grown much less rapidly than the counties in which they lie. Indeed, the outward movement of the city population has reached a point where nearly one-third of the cities of 100,000 or more inhabitants in 1940 and about one-fourth of the cities in the 25,000–100,000 size group actually lost population during the last decade.

The most dramatic expression of this trend is to be found in those urban complexes which the Census has designated as "metropolitan districts." Whereas the central cities, constituting the core of these metropolitan districts, have grown only 6.1 per cent during the last decade, the outlying areas on the periphery of the central cities have grown 16.9 per cent, as Table 1 indicates. Thus nearly one out of six Americans is a suburbanite, and there is one suburban dweller for every two inhabitants of a metropolitan city. That the flight from the central cities to the rims of the metropolitan areas is continuing is shown by the fact that while in 1930, 30 per cent of the population of metropolitan

2   See Louis Wirth, "Urban Communities," *American Journal of Sociology*, XLVII (May, 1942), 833 ff.

districts lived outside the central cities, in 1940 there were 32
per cent outside. For the 133 comparable districts, the centers
grew 5.0 per cent and the peripheries 15.8 per cent. Of the 140
metropolitan districts, 36, or 25.7 per cent, lost population in
their central cities during the decade 1930–40 and only 7 gained
as much or more in their central cities as in their outlying sections. The implications of this suburban trend for local government, the physical structure of cities, housing, industry, taxation,
real estate values, and ways of living are already becoming apparent. The fact that nearly half of the nation's total population
is concentrated into 140 metropolitan areas is in itself impressive,

TABLE 1
POPULATION OF METROPOLITAN DISTRICTS, 1940 AND 1930

	POPULATION		INCREASE	
	1940	1930	Number	Per Cent
Total (140 districts)	62,965,773	57,602,865	5,362,908	9.3
In central cities	42,796,170	40,343,442	2,452,728	6.1
Outside central cities	20,169,603	17,259,423	2,910,180	16.9

Source: U.S. Bureau of the Census, *Sixteenth Census of the United States: 1940, Population: Number of Inhabitants, United States Summary* (1st ser.; Washington: Government Printing Office, 1941),
p. 71.

indicating that, although dispersion of the population and industries from the central cities is under way, this does not spell the
end of urbanization but means, rather, a new type of decentraliza-
tion within more inclusive metropolitan areas. The importance of
dense concentrations of people and industries in a few urban
areas is shown by the fact that the 33 "industrial areas" recognized by the Census of Manufactures, comprising 97 counties with
only 1.7 per cent of the total land area and 35.4 per cent of the
total population of the United States, accounted for 54.7 per cent
of the total number of wage earners in 1939.[3]

Nearly 60 per cent of the 184,230 American manufacturing
establishments producing in 1939 goods valued at 56.8 billion

[3] U.S. Bureau of the Census, *Census of Manufactures, 1939. Distribution of Wage Earners in the United States by Counties* (released November, 1941).

dollars were concentrated in these 33 industrial areas comprising the chief metropolitan cities of the country. Each of the 14 American cities with a population of over a half-million is the center of an industrial area. Together they accounted for 26.1 per cent of the value of all manufactured products produced in the United States. New York and Chicago together accounted for nearly half of this. Although the metropolitan areas seem to have lost something of the momentum of growth which they showed in the past, they still comprise the concentrated workshops and habitations of the nation.

The serious problems which the flight of industry and people into the suburban fringe creates for the central cities can be more adequately appraised if the suburban trend is seen as operating in combination with the outward movement of residential and business districts within cities themselves. The inner core of the cities have been threatened by depopulation, blight, and decay.

Some of the major cities of the country have been faced with the problem of maintaining urban public services such as policing, fire protection, sanitation, education, and recreation at constant or increasing costs in the face of declining income from taxation because of a drop in the value of taxable property and increasing tax delinquency. The efforts that have been made by the public housing agencies to check blight and to construct low-cost housing in the slum sections near the centers of cities have not been on a sufficiently large scale to reverse the trend of migration toward the fringe of the cities and have not effectively halted the obsolescence of public facilities and private structures in the inner and older built-up areas of our cities. Commendable as the efforts to rehabilitate the deteriorated areas are, they have to a large extent been offset by the activities of the lending agencies of the federal government, which have looked upon the older areas as poor risks and have favored the outward movement of new residential construction. Increasing traffic congestion at the city centers, coupled with increasing emphasis upon high-speed, through-traffic lanes to the outskirts and the suburbs, has accentuated the tendency to create residential vacuums at the hearts of cities.

Defining the Planning Area

One of the first problems which confronts the planner is the delineation of the area to be planned. Much as he would like, he cannot avoid formulating somewhere near the start of his procedure a definition of the scope of his activities, for unless he does this he will not even know how to limit the range of his observations and the ramifications of the factors and forces he seeks to analyze and control. It is a good rule here as elsewhere to start with the ideal of approximating the total situation. But it is a well-known fact that we can never approach the whole and always must content ourselves with a more or less incomplete and circumscribed part. As the poet put it:

All things by immortal power
Near or far,
Hiddenly
To each other linked are,
That thou canst not stir a flower
Without troubling of a star.

FRANCIS THOMPSON

Even the planner must choose, but let us hope that he will choose as wisely as possible, and that in seeking to discover a practicable planning area he will consider both the range of the problems with which he deals and the scope of potential control that is to be exercised.

It may be well at the outset to indicate that there are several distinct approaches to a region. First, we may conceive a metropolitan region as an area containing a dominant central city exercising a progressively diminishing influence upon a territory the outer boundaries of which are indeterminate. Second, we may think of a metropolitan region as an area containing a central city exercising a dominant influence over a territory the periphery of which is marked by the zone where the dominance of another competing metropolitan region becomes apparent. Third, we may visualize metropolitan regions as more or less arbitrarily fixed areas into which the country as a whole has been divided for various administrative purposes.

The first type of region is largely determined by the size and importance of the city as an economic and social entity, the degree to which it is dependent for its life upon a hinterland, and the degree to which the life of the hinterland is dependent upon and integrated with the central city. Obviously this will vary for different functions. The boundaries of such a region may be conveniently drawn along a line where the central urban influences fade out and become indistinguishable. Beyond this area there may lie an indefinitely extended no man's land which is either distinctly rural or which at any rate is not the recognized domain of any other metropolitan region. Because until recently in many parts of our country there still existed vast wide open spaces, the metropolitan regions have not been under the necessity of staking out their respective imperial domains.

The second type of metropolitan region is one which may be thought of as constituting a sort of socioeconomic watershed the boundaries of which are drawn along a line in each direction where lines of interdependence flow more predominantly toward one rather than another metropolitan center. Such a line might be determined on the basis of the flow of trade, of newspaper circulation, of commutation, or of the labor flow. Particularly in the highly urbanized sections of the nation does this type of region emerge as an important unit.

The third type of region is the product largely of administrative controls, particularly federal controls, which have progressively become more important as the functions of our national government have multiplied. The administrative areas of which a given metropolitan city is the center may vary enormously, but by virtue of the establishment of such centers and the delineation of their regional domains the country as a whole is carved into significant regional units.

It would indeed be fortunate if each of these three types of areas were internally consistent and clearly defined, not to speak of being consistent with one another. Unhappily for the planners, however, this is far from true and poses a problem which taxes the ingenuity of the best of them. The sad fact is that cities and regions are products of growth rather than of design and what is more they are fluid rather than static. As a wise observer has said: "To ingenious attempts at explaining by the light of reason things that want the light of history to show their meaning, much of the learned nonsense of the world has indeed been due."[4]

We should note, however, that we need not accept the chaos that we have inherited from history as an immutable and inflexible fact before which we can only stand in awe and reverence. The rationale of planning is that even if we must accept the past as given, and read its lessons, the future is ours to influence if not to make. If I may quote another poet: "All other things *must,* man is a being who wills." The way in which we conceive of the planning area may in itself become an important factor in the shaping of the cities, the regions, and the nation of the future.

You will ask, and you have a right to ask, whether there is an optimum planning region, one which better than all the others lends itself to the uses of the planner. Regretfully I must admit that life for the planner as for all the rest of us is full of compromises; but in planning, as in other fields, let us not make our compromises before the battle, during the battle, and after the battle again, for if we do we will have precious little left of what originally drove us to do battle with the enemy. If it is true that the perfect is the enemy of the good, the good is no less an enemy to the perfect.

The search for an all-purpose planning area may be as futile as the search for the Holy Grail, but the search for an approximation to such an area is the categorical imperative of the planner. Even if he does not reach it, the educative influence which the search for it is likely to bring will make his work more productive and more intelligent and will at the least lift him out of the level of quackery to the uncomfortable plane of the sciences.

Obviously the determination of the planning area depends in some measure upon what is to be planned. There may be purposes for which the corporate city, or even a subdivision thereof, may be quite adequate. For smaller towns and cities the county may

4   E. B. Tylor, *Primitive Culture* (London, 1871), p. 17.

be enough. And for some of the larger urban centers the areas which have been designated by the Census of Population as metropolitan districts and by the Census of Manufactures as industrial areas may be quite adequate. If the planning is of a circumscribed, segmental character, the scope of the area may very properly be the scope of the function. But most planning is not, or should not be, unifunctional but comprehensive, and while there are certain interconnections between functions which express themselves in comparable areal scope, there is no assurance that a functional area that may be chosen by the planner on the basis of hunch or tradition will yield an adequate basis for comprehensive urban planning. If the planner must err, let him err on the side of taking in more rather than less of the periphery of the city. If he must map the planning area, let him touch his pencil lightly as he defines its outer rims—to remind him that as far as possible they should forever remain fluid. If he must be specific, let him draw his lines of demarcation in such a way that they will represent the coincidence of the most vital zones of influence of the city upon its hinterland—that he can ascertain after examining both what is and the fundamental factors that have brought it about and that are likely to change it.

An Empirical Basis for Defining the Planning Area

Even the smallest hamlet tends to maintain itself and to grow, to take on structure and to metamorphose, because of forces not contained within itself. In any city of any size, and particularly in cities of metropolitan proportions, the lines of mutual influence between the city and the outside world are so complex as virtually to defy orderly statements. Nevertheless an attempt must be made at least to outline some of the principal criteria of interdependence and integration that should furnish a basis for the empirical determination of the metropolitan planning area.

Whatever else the city may be, in our kind of civilization it is first and foremost a human settlement resting upon an economic base with more or less widespread economic ramifications.

If the planner therefore would delineate his planning area in such a way as to conform as nearly as possible to the definition of the region as an economic unit, he must take account of the interaction between the city and the outside world which flows from the fact that the city is not merely the dwelling place of man but the workshop and the center of interchange of goods and services.

Among the facts to be considered in delineating the boundaries of the planning region, therefore, is first the area from which the city draws the raw materials which it in turn processes, stores, and distributes. It may not be possible to do this for all of the basic raw materials which the city so uses, but it should be possible to do it for those which constitute the most important base for the city manufacturing activities. There is secondly the fact that the city ships its products to the outside world and is therefore dependent for its economic prosperity upon a market which may be regional, national, or world-wide. Obviously here again it would be impossible and impracticable to draw a line demarcating an area comprising all of the seller relationships that the city has to its market. It will be sufficient, however, to note the area over which the bulk of its most significant products is distributed. Two distinct areas of this sort are commonly noted: (*a*) the retail-trade area, comprising the more or less immediately adjacent territory, the outlying boundaries of which are roughly determined by the area over which retailers advertise, over which a regular free-delivery route is maintained, over which local newspapers circulate their retail ads, and over which the chain stores maintain approximately the same price; (*b*) the wholesale area, which has been fairly well sketched by the Census of Business for the larger communities, comprising of course a much wider area, delineated again by the territory over which the wholesale houses maintain regular sales and delivery routes, maintain a common price structure, and maintain a dominance which another wholesale center would find it difficult to challenge.

Such interconnections of an economic sort as banking, particularly the delineation of the area over which outlying banks maintain depositories in central banks, must be taken account of.

Since much of our economic life depends upon the circulation of news, the newspaper circulation area covered by the metropolitan press constitutes a significant orbit of influence. The same has lately come to be true of radio-listening areas. One of the most important criteria for determining the metropolitan planning region, however, and one which can be easily ascertained on at least a sampling basis, is the area from which the urban community draws its labor supply. This is the area defined by the territory over which people living in the cities go to work and the area outside the city from which workers are drawn to urban establishments. The routes of automobile transport and the commutation zones may be found roughly to approximate this area.

There are in addition such factors as the extent of the local freight-rate zone, the local switching area, the area over which local postal rates prevail, the area over which belt-line railroads operate, the area served by urban public utilities, and the area of local telephone rates, which can be used to check on and to correct the boundaries of the metropolitan region arrived at by other criteria such as those mentioned above.

What has made the city the vital force in the national life that it is, however, is not merely the fact that it performs certain economic functions but also that it is enmeshed with a hinterland of varying scope in countless social activities. Among these are: the area over which such urban institutions as hospitals, schools, churches, theaters, and clubs are patronized by the people of the hinterland; the area over which the professional services which urbanites perform are sought by an outlying clientele; the area over which urbanites seek recreation in the form of golf clubs, forest preserves, and camp sites; and the area over which a substantial proportion of outlying residents maintain intimate social connections with people in the city. It may even be true that the area over whch the inhabitants of the region think of themselves as belonging to or being a part of the city constitutes a crucial criterion for the definition of the planning area. This may be ascertained by their contributions to urban philanthropic activities and the interest they take, however slender, in civic affairs. It should be recognized, of course, that the area over which a given urban state of mind prevails is difficult to ascertain, although the circulation figures of the metropolitan newspaper may give us a rough index. There are other more or less arbitrary criteria which may be taken account of. Among them are the extent of urban land uses, the area of continuous urban population density, and the area over which urban real estate firms operate subdivisions.

Although the planner will be cautious in accepting any arbitrarily laid out or historically constituted governmental units as his planning area, he cannot fail to take account of the existence of these governmental and administrative units and their interrelationships. Besides the corporate entity which is the city, it will be necessary to take account of township and county lines, tax districts, police districts and judicial areas, voting districts, and similar administrative units. These will generally not cross state boundaries, and yet such services as sanitation, health services, fire services, and police services which the central city renders may frequently spill over not only local administrative lines but even state boundaries. Of late the areas over which contracts for joint services between different administrative units are made have become increasingly important. That the outward movement of municipal boundaries does not keep pace with the actual spread of services is perhaps most dramatically illustrated by the extent to which extensive rural areas constituting the milkshed of central cities have subjected themselves to the control of urban sanitary inspection. In not a few metropolitan areas, especially in those marginal regions where otherwise chaotic developments would take place on the peripheries of cities and of suburbs, the cities have been able to obtain such concessions from their suburban neighbors as the power to control zoning of land uses, the regulation of building construction, and even planning.

In recent years one of the most revolutionary developments in the structure of metropolitan regions has come through the expansion of the services of the federal government to local communities and the multiplication of federal administrative authorities operating outside of Washington. The federal reserve districts, the Army corps areas, the housing, works, and security agencies, by the very fact that they have set up district offices and divided the country into administrative regions, have brought about a certain degree of integration which a few years ago would have been considered as utopian. The National Resources Planning Board's report of a few years ago on *Regional Factors in National Planning and Development* listed well over a hundred such administrative areas into which the country was divided. Since that time these administrative units have multiplied enormously, and there were added to them the numerous agencies connected with defense and war activities, such as the War Production Board areas, the defense areas as constituted by the defense, health, and welfare services, and the rent control and rationing areas with which we are familiar. It is of course a regrettable fact that the federal government itself has apparently not been able or not been willing to adopt a more or less standardized set of areas the country over. Here one of the most colossal tasks of co-ordination on the federal level remains to be undertaken. If this task can be adequately performed, it might set an example to state and local authorities and contribute immensely to the progress of regional planning. One contribution, however, which particularly the federal defense and war agencies made in a number of instances, was to recognize metropolitan regions as distinct administrative areas separate from the states to which they belong and sometimes comprising sections of several states. This step may do much toward rationalizing metropolitan administration.

It should, of course, be recognized that not all of the criteria for delimiting a planning region sketched above are of equal importance. Nor does each stand as an isolated fact. It is one of the tasks of the planner, therefore, to evaluate the significance of these several criteria and to understand their interrelationships. In this way he may ultimately arrive at the point where the countless possible definitions of metropolitan regions can be reduced to a few, and by working out the approximate coincidence of these boundaries they may be actually further reduced to two: (1) the immediate planning area constituting the region of daily intimate and vital interrelation between the city, its suburbs, and periphery; (2) the wider planning region which takes account of the city's and its surrounding areas' place in the national world economy.

The Metropolitan Region Challenges the Planner

Just as gunpowder spelled the end of the walled medieval city, so the automobile, electricity, and the technology of modern industrial society have blasted the barriers of city charters and of the traditions and laws and grooves of thinking which have hitherto prevented a rational approach to city planning. We live in an era which dissolves boundaries, but the inertia of antiquarian lawyers and lawmakers, the predatory interests of local politicians, real estate men, and industrialists, the parochialism of suburbanites, and the myopic vision of planners have prevented us from a full recognition of the inescapable need for a new planning unit in the metropolitan region. As more and more of our services in everyday living become affected by the operations of government, as more of our governmental functions become managerial, it is becoming ever more necessary that the planning unit actually become the governmental unit.

It is not the planners who have invented the new leviathan. But it is for the planners to recognize the actuality of the new leviathan that has been created by the economic, social, and political forces of our time. It is of the utmost importance for the future of a democratic order that plans and decisions be made by those who have a stake in their effect. The area of control must be the area of interdependence, in which an aggregate of people have a common stake; but the area of local interdependence has grown ever larger, whereas the area of control has lagged behind. In determining the new area of local autonomy, therefore, it is well to remember that "in a national state, and especially in a democracy, it is of the highest importance that the necessary role of local self government in matters that are really local should be protected and preserved."[5] This requires the invention of a

[5]   Charles E. Merriam, "Urbanism," in *1126: A Decade of Social Science Research* (Chicago: University of Chicago Press, 1940), p. 32.

new unit for planning which will make local autonomy in the enlarged regional sense possible.

As a young English writer reviewing the effect of war upon the communities of his country has said, "National Planning, even in the physical sense, will be impossible if we tolerate the existing definitions of Local Government and municipal boundaries."[6] We might add that without the recognition of the metropolitan region as a planning unit it will be impossible to plan either the city or the country.

6   Ritchie Calder, *Start Planning Britain Now: A Policy for Reconstruction* (The Democratic Order, No. 5 [London: Kegan Paul, 1941]), pp. 33–34.

21

WORLD COMMUNITY, WORLD

SOCIETY, AND WORLD

GOVERNMENT:

AN ATTEMPT AT

A CLARIFICATION OF TERMS

I

THE QUEST for a free, peaceful, and just world in which all men can develop their capacities to the fullest and enjoy the blessings of an advancing civilization is the professed aim of more than a few Americans and other members of the human race. This goal has been variously formulated, sometimes as the building of a world community or world society, and sometimes as the construction of a world government or world state.

These terms, while designed to aid us in defining the objective toward which we are to move, themselves introduce an element of

Reprinted from *World Community*, ed. Quincy Wright (Chicago: University of Chicago Press, 1948).

confusion into programs of action and thus become obstacles to the realization of the ends which they symbolize. There are those, for instance, who believe that we already have a *world community* and that what is necessary is to develop a corresponding *world society*. There are others who take the existence of a world society—or at least an embryonic world society—for granted and regard the creation of a world government or world state as the urgent need of the present. And since a regime of law and order is the characteristic mark of government and is indicative of the existence of a state, they would proceed to formulate such a body of basic law or a constitution for the governance of the world and thus bring a world state into being.

Clearly, if a world community already exists, it is superfluous to spend effort to bring it into existence. If a world society is already at hand, it is obviously stupid to be waiting for it to emerge. This, of course, still leaves open the question of whether a world community or society is a necessary prerequisite for the effective operation of world government and the effective functioning of a world state. It also leaves open the question of whether the framing of a world constitution is a necessary or desirable step in the building of a world community. Furthermore, it leaves unanswered the question as to whether a world community can be deliberately built, or whether it is the unwitting product of growth and unintended activity. It also leaves open the issue as to whether, if a world community or society were in existence, a world government or state would be necessary at all for the attainment of a free, peaceful, just, and prosperous humanity.

Disagreements as to the ends to be striven for as well as to the most appropriate means to be employed in the pursuit of the ends will persist as long as this confusion continues to plague us. The confusion, however, by which mankind and the intellectual leaders of mankind are beset in the attempt to work out the problems of the contemporary world are of two kinds: (1) the ambiguity of the terms of discourse and (2) the differences in judgments concerning the facts and the relations between the facts. It is the purpose of this paper to deal only with the former, although it will be difficult to avoid at least some reference to the latter, especially since it is impossible to discuss terms and the relations between terms without alluding to the objects or phenomena which they designate and the relations that are supposed to exist between these objects or phenomena.

Agreements regarding objectives and programs of action will obviously be impeded as long as the parties to the debate talk *past* one another instead of *to* one another. There may still be disagreement as to the values to be achieved and the procedures to be employed to achieve them even after the terms used in discourse have been clarified, because there may still be errors of fact, of logic, and of theory. But the least we can do to facilitate the realization of such hopes as we share is to provide ourselves with fairly precise categories of thought and of communication in terms of which we understand ourselves and our fellows.

II

The controversy that exists concerning whether a world community must precede a world state, whether the two develop simultaneously, or whether the world community may be expected to arise out of a world government rests to a large extent upon the meaning ascribed to the term "world community." Though the terms "state" and "government" are by no means unambiguous, there is on the whole less confusion incident to their use than there is in the case of the term "community." The confusion in all these instances is, of course, largely due to the circumstance that these and most other words we use in social-science discourse are also terms current in common speech and often reflect the universe of "common sense."

But even the common-sense meaning of the terms "state" and "government" carry the connotation of more or less formal organization, whereas the term "community" connotes, if it does not actually denote, the absence of formal association and organization and of legally sanctioned or regulated living-together of men. Indeed, we even speak of plant and animal communities, where formal, deliberately contrived, and legally sanctioned organization is precluded.

When the plant and animal ecologist talks about a community, he is referring to the aggregation of living forms knitted together by symbiotic ties into a web of life. Through their involvement in the struggle for existence in a given habitat, the various individual members and species of organisms acquire a spatial position and a place in the division of labor which gives to each its peculiar character and function and to the total community the semblance of an equilibrium.

The sustenance and reproductive relationships which the individual organisms and types of living things develop with one another and with the habitat as a whole give the plant and animal community an internal interdependence and a distinctiveness from other communities which leave the external observer with the impression of the separate identity of each community. The bonds that bind the individual organisms and varieties of plant and animal organisms together are the functional interrelationships which are essentially competitive. When we talk about the "law of the jungle," we mean the war of each against all. This state of existence, if it can at all be called social, rests on what Kant has called man's "unsocial sociability," that is to say, upon a set of conditions under which each organism strives to achieve its own ends and only inadvertently confers some benefit upon other organisms, but through this inadvertent by-product of its own selfish striving creates ties of mutual interdependence with others. Such a condition of interdependence does not call for either awareness, communication, or the existence of or agreement on norms.

The symbiotic relationships which underlie every plant and animal community are either those of (1) *mutualism*, where the functions of one organism or variety of organisms are beneficial to others and vice versa; (2) *commensalism*, where the benefits derived by one are a matter of indifference to the other; or (3) *parasitism*, where the benefits derived by one imply harm to the other. Classical examples of each type of symbiotic relationship are readily available from plant and animal ecology.

A special case of an animal community often cited as a model for mankind is the peculiar symbiotic relationship obtaining among the members of colonies of social insects. Even there, however, the order and cohesion that prevail are based not upon communication, mutual awareness, and the acceptance of social norms but rather upon the morphology and elementary reflexes or instincts which are built into the organisms and which operate automatically.

III

The human community, too, rests upon a similar ecological base, but it should be noted that human communities are never merely ecological units. Upon the ecological base there are always superimposed economic, cultural, political, and moral or ethical levels of interdependence. The human economy is never without some rules of the game. There is always present some degree of awareness of the other. There is always some measure of conscious control. There is language, symbolic communication, and some approximation to mutual understanding. There are rights and duties, claims and expectations. There are not merely tropisms and reflexes but also habits and sentiments, customs, institutions, shared norms, and values. In short, there is not merely symbiosis but also some degree of consensus.

One of the persistent interests, however, among students of man is the attempt to differentiate between a community and a society. In a sense these two terms have become polar concepts in the efforts to understand human social life. When we use the term "community," we seek to isolate and to emphasize the physical, spatial, and symbiotic aspects of human group life, whereas by the term "society" we wish to bring into focus and to stress the psychic, deliberative, rational, normative, and consensual phases of group existence. When we are dealing with human beings as aggregates of population distributed in space and in relationship to resources, it is useful to employ the concept "community." When, on the other hand, human groups are thought of as held together by communication, by the bonds of interest, and when they move toward common collective goals for which they require a common understanding of symbols and a sharing of common norms, we are dealing with a society.

It should be noted, however, that every human community is always something of a society. It is difficult to conceive of human beings living together in close physical contact with one another without engaging in communication, especially if the physical contact persists over a considerable time. And, as Dewey has pointed out, there is "more than a verbal tie between the words *common, community, and communication.* Men live in a community in virtue of the things which they have in common; and communication is the *way in which they come to possess things in common.*"[1]

We do occasionally find instances of two or more groups of people living next to one another but having little if any direct physical contact. The etiquette of the classical caste system was a case in point, as was the "silent trade" in the course of which adjoining communities exchanged goods without communication or direct physical contact. The diffusion of modern technology through the more or less impersonal market on a world scale is another approximation to such a case. Although the market mechanism does involve communication of some sort among the participants in commerce, the physical and social distance between producers and ultimate consumers is immensely greater in the modern world market in capitalistic civilization than it was in earlier times. This is not to say that there are not some survivals of the intimate, personal market to be found today; but it certainly is not representative of typical economic relations in the modern world.

While every community tends to generate some element of society, the reverse is not so obvious. The people scattered over the face of the earth who share, let us say, a common interest in some esoteric belief or body of knowledge but who may never have met can perhaps be said to live in a simulated community, but the ties of such a community will at best be tenuous. In such instances where the bond of cohesion among individuals rests upon shared beliefs based upon communication, it is proper to put the accent upon the polar concept of society. Conversely, where the bonds linking individuals rest upon spatial contiguity,

1   John Dewey, *Democracy and Education* (New York, 1915), p. 5.

upon a division of labor, and upon competition in the market, it is preferable to put the stress upon community. What makes every community at least an embryonic society, however, is the fact that any involvement in reciprocal relations among human beings calls for some kind of communication and generates some degree of consensus.

IV

In a sense, the concept "world community" is a contradiction in terms, for the community is most frequently conceived as a territorially limited *local* unit. We do not ordinarily speak of an individual as belonging "to more than one community, except in so far as a smaller community of which he is a member is included in a larger of which he is also a member."[2] More particularly, it has been taken as the mark of a community that "one's life may be lived wholly within it, that all one's social relationships may be found within it."[3] In that sense a community is an inclusive, relatively integrated territorial group as distinguished from the segmental and widely ranging ties and identification of society.

It appears, therefore, that in the traditional conception of community there are implicit the notions of territorial compactness and closeness, intimacy of contact, and relative self-sufficiency. These criteria apply readily enough to most human settlements in an earlier stage of civilization; but it is difficult to find modern communities which in their economic, social, and political life can be sharply delineated by narrow local bounds. Modern technology, economy, political organization, and even culture tend to encompass the earth. We can see this more clearly if we recognize and attempt to trace the intricate and far-flung networks of interrelations which are associated with such a relatively compact unit as a metropolitan region. The limits of such a region must be more or less arbitrarily defined in terms of retail and

2   Robert E. Park and Ernest W. Burgess, *Introduction to the Science of Sociology* (Chicago: University of Chicago Press, 1921), p. 163.

3   Robert M. MacIver, *Society: Its Structure and Changes* (New York, 1931), p. 9.

wholesale trade area, commutation area, newspaper-circulation area, and service area of the central city. To delineate the "communal" boundaries of an entity as large as a national state would obviously lead to even greater complications.

Barriers to the universal spread of technology, science, and culture are, of course, still formidable. Tribal, racial, national, linguistic, religious, economic, political, and other differences do still divide the world into separate regions. But, on the other hand, there remain few self-sufficient, internally homogeneous islands some inhabitants of which, at least, have not been drawn into the universal currents of modern life; and these few remaining islands are being rapidly submerged.

The overwhelming trend is from *Gemeinschaft* to *Gesellschaft*;[4] from social groupings based upon "status" to those based on "contractual"[5] relations; from homogeneous aggregates held together by "mechanical solidarity" to heterogeneous aggregates based upon "organic solidarity" and a division of labor;[6] from "primary groups"[7] to secondary groups; and from the "folk culture"[8] to urban industrial civilization.

The bonds of the market certainly are not so personal and intimate as are those of *kinship* and close local association, but they do organize life over ever wider areas approaching the limits of the universe. There are still local dialects, but there are also world languages. There still is rumor and gossip, but there also is ever greater reliance on news. There still are local cultures, but there is also an approximation to world civilization. There still

4   See Ferdinand Tönnies, *Gemeinschaft und Gesellschaft* (5th ed.; Berlin, 1922).

5   See Sir Henry S. Maine, *Ancient Law* (London, 1861) and *Village Communities in the East and in the West* (New York, 1889).

6   See Émile Durkheim, *The Division of Labor in Society* (New York, 1933) and *Elementary Forms of Religious Life* (New York, 1915).

7   See Charles H. Cooley, *Social Organization* (New York, 1909).

8   See Robert Redfield, *The Folk Culture of Yucatan* (Chicago: University of Chicago Press, 1941).

are local, county, state, and national governments, but there are also emerging world political institutions, however feeble. We even find more or less successful appeals made by statesmen to the court of "world opinion," to the "conscience of mankind," and to the loyalties and duties of "world citizenship." These phrases may as yet be merely figures of speech, but in critical situations in the recent past they have demonstrated their power to move men's thoughts and actions.

V

The central issue which makes the concept "community" relevant to the problem of peace, world order, and progress is the indispensability of a basis for effective co-operation and collective action among the nations and peoples of the world. In this connection it might be pointed out that the cohesiveness of a group derives, or is widely believed to be derived, in part from its antagonism to other groups. This function of external conflict as a factor making for internal integration has been dramatized by William Graham Sumner, and others before him, notably Gumplowicz, as the in-group versus out-group relationship. It has been suggested that if the whole world were to become a single community, the organizing and beneficent effect of conflict would be lost and, hence, that such a world could not long remain an integrated unity unless it picked upon some extra-mundane body for its opposition.

Here it may be in point to emphasize that such local community cohesion as we now have is sustained only in negligible degree by conflict with other communities. There is no evidence available to me on the basis of which students of local communities could arrive at the conclusion that intracommunity solidarity is significantly furthered by intercommunity conflict. It is highly questionable whether external conflict is an essential ingredient of internal community cohesion, and it is at least plausible that adequate equivalents for external conflict can be found in what Simmel calls the war against "inner enemies." And if we do not actually have ready-made "inner enemies" at hand, we can always invent them. We have, of course, a considerable literature tending to support the proposition that nation-states are never so strong as when they are threatened by external enemies. Whatever the facts may be on a national and international level, there is nothing to support the assumption that local communities gain an appreciable *measure of their internal integrity through external conflict.*

VI

If we are to apply the lessons we have learned from the structure of community life on a local scale to the problem of organizing the world, it will be helpful, then, to think of the community in terms of a series of processes and levels of interaction.

In its most elementary sense the community is a habitat which sustains a population. The symbiotic relationships or the competitive co-operation which the occupancy of a common habitat demands creates a common ecological base upon which social relationships may develop.

Upon this ecological base human beings tend to build a technological order, a division of labor, and an economy. Such an order inevitably calls forth a set of norms and institutions which control the participants. These controls are initially for the most part unconscious. Later they tend to become conscious and formal. When such an order becomes crystallized, it takes on political forms, of which the law, the state, and the police are symbolic. Throughout this process communication goes on, and a set of common understandings, values, and ideals and a body of loyalties develop, based upon participation in common experiences and the generation and dissemination of common symbols. From this foundation there emerges the beginning of a moral order in which individual and group conduct is controlled not so much by external coercion as by uncoerced consensus.

Thus we pass along the continuum from community to society, from a form of living together in which the members of the aggregate have not merely conflicting and parallel interests but also common or shared interests. A community thus might be regarded as a state of existence, whereas a society is a state of mind.

VII

A serious misunderstanding often stands in the way of rational discourse about the world community. It is naïvely assumed that likeness of characteristics makes for integration, whereas heterogeneity impedes integration. The fact is that similarity of traits may also be the occasion for more intense antagonism, whereas differentiation of traits may be the basis for a mutually beneficial division of labor. We see this situation in the plant and animal world, where we have what is known as "like commensals" and "unlike commensals." The hardest wars are often fought between "like commensals." If the trait of belligerency were universal among men, it surely would not make the creation of a peaceful world easier. All depends, therefore, upon what traits are similar and what traits are different.

Similarly, it is often naïvely assumed that the more contacts we have with one another and the more intimate these contacts, the less occasion there will be for conflict. It should be noted, however, that frequency and intimacy of contacts can become the basis of conflict as well as of harmony. To know one another better is often to hate one another more violently. To be sure, a common language and a common culture facilitates mutually intelligible communication, but it also makes possible conflict in areas of life in respect to which we were formerly indifferent. The more we know one another and the more frequent and intimate our relations with one another are, the more opportunity there also exists for disagreement, for irritation, and for overt conflict.

VIII

In building a world community or world society, we encounter the problem of "community organization." From what has been said before, community organization is in part an unconscious development in interaction on a symbiotic basis of competitive co-operation, but it is in part also a product of deliberate construction, of education, of facilitation, of communication, of the building of institutions and other formal controls, and of participation in organized life. Attention might be directed at this point to the history of the community organization movement. In the United States this movement is about two generations old. It began with the surveys and studies of actual communities as they existed in England and America, such as Charles Booth's survey of London. In the course of these studies it was found that communities had organization or structure quite apart from any deliberate and concerted effort to create such structure. The actual problems of social life of these communities were discovered, and organized efforts were undertaken to remedy some of these undesirable conditions of life by bringing incongruities into mutual accord and by building new programs of action and initiating new control devices. It was the deliberate effort to create and manipulate the institutions and services of communities in the interests of more wholesome life that became known as the community organization movement.

This takes us back to an interesting discussion which went on during the eighteenth century among the Scottish moralists concerning the relations between the "natural order" and the "civil order." They raised the question as to the extent to which a community was an organism or a natural entity, as over against the extent to which a community was an artifact, that is, a contrived entity. While a full discussion of this problem would take us too far afield, it is an issue of significance in the light of present-day discussion concerning the need for building a world society. It has been argued, for instance, that it is useless to attempt to build a world society, for, if one is to exist, it will come into being as the unintended end product of the participation of people in some common enterprses on a world scale. I am skeptical of this argument because we have learned from local experience that, whereas sometimes a formal organization may impede a natural development, it is also true that formal organization may facilitate and guide such natural processes.

In struggling for the emergence of a world community and a world government, therefore, it is well to keep in mind that we already have much to build upon. In many respects the world is already drifting toward a community. In other respects it can be helped to do so or can be impeded in this process.

There is, for instance, a reciprocal relationship between world trade and world political organization. The more trade we have, the more rules and regulations we will need and develop for carrying it on; and, in turn, the more we subject ourselves to commonly accepted rules and regulations, the more easily world trade can be carried on. I do not mean to suggest, of course, that these rules and regulations are always beneficent; they may be stupid and lead to the emergence of trade barriers. Similarly, the more of a common culture we have, the less we need formal law and the easier it is to enforce such law as there is. On the other hand, the attempt to create a common rule of law in areas where no such law existed before itself enlarges and deepens the sphere of a common culture. The formulation and adoption of the Constitution of the United States has probably been an important factor in the emergence of a "national community."

Even in highly integrated local communities we find some deviations from the accepted norms in the form of crime and other forms of social disorganization. The very issues, however, for public discussion and public action which such deviations pose furnish occasions for increasing community solidarity. Indeed, it has been pointed out by Durkheim that it is precisely in the attempt by communities to prevent and punish infractions of social rules that these communities reaffirm and strengthen their solidarity. We should not expect, therefore, on a world scale any more than on a local scale, to find complete and unvarying adherence to existing social norms. Rather, we should be prepared to use these occasions as opportunities for creating a world opinion, a world conscience, world-wide concerted and collective action, and a sense of belonging to a world entity.

In building the world of tomorrow, therefore, we must start with what we have. We must take the world as it is. We cannot expect to start with a clean slate. If we see the ingredients of a world community in a series of forms of interaction on a universal scale—actions which formerly for the most part were carried out on a local, regional, or national scale—we can measure the progress in world solidarity and integration as we go along. The world community upon which a world society will ultimately have to rest will not automatically come into existence by making a world constitution or even by having such a constitution formally accepted; but, on the other hand, neither need we wait until the world is ready for a universal regime of law before making progress toward peace and order. Between the inevitable and the impossible there lies a realm of the feasible. On this we must keep our eye, for it is this area that provides the opportunity for deliberate intervention and sets the limits for such intervention.

We have already a number of embryonic world institutions. They are indicative of the degree to which we have achieved a world community. For the time being they are still feeble; but they represent a great advance over what we have had before. We shall probably not achieve in our lifetime anything even approximating the ecological, the economic, the cultural, the political, and the moral integration which we have achieved in communities on a local scale. But even some progress in that direction on a world scale is better than war or the permanent division of the world into two potentially warring camps.

Louis Wirth: A Biographical Memorandum

By Elizabeth Wirth Marvick

Louis Wirth was born on August 28, 1897, in the village of Gemünden in the Rhineland district of Germany. The oldest son, he was the second surviving child of Joseph and Rosalie Lorig Wirth. Louis' birth was followed over a period of ten years by that of three brothers and two sisters.

Wirth's father was a relatively prosperous member of the Jewish community of this small village in the Hunsrück district near Coblenz. The family lived in a house that had belonged to Wirths for at least four centuries. Like his grandfather and father, Joseph Wirth was a cattle merchant and farmer on a small scale—as were most Jews in rural areas of the Rhineland and Westphalia.

Louis Wirth's mother was also the child of a Jewish cattle dealer who headed an old and respected family in a neighboring town. Her mother, however, was the daughter of a well-to-do family of merchants and rabbinical scholars and came from a town in the Saar region. Rosa Victor Lorig, Wirth's grandmother, had several brothers who emigrated to America in the first half of the nineteenth century and settled in Missouri. When the four Lorig brothers, Wirth's maternal uncles, approached military age they also migrated to America, settling in Kansas, Nebraska, and Colorado.

For Wirth, Gemünden, a settlement of only nine hundred persons, was always an exemplification of the narrowness and monotony of village life. In "Urbanism as a Way of Life" (1938) and other writings he was later to pay tribute to urban civilization, which he contrasted implicitly with the deficiencies of the rural setting.

Although Joseph Wirth was well off compared with most of his neighbors, his land holdings comprised only about twelve acres. These were mostly given over to cattlefeed crops, and the whole family had to work in the fields. One of Louis' brothers recalls that ". . . The city appeared to us as the incarnation of the good life—less toil and more leisure to pursue intellectual interests." Certainly Wirth was never tempted to romanticize rural life or to bemoan the rural-urban migration.

The Jewish community in Gemünden was composed of between eighteen and twenty families, mostly of old standing. The Wirth household was a social center for this group. Card-playing was the chief evening recreation and on Saturday morning after service in the synagogue the members congregated at the Wirths' for talk. While Joseph Wirth was orthodox in religion he had a critical intelligence in worldly affairs and specially admired business acumen. His strong sense of humor and tolerance for differences in others modified any picture of a stern patriarch. Wirth's mother had a reputation for piety and for a broad-minded good nature. Her optimism concerning her fellows became legendary in the family.

Jewish children in Gemünden attended the evangelical *Volksschule* for secular subjects, Monday through Friday, and the religious school, taught by the rabbi, on Sunday. Both courses were compulsory for eight years. At the time Wirth attended these schools few Gemünden youths had been sent to a *Gymnasium.*

Wirth's mother, however, had higher educational aspirations for her children and it was she who persuaded her husband to provide further tutoring by the village teacher for Louis. When her twin brother Isaac visited Gemünden in 1911 his offer to take Louis and his older sister Flora back to the United States was particularly welcomed by her because of the educational opportunity it would bring. Without it, Wirth would probably have been apprenticed to a merchant in Frankfurt or another city and have followed a commercial career, as did all but one of his younger brothers.

After the young Wirths were taken to Omaha, Nebraska, they joined the household of Emanuel Lorig, who had a family of his own. Thereafter, Uncle Isaac, a bachelor adventurer, migrated to Costa Rica, where he ran a coffee plantation and acquired a reputation in Gemünden for pecuniary success which years later turned out to be wholly unfounded.

Wirth regarded several of his experiences in the public schools of Omaha as turning points in his life; particularly with an elementary-school teacher who labored to teach him English after school hours. He became fluent not only in written but also in spoken English and as an adult had no trace of German accent. This was the second time in his life that a major shift was required in his communication techniques, for the *Evangelische Volksschule* had already taught him, though he was strongly left-handed, to write a fine script with his right hand.

In high school Wirth was influenced strongly by an outspokenly liberal and agnostic teacher of history. He became a successful high-school debater and by this means on one occasion earned a ceremonial dinner at the house of William Jennings Bryan. Here he and other guests were obliged to sign a temperance pledge.

Wirth was again to be "rescued" from a commercial career. It was planned for him to join the small retail business of his uncle, with whom his relations were not congenial. However, he won a regional scholarship to the University of Chicago, edging out his nearest competitor by a very small margin. Thus he was able to leave Omaha for good.

Wirth arrived in Chicago at the beginning of the First World War. Here his tendency to radical protest took a political turn. In these years the University of Chicago was one of the few American academic centers where Marxism and later Leninism were the subject of intellectual scrutiny, partly due to the interests of Albion W. Small. After America entered the war, Wirth participated in anti-war activities of Marxist groups on the campus which purported to follow the line of the Third International. His radicalism may have been related to his uncomfortable position as a

German national as well as to his anti-commercial prejudices. In any case, Wirth's commitment to Marxist ideology—as to any ideology—seems never to have been very deep. His strong reaction against theology of any kind had earlier led to his rejection of his parents' religion. His generalized skepticism (later to be directed against "general" theory-building) found guidance under Park, Burgess, and Thomas, who together with Small and G. H. Mead, all taught undergraduate as well as graduate students.[1]

For Wirth, Chicago always had the romantic connotations of a new life. His lasting identification with that city was further encouraged by the interests of Park, Burgess, and Thomas in German sociology and empirical research on city life. At this time also Park's connection with Booker T. Washington helped to form another identification of Wirth—with the American Negro. Wirth himself remembered that, when he was a student, reading W. E. B. DuBois' *The Souls of Black Folk* had been an important and moving experience for him.

After Wirth took his undergraduate degree he went to work for the Bureau of Personal Service of the Jewish Charities of Chicago as a director of the division for delinquent boys.

In 1922 the German inflation made possible a return to Germany for a few months—his first visit to his family since 1911. This was also an occasion to introduce to his family Mary Bolton, whom he married in Chicago in 1923. Miss Bolton, whom he had met as an undergraduate through the University German Club, was trained as a social worker at Chicago. From Paducah, Kentucky, she was the daughter of a harness salesman of moderate means with rural ancestry of English origin and status about

[1] Veblen, of course, had been gone from Chicago for a long time, but Wirth met him about 1920 under interesting circumstances. Veblen had taken a lodging in Chicago. A. W. Small heard of this and sent Wirth to extend an invitation to dinner on Small's behalf. This was a propitiatory gesture as Small had been Dean at the time of Veblen's dismissal and considered himself responsible for it. Veblen declined the invitation on the grounds that he had no respectable clothes, and later declined an offered loan, at the same time sending the message through Wirth that he now understood Small's position at the time of the dismissal and could no longer blame him for it.

equivalent to Wirth's family. She had been raised in the conventions of the Baptist Church of a small town under the scrutiny of a Fundamentalist father, a follower of Bryan with a better than average education and some political ambition. His aspirations came to focus upon his daughter, and his choice of the University of Chicago for her as the nearest great center of learning (under the safe leadership of good Baptists) was her rescue from the narrowness of small town life and dogmas as Wirth's emigration and scholarship had been for him. In marrying her, Wirth was the first member of his family to marry a non-Jew. (Others of his generation were to follow suit however.) Wirth's assimilationist inclinations and principles, like those of his wife, partly derived from their common reaction against dogmatism and provincial ethnocentrism. Their two daughters were to be encouraged in agnosticism with audible atheistic overtones, at the same time that they were to acquire a "generalized minority" ethnic identification.

In the three years following his return from Europe and his marriage, Wirth's wife's salary as social worker made it possible for him to resume academic work as a graduate student. *The Ghetto*, his doctoral dissertation, was completed in 1925. During this time he also taught part-time at the University of Chicago and at the YMCA college. A temporary appointment as assistant professor at the University in 1926 was followed by an appointment in 1928 to the Department of Sociology of Tulane University in New Orleans. At that time the faculty of this private university were not only under the scrutiny of segregationists, but also subject to pressure from the locally influential Roman Catholic church. Wirth's role in New Orleans as a consultant to a social agency devoted to child guidance and his speeches to private groups were publicized as "pro– birth control" and despite his appointment to an associate professorship in Tulane in 1929, his contract was not to be renewed again. At this time he won a fellowship from the Social Science Research Council for research on the sociology of knowledge. Thus during 1930–31 he was able to travel with his family in France and Germany. Here he had conversations with W. Sombart, K. Mannheim, L. von Wiese, and others. Shortly thereafter started the correspondence with Mannheim that resulted in the English edition of *Ideology and Utopia* (1936).

The year of Wirth's fellowship was a critical one in Germany —Nazi gangs of youths were in evidence even in Wirth's home village of Gemünden. It is interesting that his optimism, usually very pronounced, did not prevent him from expecting the Fascists to capture power. An early move on his return to the United States was to take the first steps to resettle the entire Wirth family in America. In the years between 1932 and 1937 every member of the family left Germany and most eventually re-established themselves in the United States.

During Wirth's stay in Europe, Park became temporary chairman of the Department of Sociology at the University of Chicago, and Wirth was offered an associate professorship there to be taken up on his return in 1931.

The advent of the Roosevelt Administration gave to American sociologists and intellectuals a new and unprecedented role to play in government. At the University of Chicago, Wirth, his colleagues, and graduate students prepared testimony for congressional committee hearings on unemployment and urban conservation. In 1935 he was appointed consultant to the National Resources Planning Board on which he served until 1943, the last year as regional chairman. In this capacity he was co-author of *Our Cities: Their Role in the National Economy* (1937), one of the first efforts to bring empirical evidence collected by professional sociologists directly to bear on federal policy-making.

During the early 1930's Wirth worked closely with graduate students Horace Cayton, Herbert Goldhamer, and Edward Shils; each collaborated with him on various projects. Philip M. Hauser, another graduate student, went to the Bureau of Census on a full-time basis. Increased opportunities for data collection, field work, and influence in powerful circles seemed to give Wirth cause for optimism concerning social reform.

During these same years Wirth also played a considerable part in the organization of an introductory course in the social sciences in the newly developing College of the University of Chicago.

This course and its sequels gave undergraduate students an opportunity for social science study beyond anything then available in the country.

During the late thirties Wirth was increasingly involved in community affairs in Chicago. He was more and more often called upon to give speeches to lay groups, usually on urban planning or race relations. Adept as a moderator and discussant on radio panels, between 1937 and 1952 he participated in sixty-two University of Chicago "Round Tables."

Wirth's effectiveness as a radio speaker is impossible to measure, but as a lecturer in personal contact with his listeners he had an unusual gift. Many witnesses and incidents attest to the fact that his oratorical powers in face-to-face addresses were of that rare kind which could actually persuade those who heard him to change their conduct. This exceptional effectiveness was no doubt gratifying to Wirth and may account for his willingness to speak to many groups. He diverted increasing time and energy to playing the role of persuader. Unfortunately, most of these addresses were unwritten and unrecorded ("Chicago: Where Now?" [1944] is one of the few exceptions). It is doubtful in any case whether his ability to identify with and reinforce the "better nature" of his listeners could be communicated through a text. Since this was nevertheless one of his striking capacities it is tempting to speculate on its sources in his personality. He combined ingenuousness with skepticism and sternness. His personal attraction for a wide variety of people may have lain in the coupling of a manifest integrity with the reassurance of an obvious and direct pleasure in people with personalities quite different from his own. He himself was not a specially good storyteller, but he enjoyed being told jokes and anecdotes. Those with whom he seemed best able to relax in an atmosphere of intimacy were not his colleagues but his brothers and sisters and social workers and administrators who were also friends of his wife. With these he played occasional card games.

Wirth was early to see that the aftermath of the Second World War would open up a "revival of conscience" and increase the militancy and power of minority groups. He hoped for an acceleration of the demand for reform in urban living conditions and minority rights. His interests and energies were almost entirely absorbed by practical efforts to promote these changes. Academically he continued to offer courses in the sociology of knowledge and in the history of sociological theory, as well as courses more closely related to his immediate interests.

Toward the end of the war he collaborated with Ernest Grunsfeld, a Chicago architect, in developing a plan for the physical rehabilitation of Chicago. In 1944 Wirth was appointed Director of Planning for the Illinois Post-War Planning Commission. As director of the American Council on Race Relations he played a leading part in drawing up a brief submitted on behalf of "friends of the court" which was quoted in the majority decision invalidating restrictive covenants (the Morgan Case). After his death some of the data he had prepared were used in the Supreme Court decision of 1954 on school segregation. In this decision (Baker vs. United States) one of Wirth's objectives of longest standing was virtually realized: the Court acknowledged that "separate but equal" was a contradiction in terms when it involved the educational segregation of a weak and disadvantaged minority from a dominant and more prosperous caste.

Wirth was formal or informal adviser to many groups devoted to social action. After 1945 he wrote scarcely any article that was not to be presented before a particular group on a specific occasion. During the last decade of his life he projected a major scholarly work on the city. A few chapters were drafted and an outline prepared as a basis for filing large quantities of material, but the work did not advance beyond this stage.

Wirth was elected president of the American Sociological Association in 1946. His work in connection with the establishment of the International Sociological Association and his installation as its first president in 1950 meant that from 1948 he made several trips to Europe. He had not visited there since 1931.

He died suddenly of a coronary thrombosis after making a speech at a conference on community relations on May 10, 1952, in Buffalo, New York.

The Bibliography of Louis Wirth

"Culture Conflicts in the Immigrant Family." Unpublished Master's thesis, University of Chicago Library, 1925.

"A Bibliography of the Urban Community," in R. E. PARK, E. W. BURGESS, and R. D. McKENZIE, *The City*. Chicago: University of Chicago Press, 1925.

"The Sociology of Ferdinand Tönnies," *American Journal of Sociology*, XXXII (November, 1926), 412–22.

"Some Jewish Types of Personality," *Publications of the American Sociological Society*, XXXII (1926), 90–96.

The Ghetto. University of Chicago Press, 1928.

"Sociology for Nurses," *American Journal of Nursing*, XXVIII (November, 1928), 1131.

"Culture Conflict and Misconduct," *Social Forces*, IX (June, 1931), 484–92.

"Clinical Sociology," *American Journal of Sociology*, XXXVII (July, 1931), 49–66.

Sociology: Vocations for Those Interested in It, ed. ROBERT C. WOELLNER. Chicago: Board of Vocational Guidance of the University of Chicago, 1931.

"The Meaning of Environment," *Introductory General Course in the Social Sciences*. 2d ed. Chicago: University of Chicago Bookstore, 1932. Pp. 178–79.

Reprinted from *Community Life and Social Policy*, ed. Elizabeth Wirth Marvick and Albert J. Reiss, Jr. (Chicago: University of Chicago Press, 1956), pp. 409–16.

"The Scope and Problems of the Community," *Sociological Problems and Methods* ("Publications of the American Sociological Society"), XXVII (May, 1933), 61–73.

"Race and Nationalism," *Introductory General Course in the Study of Contemporary Society.* 4th ed. Chicago: University of Chicago Bookstore, 1934. Pp. 393–413.

"Segregation," *Encyclopaedia of the Social Sciences,* XIII (1934), 643–47.

"Albion Woodbury Small," *Encyclopaedia of the Social Sciences,* IV (1934), 98–99.

"The Nature, Scope and Essential Elements in General Education," *General Education,* ed. WILLIAM S. GRAY. ("Proceedings of the Institute for Administrative Officers of Higher Institutions," Vol. VI.) Chicago: University of Chicago Press, 1934. Pp. 25–35.

"Chicago: The Land and the People," *Survey Graphic,* XXIII (October, 1934), 468–71, 520–25.

"The Prospects of Regional Research in Relation to Social Planning," *Publications of the American Sociological Society,* XXIX (August, 1935), 107–14.

"The Literature of Sociology," with EDWARD A. SHILS, *Social Studies,* XXVI (November–December, 1935), 459–75, 525–46.

KARL MANNHEIM. *Ideology and Utopia.* Translated with EDWARD A. SHILS, with an Introduction by LOUIS WIRTH. New York: Harcourt, Brace & Co., 1936.

"Does Chicago Know Itself?" *Polity,* IV (January, 1936), 5–9.

"A Glimpse of Chicago's Changing Population," with RICHARD LANG, *Polity,* IV (February, 1936).

"Types of Nationalism," *American Journal of Sociology,* XLI (May, 1936), 723–37.

"Symposium on Present Trends in Guidance: Part III," *Purdue University Studies in Higher Education.* ("Proceedings of the 2nd Annual Guidance Conference" held at Purdue University, November, 1936, Vol. XXX.) Pp. 63–78.

LOUIS WIRTH *et al.* "Our Cities: Their Role in the National Economy," *Report of the Urbanism Committee to the National Resources Committee.* Washington: Government Printing Office, 1937.

"The Interrelation of Cultures," *Social Research,* IV (September, 1937), 328–32.

"Some Criteria for the Selection of Research Projects in the Social Sciences," *Conference of Representatives of University Social Science Research Organizations.* New York: Social Science Research Council, 1937.

"Localism, Regionalism and Centralization," *American Journal of Sociology*, XLII (January, 1937), 403–509.

"The Literature of Sociology, 1935 and 1936," with EDWARD A. SHILS, *Social Education I* (October–November, 1937), pp. 499–511, 575–85.

"The Urban Mode of Life," *New Horizons in Planning*. American Society of Planning Officials, 1937. P. 23. Also as "What of the City?" *American Planning and Civic Annual*. Washington, D.C.: American Planning and Civic Association, 1937. Pp. 374–79.

"Local Community Fact Book: 1938," with MARGARET FUREZ. Chicago: Chicago Recreation Commission, 1938.

"Metropolitan Regions," with LEWIS C. COPELAND, *Population Statistics*. (For the National Resources Commission, Part III.) Washington, D.C.: Government Printing Office, 1938. Pp. 1–52.

"Urbanism as a Way of Life," *American Journal of Sociology*, XLIV (July, 1938), 1–24.

"Public Safety," with MARSHALL B. CLINARD, *Urban Government* (Supplementary Report of the Urbanism Committee to the National Resources Committee, Vol. I, Part V.) Washington, D.C.: Government Printing Office, 1939. Pp. 247–303.

"Federal Reporting of Urban Information." (Members of the Urbanism Committee to the National Resources Committee, Vol. I, Part III.) Washington, D.C.: Government Printing Office, 1939. Pp. 161–77.

"Social Interaction: The Problem of the Individual and the Group," *American Journal of Sociology*, XLIV (May, 1939), 965–79.

"Housing," *Contemporary Social Problems*, ed. with an Introduction by LOUIS WIRTH. Chicago: University of Chicago Press, 1940. Pp. 1–13, 22–68.

"The Urban Society and Civilization," *1126: A Decade of Social Science Research*, ed. LOUIS WIRTH. Chicago: University of Chicago Press, 1940.

"Ideological Aspects of Social Disorganization," *American Sociological Review*, V (August, 1940), 472–82.

"Biases in Education for Business," *Business Education for What?* ("Proceedings of the University of Chicago Conference on Business Education," 1940.) Pp. 1–10.

"Prerequisites for Peace," *Unity*, CXXVI (February 17, 1941), 182–85.

"The Present Position of Minorities in the United States," *Studies in Political Science and Sociology*. (University of Pennsylvania Bicentennial Conference.) Philadelphia: University of Pennsylvania Press, 1941. Pp. 137–57.

"Advertising for the Sophisticated," *Bulletin* (Financial Advertisers Association), XXVI (January, 1941), 112–13.

"Problems and Prospects of the Social Science Curricula," *Administrative Adjustments Required by Socio-Economic Change*, ed. WM. C. REAVIS. ("Proceedings of the Tenth Annual Conference of Administrative Officers of Public and Private Schools.") Chicago: University of Chicago Press, 1941.

"The 1940 Census Forecasts the Future," *Real Estate* (September 20, 1941), pp. 7–9.

GEORGE C. ATTERBURY, JOHN L. AUBLE, ELGIN F. HUNT. *Introduction to Social Science: A Survey of Social Problems*. With a Foreword by LOUIS WIRTH. New York: Macmillan, 1941. Pp. ix–x.

"Appearance of Harmony," *Notes and News* (Council of Jewish Federation and Welfare Funds) (January 15, 1941), pp. 8–9.

"Morale and Minority Groups," *American Journal of Sociology*, XLVII (November, 1941), 415–33.

"The Composition of Our Population Is Changing," *Real Estate* (September 27, 1941), pp. 14–19.

"Urban Communities," *American Journal of Sociology*, XLVII (May, 1942), 829–39.

Review of SALO W. BARON's *The Jewish Community*, in *Historia Judaica*, VI (April, 1944), 83–86.

"The Metropolitan Region as a Planning Unit," *National Conference on Planning Proceedings, 1942*. Chicago: American Society of Planning Officials, 1942. Pp. 141–51.

Review of ERICH FROMM's *Escape from Freedom*, in *Psychiatry*, V (February, 1942), 129–31.

"The New Birth of Community Consciousness," *Community Life in a Democracy*, ed. FLORENCE C. BINGHAM. Chicago National Congress of Parents and Teachers, 1942. Pp. 11–23.

"Problems in American Life," *Unity*, ed. LOUIS WIRTH and PAUL B. JACOBSON. Washington: National Education Association, 1942–43. Pp. 6–16.

Review of SEBA ELDRIDGE & ASSOCIATES' *Development of Collective Enterprise*, in *Public Administration Review*, III (autumn, 1943), 369–74.

"Powers and Services of Government in the Post-War Periods," *War and Post War Responsibilities of American Schools*, ed. WILLIAM C. REAVIS. ("Proceedings of the Twelfth Annual Conference for Administrative Officers of Public and Private Schools," 1943, Vol. VI.) Pp. 57–70.

Review of STANLEY P. BRAY's *Jewish Family Solidarity: Right or Fact?* in *Jewish Social Studies*, V (January, 1943), 80–81.

"The Post-War Situation," *Education on the Air*, ed. JOSEPHINE H. MACLATCHY. ("Fourteenth Yearbook of the Institute for Education by Radio.") Columbus: Ohio State University, 1943. Pp. 14–30.

"Education for Survival: The Jews," *American Journal of Sociology*, XLVIII (May, 1943), 682–91.

"Effect of War on American Minorities." New York: Social Science Research Council, 1943.

"The Urban Community," *American Society in Wartime*, ed. WILLIAM F. OGBURN. Chicago: University of Chicago Press, 1943. Pp. 63–81.

LOUIS WIRTH *et al.* "Preparing for War Contract Termination." Illinois Post-War Planning Commission, 1944.

———. "Your Business after the War." Illinois Post-War Planning Commission, 1944.

———. "Illinois Prepares for Peace." Illinois Post-War Planning Commission, 1944.

"Needs for Social Planning," *American Library Association Bulletin*, XXXVIII (March, 1944), 112–14, 118. Reprinted in *Educational Digest*, 1944.

"Life in the City," in LEON CARNOVSKY and LOWELL MARTIN, *The Library in the Community*. Chicago: University of Chicago Press, 1944. Pp. 12–22.

"What Causes Unemployment," *What Causes Unemployment*. (Forum sponsored by the Industrial Relations Committee of Champaign County, Illinois.) Champaign: Bartlett Foundation, Inc., 1944. Pp. 16–18.

"Postwar Political and Social Conditions and Higher Education," *Annals of the American Academy of Political and Social Science*, CCXXXI (January, 1944), 154–62.

"Race and Public Policy," *The Scientific Monthly*, LVIII (April, 1944), 302–12.

"Illinois," *State Government*, XVII (October, 1944), 418–19.

"The Social Setting of Postwar Higher Education," *Higher Education in the Postwar Period*, ed. JOHN DALE RUSSELL. ("Proceedings of the Institute for Administrative Officers of Higher Institutions.") Chicago: University of Chicago, 1944. Pp. 1–13.

"The Hybrid and the Problem of Miscegenation," with HERBERT GOLDHAMER, *Characteristics of the American Negro*, ed. OTTO KLINEBERG. New York: Harper & Bros., 1944.

"The Bearing of Recent Social Trends upon Attainable Programs for Peace and World Organization," *Approaches to World Peace.* (Fourth Symposium Conference on Science, Philosophy and Religion in Their Relation to the Democratic Way of Life, Inc.) New York: Harper & Bros., 1944. Pp. 110–24.

"Urban and Rural Living." National Council in the Social Studies, National Association of Secondary School Principals, 1944.

"City Planning and Racial Policy," and "Positive and Negative Aspects of Present Day Race Relations," *Race Relations in Human Relations.* ("Summary Report, Second Annual Institute of Race Relations" [Fisk University, Nashville, Tennessee], July, 1945.) Pp. 31–32; 119–23.

"Effect of Recent Social Trends in Urban Planning," *Public Management,* XXVII (January, 1945), 10–13.

"Planning of Modern Urban Communities," *Forthcoming Developments in American Education,* ed. WILLIAM C. REAVIS. ("Proceedings of Fourteenth Annual Conference for Administrative Officers of Public and Private Schools, 1945," Vol. VIII.) Chicago: University of Chicago Press, 1945. Pp. 154–67.

"Human Ecology," *American Journal of Sociology,* L (May, 1945), 483–88.

"The Social and Cultural Make-Up of Chicago," *Unity.* ("Proceedings of the Conference on Home Front.") Chicago: Mayor's Committee on Race Relations, 1945. Pp. 8–9.

"Social Science Research," *Report of the Third Conference of Negro Land Grant Colleges for Co-ordinating a Program of Co-operative Social Studies,* ed. E. FRANKLIN FRAZIER. Washington, D.C.: Howard University Press, 1945.

"Negro Life in the Urban North" (review of ST. CLAIR DRAKE and HORACE CAYTON's *Black Metropolis*). *The New York Times Book Review,* November 4, 1945, p. 5.

"Does the Atomic Bomb Doom the Modern City?" ("Proceedings of the 22nd Annual Conference of the American Municipal Association," Report No. 159, December, 1945.) Pp. 30–33. Reprinted in League of Iowa Municipalities' *Monthly Magazine,* No. 5 (July, 1946), pp. 17–24, and other journals.

"The Alternative to World Atom Control," *Sci-En-Tech News,* II (December, 1945), 1–3, 7.

"The Problem of Minority Groups," *The Science of Man in the World Crisis,* ed. RALPH LINTON. New York: Columbia University Press, 1945. Pp. 347–72.

"Group Tensions and Mass Democracy," *American Scholar*, XIV (spring, 1945), 231.

"The Federal Government and Research in the Social Sciences." Memorandum of the S. S. Research Council, October, 1945.

"Rebuilding Metropolitan Chicago," *University of Chicago Magazine* (May, 1946), pp. 5–6.

"The Unfinished Business of American Democracy," in "Controlling Group Prejudice," *Annals of the American Academy of Political and Social Science*, CCXLIV (March, 1946), 1–10.

"Community Planning for Peacetime Living," ed. with ERNEST R. HILGARD and I. JAMES QUILLEN. Stanford University Press, 1946. Part I, chaps. 1–3.

Review of BUCKLIN MOON's *The High Cost of Prejudice*, in *New York Times*, June 1, 1947, p. 20.

"Planning for Freedom." ("Proceedings of the Institute of Community Planning.") University of Oklahoma, 1947. Pp. 14–26. Also in *Planning*, 1947. Pp. 3–19.

"American Sociology–1915–47," *American Journal of Sociology*, Index to Volumes I–LII (1895–1947), pp. 273–81.

"Karl Mannheim (1893–1947)," *American Sociological Review*, XII, 356–57.

"Ideas and Ideals as Sources of Power in the Modern World," *Conflicts of Power in Modern Culture*. (Seventh Conference on Science, Philosophy and Religion in Their Relation to the Democratic Way of Life.) New York: Harper & Bros., 1947. Pp. 499–509.

"The Price of Prejudice," *Survey Graphic*, XXXVI (January, 1947), 19–22.

"Responsibility of Social Science," *Annals of the American Academy of Political and Social Science*, CCXLIX (January, 1947), 143–52.

"The World in an Atomic Age," with H. C. UREY and CLYDE HART, *Assembly Papers*. New York: Council of Jewish Federation and Welfare Funds, 1948.

"International Tensions as Objects of Social Investigation," *Learning and World Peace*. (Eighth Conference on Science, Philosophy and Religion in Their Relation to the Democratic Way of Life.) New York: Harper & Bros., 1948. Pp. 45–54.

"Consensus and Mass Communication," *American Sociological Review*, XIII (February, 1948), 1–15.

"Housing as a Field of Sociological Research," *American Sociological Review*, XII (April, 1947), 137–43. Reprinted in *Journal of Housing*, V (June, 1948), 154–60.

"Research in Racial and Cultural Relations," *Proceedings of the American Philosophical Society*, XCII (1948), 381–86.

"World Community, World Society, and World Government: An Attempt at a Clarification of Terms," *World Community*, ed. QUINCY WRIGHT. Chicago: University of Chicago Press, 1948. Pp. 9–20.

"Sociological Factors in Urban Design," *1948 Convention Seminars*. American Institute of Architects, 1949.

"Comment on *Factors in Race Relations*." Comment on paper by GUSTAV ICHHEISER. Rejoinder by ICHHEISER. *American Journal of Sociology*, LIV (March, 1949), 399.

"Comments on the Resolution of the Economic and Social Council on the Prevention of Discrimination and the Protection of Minorities," *International Social Science Bulletin*, I, Nos. 3–4 (1949), 137–45.

"Social Goals for Nation and World," *Survey*, LXXXV (July, 1949), 386–88.

"Domestic and International Inter-Group Relations," *Build the Future*. (Addresses celebrating the inauguration of Charles Spurgeon Johnson, sixth president of Fisk University.) Nashville, Tenn.: Fisk University Press, 1949. P. 77.

"Chicago: A Big City Has Big Problems," *Woman's Press*, February, 1949.

"Consensus and Mass Communication," *Mass Communication*, ed. WILBUR SCHRAM. Urbana: University of Illinois Press, 1949.

"Local Community Fact Book of Chicago," with ELEANOR H. BERNERT, *Chicago Community Inventory*. Chicago: University of Chicago Press, 1949.

"Problems and Orientations of Research in Race Relations in the U.S.," *British Journal of Sociology*, I (June, 1950), 117–25. Reprinted as "Research in Intergroup Relations," *One America*, ed. F. J. BROWN and J. S. ROUCEK. New York: Prentice-Hall, 1952.

"Integrative Tendencies in International Relations," *Perspectives on a Troubled Decade: Science, Philosophy and Religion, 1939–1949*, ed. R. M. MACIVER *et al.* New York: Harper & Bros., 1950. Chap. xvi, pp. 267–77.

"Social Goals for America," *Social Welfare Forum*. ("Proceedings, 76th Annual Meeting, National Conference of Social Work.") New York: Columbia University Press, 1950.

"The Significance of Sociology," *International Social Science Bulletin*, III (1951), 197–200.

"The Limitations of Regionalism," *Regionalism in America*, ed. MERRILL JENSON. Madison: University of Wisconsin Press, 1951.

"The Social Sciences," *American Scholarship in the Twentieth Century*, ed. MERLE CURTI. Cambridge: Harvard University Press, 1953. Pp. 33–82.

"Round Table" Publications*

The Relief Problem (April 24, 1938)
Taxes and the Consumer (October 20, 1938)
Taxes as Social Insurance (December 18, 1938)
The Progress of Man (December 25, 1938)
How Shall We Solve the Housing Problem? (January 22, 1939)
The Public Debt and the Future (February 22, 1939)
Room To Live (April 16, 1939)
Refugees (May 7, 1939)
The Place of Radio in a Democracy (June 18, 1939)
Out of School—Out of Jobs (July 23, 1939)
Is the Consumer Getting His Nickel's Worth? (August 13, 1939)
The High Cost of Living (September 17, 1939)
Testing Public Opinion (November 5, 1939)
Taxes (November 19, 1939)
When Tomorrow Comes (December 24, 1939)
The Jews (January 28, 1940)
The Census (March 31, 1940)
Babies Cost Money (May 26, 1940)
Civil Liberties and the Fifth Column (July 7, 1940)
Should America Feed Europe? (September 8, 1940)
America's Defense Policies (November 10, 1940)
Art and Our Warring World (November 24, 1940)
Is This Our War? (January 1, 1941)
Defense and America's Health (May 11, 1941)
Our Liberties—Are They in Danger? (July 5, 1941)
Anti-Semitism (October 5, 1941)
Science and War (November 2, 1941)
Morale—Ours and Theirs (January 1, 1942)
The American Temper (March 29, 1942)
Aliens in Our Midst (May 10, 1942)
Health in Wartime (August 30, 1942)
Manpower (November 1, 1942)
The Airplane and the Future (February 8, 1943)
The States and Postwar America (June 20, 1943)
The Psychiatric Cost of War (November 19, 1944)
Should We Adopt Government Health Insurance? (December 31, 1944)

* Louis Wirth *et al.*, in "University of Chicago Round Table" radio transcripts (Chicago: University of Chicago, 1938–52).

Breaking the Housing Blockade (November 24, 1945)
The Little Man in a Big Society—What Can He Do? (March 17, 1946)
Can Worldwide Income Inequalities Be Lessened? (December 22, 1946)
How Can We Get Housing? (January 26, 1947)
What Are the Implications of President Truman's Speech? (March 16, 1947)
The Social Responsibilities of Radio (May 4, 1947)
Equality of Educational Opportunity (November 23, 1947)
What Are the Hopes for Peace? (December 21, 1947)
Loyalty and Liberty in 1948 (January 4, 1948)
Higher Education for All (January 25, 1948)
What Do We Know about Prejudice? (May 2, 1948)
The Politics of Housing (July 18, 1948)
Race Relations around the World (December 5, 1948)
Equality of Educational Opportunity (December 26, 1948)
Should We Adopt President Truman's Civil Rights Program? (February 6, 1949)
The North Atlantic Pact and Russia (March 6, 1949)
Democracy: A World Hope (May 15, 1949)
The Atlantic Community Faces the Bomb (September 25, 1949)
France and the Future of Europe (October 16, 1949)
Un-American Education (November 20, 1949)
What's Past Is Prologue (January 1, 1950)
Can We Solve the Civil Rights Issue Now? (February 12, 1950)
The Census Shows Us Up (March 26, 1950)
Freedom in an Age of Danger (December 17, 1950)
What Do Americans Believe about Their Fellow-Men? (February 18, 1951)
What Is the Basic Conflict between the U.S. and Russia? (June 10, 1951)
Can the New World Make the Whole World New? (December 30, 1951)
The State of the Union (January 13, 1952)
Has the Truman Doctrine Been a Success in Greece and Turkey? (March 30, 1952)